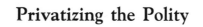

Privatizing the Polity

Privatizing the Polity

HOLONA LeANNE OCHS

Published by
STATE UNIVERSITY OF NEW YORK PRESS
Albany

For information, contact
State University of New York Press
www.sunypress.edu

Production, Laurie D. Searl
Marketing, Michael Campochiaro

Library of Congress Cataloging-in-Publication Data

Ochs, Holona LeAnne.
    Privatizing the polity / Holona LeAnne Ochs.
        pages cm
    Includes bibliographical references and index.
    ISBN 978-1-4384-5759-8 (hardcover : alk. paper)
    ISBN 978-1-4384-5761-1 (e-book)
    1. Economic assistance, Domestic—United States.   2. Poverty—
Government policy—United States.   3. Privatization—United States.
I. Title.
    HC110.P63O26 2015
    338.973'05—dc23   2014038027

10 9 8 7 6 5 4 3 2 1

Contents

Tables and Figures

Tables

Figures

Acknowledgments

Authors incur numerous debts in the process of conducting research and publishing the results, and I am indebted to so many—friends, family, and colleagues. First, I want to thank my husband, Kuroki M. Gonzalzles. He read so many drafts of this manuscript that I was afraid I might be reading something that I did not want to read if I asked him to read it just one more time. I would also like to thank the anonymous reviewers from SUNY Press who offered very specific and useful feedback that contributed tremendously to improving this project. Second, I feel as though I cannot thank enough my mentors, who have been patient, consistently supportive, and from whom I have learned so much. I sincerely appreciate the guidance of Andrew B. Whitford, Donald P. Haider-Markel, Julia Jordan-Zachery, and Laura Katz Olson. Without them, this work would not be possible. There are so many other mentors who also deserve special mention. In particular, I would like to thank Mark Joslyn, Elaine Sharp, Richard Seltzer, and Richard Fording.

Despite the time and obsessive focus spent on this book, I still have some friends. And, they have been there for me in so many ways throughout this process. I especially want to thank Hillary Watts-Bird, Beauty Bragg, Barb Childress, Vera Fennell, Kristin Handler, Julia Maserjian, Tamara Myers, Stephanie Powell-Watts, Lisa Regan, Angela Scott, Edward Lachica and all my pals in yoga who try to keep me sane. Without my friends and family, I couldn't image how this project would have ever been completed.

Over the years, a number of scholars have commented on work that contributed to this project and engaged me in conversations, debates, and presented thought-provoking critiques that have improved this research immensely. Special thanks to Michael Bennett, Armand Anthony Gonzalzles, MD, Sharon Paynter, Maureen Berner, Joe Soss, Sanford Schram, Caroline Hill, Dawn King, David Konisky, Ben Feltzer, Ray Block, Florie Bugarin, Dan Hopkins, Tom Hyclak, Judy Lasker, Eric Lawrence, Keesha Middlemass, Gordon Moskowitz, Michael Owens, James Peterson, John Pettegrew, Seth Moglen, Lavar Pope, Chris Parker, Dominic Packer, Todd Watkins, Alan Jennings, Stephan Wasby, as well as my colleagues at Lehigh University and Howard University that are not specifically mentioned here. There are so many interesting conversations and intellectual debates that have helped me formulate this story, and I appreciate each and every one of them.

Additionally, I would like to acknowledge the research support that has contributed to this work. Financial support from the Franz and Lehigh University Class of 1968 faculty research grant allowed me to compile a comprehensive dataset on poverty governance and focus on the analysis during the summer months. The generous academic leave policy and availability of funds to support conference travel for Lehigh faculty contributed to numerous improvements to this project as well. Feedback at conferences and conversations, debates, and critiques from the intellectual community on campus are essential to rigorous research. This study has benefited significantly from such collaborations. I have especially appreciated the support of the Faculty and Staff of Color Network, Circle of Sisters, the Women, Gender, and Sexuality Studies Retention Committee, and the Justice Scholars at Lehigh University.

I have thoroughly enjoyed working with SUNY Press. The interest in policy studies and openness to humanistic and scientific approaches at SUNY Press are integral to building knowledge regarding complex, multidisciplinary issues such as poverty governance. In particular, I want to thank Michael Rinella, Alan Hewat, and Laurie Searl for their competence, responsiveness, and efficiency. While I truly appreciate all the advantages of the assistance recognized here, I also acknowledge that any errors, oversights, or limitations are entirely my own.

Introduction

Over the fifty years that we have been fighting the War on Poverty in the United States, the battlefields have shifted several times. The conflict space of the American welfare state has expanded, contracted, and changed shape more than once. Lyndon Johnson's 1964 State of the Union speech defined poverty as a national problem but, notably, referenced state and local coordination and intergovernmental collaboration as essential for an effective attack. He then went on to describe battlefields in every private home and public office. Johnson proposed joint federal-local efforts using better education, job training, homes, healthcare, and better job opportunities as the weapons of war. The welfare discourse itself has changed very little, but there have been significant shifts in the authorities armed to regulate moves out of poverty. The conflict itself is repeatedly about what is better and for whom.

Devolution fundamentally changed the shape of the conflict space. The Aid to Families with Dependent Children (AFDC) program was primarily federally funded, state administered, and locally implemented. Policy experimentation using state welfare waivers justified the incremental shift to the reformed conflict space. The waves of bureaucratic reforms that coincided with the Personal Responsibility and Work Opportunity Reconciliation Act (PRWORA), or welfare reform, devolved authority over social policy to subunits of government and created the Temporary Assistance for Needy Families (TANF) program. The power to design social policy within federal guidelines and manage social service contracts was transferred to subnational units of government. This afforded the states "flexibilities" in defining what better education, job training, homes, health, and job opportunities might look like for those deemed deserving. Within federal guidelines, the states select the weapons of war and arm contractors who sort and regulate opportunities.

The private or public nature of the problem of poverty remains a point of controversy, and the battlefields cross all sectors—public, private, and nonprofit. Yet, a degree of consensus has formed, confining the conflict space to debates over the appropriate market solutions for what are widely believed to be private or individual initiatives. This consensus around neoliberal market logic or supply-side economics in the welfare conflict space means that anything perceived or effectively defined as an attack on business is also perceived as restricting opportunities for people trying to move out of poverty.

Privatization is the weapon of choice in the regulation of opportunity within the current welfare context. Privatization refers to three distinct mechanisms diffusing the government monopoly on social services: (1) vouchers, (2) welfare transfers to the private sector (e.g., Work Opportunity Tax Credits [WOTC]), and (3) contracting out social service provision. It also reflects the extent to which poverty has come to be defined as an individual problem for which the promotion of business is the purported solution.

The progressive storyline about welfare devolution and privatization is that opportunities for integrating people living in poverty into economic and social systems are maximized by the "flexibilities" of devolution and the "choices" in market logic. The conservative storyline is that devolution affords states greater flexibility in regulating people living in poverty so that institutional stability is not compromised. These intertwined story lines characterize the neoliberal paternalist logic of poverty governance.

Poverty governance is a concept that can be defined structurally, normatively, critically, and in terms of politics and ideology. Structurally, poverty governance refers to the contracting networks, intergovernmental grants, public and private sector loans and loan guarantees, and intricate interjurisdictional regulatory regimes.[1] Normatively, poverty governance refers to processes of governing carried out by laws, norms, power, or language. These processes define the boundaries of inclusion and exclusion, normalcy and deviance, and compliance and disruption.[2] In the United States, management has become the dominant language of governance guided by the principles of neoliberal paternalism. The result is the cultivation of a governing mentality that utilizes the structures of governance (both normative and institutional) to enforce the neoliberal paternalist regime through disciplinary practices that define the normative boundaries of "civil society." It is this marriage of market logic and social order that defines poverty governance in an ideological and political sense.[3] Scholars from a critical perspective contend that neoliberal paternalist poverty governance cultivates self-discipline through governing mentalities that become self-reinforcing orders, regulating the normative values and social order established under neoliberal paternalism.[4] Neoliberalism employs the instruments of governance to create market opportunities, manipulate transaction costs, and impose market discipline (Brown 2006), and paternalism capitalizes on managerial reforms to monitor behavioral expectations, discipline people to market logic, and reinforce social status (Soss, Fording, and Schram 2011a, 2011b). Neoliberal paternalist poverty governance is implemented through devolved authority, increasingly privatized, enacted through diffuse networks of contracted providers, and operates in a competitive environment in which performance metrics dominate evaluations.

The new institutional arrangements of poverty governance serve critical regulating functions at multiple levels of authority throughout the devolved and increasingly privatized system. Poverty governance in the decentralized welfare system increasingly relies on innovative market solutions to generate social value. As influence shifts to the private sector, states attempt to reassert their legitimacy. Blurring sector boundaries has resulted in state legislation authorizing new organizational forms to clarify the balance between private and public motives. The increasing enactment of public purposes by private organizations and heavy competition for revenue in the social sector has resulted in greater scrutiny of nonprofit organizations.

As the nonprofit sector becomes increasingly politicized, extremely wealthy philanthropists have public battles over the value of social wealth. In a July 26, 2013, *New York Times* article, Peter Buffet calls for a reexamination of humanism. He cautions against a charitable-industrial complex overly concerned with the Return on Investment (RoI) rather than systemic change to the processes that feed growing inequalities. Many of the editorial responses to Buffet's article defend the neoliberal rationale for social entrepreneurship, calling for an understanding of the appropriate balance between individual and social objectives in microfinance and economic development. Less than a month later, Bill Gates publicly criticized Google's efforts to enhance Internet connectivity through balloon-based networks in remote parts of the world. Gates's focus on public health priorities highlights ideological differences underlying poverty alleviation strategies.

Broadly speaking, there are three perspectives on development that result in different priorities in social wealth creation: (1) Economic Development Theory; (2) Modernization Theory; and (3) Human Development Theory. Although the strategies for capital formation and growth vary, the basic premise is that economic development is the starting point. This approach equates development with growth and industrialization and focuses on growth and capital formation as poverty alleviation strategies. Modernization Theory assumes that the state has a leading role in fostering market forces. Modern institutions are the priority from this perspective because modern institutions are believed to be the prerequisite for economic development. Proponents of Economic Development and Modernization defend the Google balloons as an effort to facilitate economic growth and modern institutions. Human Development Theory contends that capital growth is not necessarily *progress*. This approach focuses on improving human capital by prioritizing health and education for sustainable growth. The criticism of Google by Bill Gates appears to be motivated by arguments grounded in human development. However, considering the access to resources Microsoft needs to be successful, it is unlikely that Gates is referring to the humanism that Peter Buffet calls upon in his article. Buffet is calling the system into question and asking people to think about the notion of *progress for whom.*

Private actors have increasing authority over public priorities, and the ideological perspectives and attitudes that drive their investments are likely to have a tremendous impact on people living in poverty. Despite the fact that the world's wealthiest tend to be American, poverty in the United States is not the sexiest investment. Ventures in less-developed parts of the world are more appealing from each perspective based on different rationales but for the same reason. The Return on Investment (ROI) is perceived to be higher. Mutuality is assumed by the various approaches to development, and the humanist questions about the "good" of the system provide little description of a system that might be persuasively more humane. Moreover, this discourse is happening without any framework for understanding the system of poverty governance. Beyond performance metrics, little is known about how fashionable investments impact people living in poverty. Private poverty governance increases the influence of the few, but the question remains: Are those influences broadly beneficial?

A considerable body of literature explores welfare policy at various points of the policy process. Yet, there is no framework for understanding findings from these disparate points in the interjurisdictional networks that make up the devolved and privatized process of social issue identification and problem definition, welfare policy formulation, adoption, implementation, evaluation, and feedback in broad perspective. Soss, Fording, and Schram (2011a) depict in great detail the structures, processes, and practices defined by neoliberal paternalism that discipline labor to the interests of the agricultural and tourist industries and shape citizenship according to the traditional status quo in Florida. But, understanding how other states differ in terms of the structures, processes, and practices and how poverty alleviation strategies in different contexts compare requires a map of poverty governance across states. Estimating the extent to which the devolved and privatized system of welfare reform has lived up to its promise necessitates an aggregate analysis of the numbers of people moving out of poverty as a result of welfare reform strategies. This study offers a moving picture of poverty governance that assesses the impact of welfare policies across states over time and details poverty governance throughout the policy process, offering a framework for future research on the specific opportunity structures within the system of poverty governance.

Plan of the Book

The primary purpose of this book is to map the components of the system of poverty governance and assess the aggregate effects of welfare reforms on impoverishment. Mapping the components of the system involves outlining the variations in state policy choices under devolution. It also refers to outlining the emerging trends in the private sector's funding and provision of social services. What is presented here is not an argument that any one state of welfare is necessarily preferred; nor is it an argument against welfare reform or work as a means to self-sufficiency. Instead, I intend to advance the systemic approach to understanding poverty governance in the United States proposed by Soss, Fording, and Schram (2011a). Soss, Fording, and Schram (2011a) present an authoritative study of poverty governance in their comprehensive analysis of workfare in Florida. This study attempts to build on their work in two ways:

1. by outlining the range of variation in devolution and privatization across states so that future research may endeavor to test their hypotheses in other contexts in an effort to comprehensively assess the components of the system of poverty governance; and

2. by examining the extent to which different state policy choices in poverty governance resulting from the political processes evidenced by Soss, Fording, and Schram (2011a) may increase or decrease aggregate levels of impoverishment over time.

I find that the neoliberal paternalist strategies to discipline people living in poverty to markets and a morality entrenched in a history of oppression make it more difficult for people to move out of poverty. In fact, intensity of poverty expands over time as the working hours of people living in poverty increases, and programs such as Individual Development

Accounts (IDAs) and the Earned Income Tax Credit (EITC) have not significantly aided in the transition out of poverty in the aggregate. This book outlines the extent of variation within the system of poverty governance across U.S. states so that the best evidence from various levels of analysis may be compiled to assess how different policy choices, implementation structures, and enactment practices may affect change in impoverishment, and provides a framework for analyzing the increasingly privatized practice of poverty governance.

Patterns of interaction that alienate and exclude increasing numbers of people, whether ascribed or subscribed, negatively impact social, political, and economic exchange and are ultimately destructive. Durable patterns of interaction that demonstrate credible commitments to mutually beneficial exchange are constructive. Impoverishment represents a durable pattern of exclusion that may reasonably be judged destructive if policies contribute to increasing numbers of people living in impoverished circumstances. Anti-poverty policies that construct opportunities for people to move out of poverty produce more durable patterns of exchange. Understanding the present state of welfare by estimating the net effects of welfare reforms across time and space allows for reasonable judgment of the durability of patterns of exchange resulting from welfare reforms.

Chapter 1: Framing the Welfare Policy Process

The boundaries of the welfare conflict space are defined by the understandings generated through the battles over problem definition, the political negotiations over policy design and adoption, the bargaining, competition, and cooperation inherent in the implementation, and the culture and craft of enactment. The potential for learning from these conflicts is contingent upon the type of evaluation or analysis as well as the degree of opportunism. This chapter proceeds by outlining the research defining the nature of those boundaries and the interconnected processes of welfare provision. Then, I describe a theoretical framework for analyzing the impact of welfare policy that offers the potential for learning. Understanding the extent to which different policy choices provide opportunities for large numbers of people to move out of poverty by comparing how programs vary across states is a necessary but not sufficient condition for policy learning. It is essential that we also consider the nature and location of influence in order to ascertain for whom opportunities are afforded. My approach utilizes various analytical strategies to identify how opportunities can be broadly obtained and opportunism minimized. In this chapter, I also explain those analytic strategies.

Chapter 2: The Evolution of Devolution

This chapter describes the process by which the welfare policy experiments diffused welfare policy to state governments and the extent to which welfare reform led to further devolution of authority in poverty governance. The quasi-markets of the diffuse welfare states produce tremendous variation across space and time. This chapter outlines the variation in state policy choices in addressing the objectives of welfare reform and also describes changes in related welfare programs. Because welfare reform led to such an incredible amount of variation, it is impossible to cover every element of welfare devolution. However, this section does provide a thorough overview of the current state of workfare. The purposes of this chapter are twofold: (1) to map the range of variation in poverty governance and provide a frame of reference for putting the pieces of the welfare puzzle together, and (2) to describe the components of the devolved and privatized policies and practices that make up the current American welfare state.

Chapter 3: The States of PRWORA-Related Welfare Programs

This study focuses on welfare programs targeting people living in poverty. A comprehensive examination of all the variations in social policy resulting from welfare reform affecting people living in poverty is beyond the scope of this book. However, there are several changes resulting from PRWORA that are not specific to TANF but need to be considered in order to understand the now fragmented state of welfare for people living in poverty. This chapter details several PRWORA-related programs and outlines their relationship to the poverty reduction strategies of TANF, including the Earned Income Tax Credit (EITC), Work Opportunity Tax Credit (WOTC), Low Income Home Energy Assistance (LIHEAP) and State Emergency Assistance programs, Food and Nutrition Assistance, and Healthcare for low and middle-income families. It is important to consider each of these programs as a component of poverty reduction because they are intended to bridge the gaps between poverty and economic self-sufficiency. The degree of variation across states affords the opportunity for learning from state choices and investments in these programs.

Chapter 4: The Privatization of Poverty Governance

This chapter outlines the privatization of poverty governance. The nature and extent of privatization in the welfare context must be understood in relation to the political rhetoric of reform that shifted blame for social problems onto government and insisted that "the business of government is business." The managerial prescriptions for social ills challenged government to compel individuals to be self-reliant and focus on production efficiency. Consequently, the privatization of welfare has come in three forms: (1) the use of vouchers to allow "citizen consumers" to shop around for things such as training services, for example; (2) contracting out services to private for-profit or nonprofit organizations; and (3) transferring functions and assets from the public sector to the private sector. The story of welfare privatization celebrates the efficiency of competitive services that are believed to allow individuals to choose their own adventure. Additionally, the paternalist story of private ownership of social issues is fed by a long history of race-gendered oppression in contractual arrangements. New Public Management (NPM) repackages the myth of the self-made man in "responsible citizenship" stories that capitalize on historical patterns of social, economic, and political exchange that advantage those privileged by a long history of property rights. Market-oriented managerial reforms utilized outcomes evaluation to justify increasing private provision of governance. Privatization has the potential to increase the efficiency of governance and the stability of authority. However, little is known about the costs, risks, and implications of privatizing poverty governance. The purpose of this chapter is to describe the extent of privatization across U.S. states in order to assess the aggregate effects of devolution and privatization over time.

CHAPTER 5: WORKFARE POLICIES AND THE STATE OF SELF-SUFFICIENCY

This chapter provides a picture of the American welfare state over time by assessing the net effects of welfare policies and practices across U.S. states as welfare reforms have developed. The data utilized in this study represent the best available measures of each of the variables over a full cycle of the policy process (a panel of U.S. states from 1990 to 2008). A feasible generalized least squares regression with correction for heteroskedasticity tests the net effects of each of the variables on impoverishment, and the results demonstrate that welfare reforms that increasingly subsidize the private sector increase impoverishment despite high work effort among TANF participants. In fact, TANF participants working more hours increasingly intensifies poverty, and Individual Development Accounts (IDAs) and state Earned Income Tax Credits (EITCs) do not significantly ease transitions out of poverty in the aggregate. The weight of the evidence affords considerable leverage in the understanding of welfare reforms as antipoverty measures and suggests a great deal about the type of feedback that can be expected given the current state of welfare. Putting this evidence together with the existing body of knowledge on poverty governance illustrates the degenerative process outlined by Schneider and Ingram (2005). In addition, the evidence presented in this study offers recommendations regarding policy choices that might reverse the degenerative trend in poverty policy. It also identifies gaps in our knowledge of the poverty governance system that can be useful for future research.

CHAPTER 6: PHILANTHROCAPITALISM: "NEW MARKETS" FOR SOCIAL SERVICES

Poverty governance in the decentralized welfare system increasingly relies on innovative market solutions to generate social value. The instruments for creating opportunities, manipulating transaction costs, and imposing market discipline varies according to the opportunity structures designed in state welfare policies and the state laws of charitable disposition. This section describes how social entrepreneurship and venture philanthropy are "innovating" poverty governance. By outlining the variation across state contexts and capturing the wealth leveraged by new poverty ventures across the hybrid spectrum, an increasing decentralization of welfare policy is evident, as are efforts by the state to reassert its legitimacy in regulating the instruments of welfare provision as they diversify.

CONCLUSION

The concluding chapter explores the dilemmas and challenges of the privatized polity and offers directions for future research. Examining the factors that affect impoverishment across the states of welfare in the United States leads to some dilemmas. A more liberal citizenry contributes to lower impoverishment, but disciplinary poverty governance in states with higher rates of paternalism lowers voting, political participation, civic participation, and engagement (Soss, Fording, and Schram 2011a). This certainly lowers the likelihood that the perspectives of people living in poverty will influence welfare policy and may contribute to more degenerative discourse in which the expansion of private influence increasingly subjugates target groups to governing authorities. If the mobilized citizenry is less socially liberal and unrepresentative of the people at risk of impoverishment, poverty may become even more entrenched as private interests are distanced from people with low political power and low social status.

Corruption is another dilemma of the welfare state. The emphasis on the mythical welfare queen and the obsession with preventing welfare fraud under conditions in which the "undeserving" and "deviant" people living in poverty are targeted without mutual restraint on public authority poses at least a few potential problems. First, loosening the restraints on those governing poverty policy is likely to contribute to more corruption. Second, the dishonesty about the nature of welfare fraud is likely to undermine the trust essential to all forms of exchange. Third, democratic liberty and popular sovereignty promote trust (Brehm and Rahn 1997), and an erosion of widespread political influence and a concentration of influence among the few allow opportunism to flourish. Fourth, failures to affect impoverishment increase economic, political, and social distance. This divides interests and ultimately undermines the willingness to cooperate with one another.

The evidence presented in *Privatizing the Polity* provides a moving picture of how policy impacts people living in poverty. Understanding the state that we are in is a necessary first step in figuring out how to improve upon our current circumstance. Future research is necessary to understand how the increasingly privatized practice of welfare provision might serve broader interests and to critically reflect on the interests pursued. Consequently, this book concludes by outlining numerous opportunities for further research on poverty governance that may fill in the gaps in our knowledge regarding how policies and practices compare as antipoverty measures.

Framing the Welfare Policy Process

Public policy is concerned with problem definition, issue construction, agenda setting, the emergence of policy options, the actions (or inactions) of governance, and the effects and impact of such action or inaction. Welfare policy articulates values, crafts meaning, justifies political decisions, assigns or reinforces status, and may even attempt to solve social problems. The boundaries of the welfare conflict space are defined by the understandings generated through the battles over problem definition, the political negotiations over policy design and adoption, the bargaining, competition, and cooperation inherent in the implementation, and the culture and craft of enactment. The potential for learning from these conflicts is contingent upon the type of evaluation or analysis as well as the degree of opportunism.

This chapter proceeds by outlining the research defining the nature of those boundaries and the interconnected processes of welfare provision. Then, I describe a theoretical framework for analyzing the impact of welfare policy that offers the potential for learning. Understanding the extent to which different policy choices provide opportunities for large numbers of people to move out of poverty by comparing how programs vary across states is a necessary but not sufficient condition for policy learning. It is essential that we also consider the nature and location of influence in order to ascertain for whom opportunities are afforded. My approach utilizes various analytical strategies to identify how opportunities can be broadly obtained and opportunism minimized. In this chapter, I also explain those analytic strategies.

Organizing the Welfare Literature throughout the Policy Process

Welfare policy as a field of study began with the definition of poverty as a social problem. Stories of welfare practices in the United States cannot be easily untangled from the Judeo-Christian traditions that defined the worldviews of the colonists and shaped the approach that the colonies took toward the welfare of the native populations. In many respects, those stories emphasize compassion, but the practices reveal patterns of compassion for those deemed worthy. In the European Christian worldview, God's will was invoked to enrich and empower Christian followers. Consequently, Native Americans represented an opportunity to convert more souls and justify the taking of native lands in the name of God and the monarchy. Alternatively, the concepts of reciprocity and the practice of gift exchange were the central tenets of building relationships, forming alliances, addressing disparate needs, and established the welfare customs of the North American Indians. Reciprocity and gift exchange are based on the behavior of the "other" and maintain an emphasis on long-term objectives. These practices represent fundamental differences in the worldviews of the colonists and the indigenous population regarding human welfare. Attempts to enslave Native North Americans were unsuccessful, so contracts for indentured servitude, primarily performed by African slaves, convicts, paupers, and servants from the British Isles and throughout the continent of Europe, were sanctioned by colonial authorities. The contracts often provided the prospect of land ownership as an incentive at the end of the period of service, but the condition of servitude also often required conversion to Christianity and was justified as a charitable act by Christians.[1]

In the early colonial period in America, Christians were legally defined as worthy of the protections of the state. The word *Christian* in the legal code defined the rights and obligations of citizenship. The legalization of the institution of slavery in New England in 1641 shifted the legal discourse to an emphasis on "Black[ness]" identifying the subjects of private property, making slavery perpetual and inheritable in the North American colonies and subsequently the United States while retaining the proceeds of the Christian identity.[2] The legacy of stories of compassion and the practices of judging the worthiness of the "other" viewed through the lens of religion and race continue to affect the character of welfare in the United States as the "problem of poverty" is constructed and reconstructed.

The development of the various stages of the American welfare system begins on a path set by the English Poor Laws.[3] During the Tudor period (1485–1603), fundamentalist battles between conservative Catholics and Reformers contributed to increasing the challenges of poverty as the closing of the monasteries in the 1530s limited the help available to people living in poverty. Demographic changes, high rates of poverty, and power politics during this period also resulted in increasing migration to the American colonies by Reformers in particular. Two years prior to the end of the Tudor dynasty, the Act for the Relief of the Poor (1601), commonly referred to as the Elizabethan Poor Law, was passed by Parliament formalizing the practices of poor relief and refining the Act for the Relief of the Poor (1597). In the state-centric view, this is the origin of the legal construction of poverty as a social problem necessitating the use of governing authority.

The English system of poor relief was imported during the colonial period and has since been characterized by localism in implementation and in the moral justifications for definitions of deservingness (Handler and Hasenfeld 1991; Katz 1989; Quigley 1999), which have always included gender, race, ethnic, and religious dimensions (Gordon 2002). Participation has been marked by stigma (Handler and Hasenfeld 1991), and the welfare state federally structured by the New Deal institutionalized the race-gendered, Judeo-Christian justifications regarding who is deserving and who is undeserving (Lieberman 1998; Mettler 1998). The federal programs for the "deserving" included Social Security Old Age Insurance, Unemployment Insurance, Old Age Assistance, Aid to the Blind, and Aid to the Permanently and Totally Disabled. Separate state and local aid programs were widely perceived as inferior (Heclo 1994) and targeted those who did not fit the "white male breadwinner" model. However, state and local policy choices regarding job category eligibility were often designed to exclude women and people of color (Liberman 1998; Mettler 1998).

The role of mass pressures and resistance as a factor in the expansion of welfare coverage is fairly well established by scholars using the comparative method (Fording 1997; Piven and Cloward 1971; Schram and Turbett 1983). Additionally, beneficent responses to black insurgency specifically have been contingent upon electoral access and political mobilization as well as the black share of the population (Fording 2001). In other words, when black citizens did not have adequate access to electoral institutions and strong political mobilization or where the black population represented a smaller share of the state population, increases in incarceration rates with few concessions for welfare relief were evident in response to mass insurgency.

Stories of provider corruption and claimant fraud have their roots in the patronage practices characterizing Civil War Pensions (Skocpol 1992), and using these stories as a strategy for discrediting welfare has long been a conservative strategy for dismantling the welfare state (Piven and Cloward 1971). Anti–welfare fraud campaigns were especially common and particularly effective in the South by focusing on black caseloads and calling upon the myth of black criminality and the myth of black laziness (Gustafson 2009; Jordan-Zachery 2009; Kohler-Hausmann 2007; Reese 2005; see also

Mendelberg 2001; Schram, Soss, Fording 2001). Political rhetoric and mass media framed welfare politics with a black face. In the 1960s, race dominated the welfare politics conflict space, and myths of black laziness, criminality, and irresponsibility were used to recast welfare policy as the problem rather than poverty (Gilens 2000; Peffley and Hurwitz 1999). The welfare policy process—from problem definition and issue framing, policy formulation, adoption, implementation, to feedback—thus cycles around patterns of historical disadvantage.

When an issue finds a frame that situates it within the public purview, it may gain attention in a number of ways. Poverty may gain attention in the media and from the public when white males experience widespread unemployment or when a pervasive economic crisis challenges stereotypical representations of poverty.[4] Furthermore, racial isolation and chronic subordination locate poverty outside of the dominant American consciousness in the absence of a focusing event that receives widespread national attention (such as a natural disaster).[5] It is also the case that the episodic framing of poverty has been shown to privatize the scope of welfare conflict; while thematic framing tends to encourage social attributions to the causes of poverty.[6] The process of framing poverty as a particular kind of problem is constructed within the existing policy context, and the current context framing poverty policy is one in which political opportunism and negative, stereotypical representations of people living in poverty limit participation and debate.[7]

The opportunistic and stereotypical framing of poverty in the current context has restricted participation and debate to the extent that neither party is aligned with the preferences of low-income constituents (Rigby and Wright 2013). People living in poverty do not appear to influence social policy, and the interests of people living in poverty are left off the active agenda when they diverge from the interests of those with higher incomes (Rigby and Wright 2013). Among elected officials, black women tend to give the most attention to the issue of poverty, and the ability of politicians concerned with poverty to influence the institutional agenda regulates poverty as a public priority.[8] If poverty reaches the institutional agenda, the race-gendered representation of the policy target affects the options considered. Public attitudes toward welfare are conditioned upon the race and gender of the perceived beneficiaries,[9] and media framing of "welfare queens" shifted public opinion against welfare based on false notions that undeserving women of color were the primary beneficiaries.[10] Women of color are framed as undeserving and deviant, so when attempts to make poverty policy a priority are met with negative race-gendered associations, the issue of poverty is not likely to become a priority.[11] In fact, race and gender have been manipulated to systematically associate public policies with "undeserving" groups in efforts to undermine or dismantle social programs.[12]

The race-gendered nature of welfare discourse also influences policy formulation and design.[13] When poverty moves up the institutional agenda, the potential policy remedies are contingent upon the policy target.[14] Those advantaged by positive social constructions and political power receive welfare benefits that tend to be oversubscribed, often unquestioned, and sometimes even not conceived of as welfare. For example, one man at a political gathering in Simpsonville, South Carolina, in 2009, yelled at Republican representative Robert Inglis, "Keep your government hands off my Medicare!" His misguided statement aptly characterizes the wider Tea Party resistance to perceived "government takeovers" of healthcare and student loans. The political mobilization of these widening demographics are likely to maintain the political power of both the aging and student populations, but the framing of one or the other as greedy or deviant might shift that group to contenders. Contenders in welfare policy have political power but are negatively socially constructed. Dependents, on the other hand, lack political power but are constructed as basically good people. For example, people receiving food stamps tend to lack political power as they are less likely civically engaged; while there is a stigma associated with participation in the program, participants are generally described as in need and not taking advantage. This is increasingly the case as more middle-class educated whites find themselves turning to food assistance during the long Great Recession. Alternatively, those who lack political power and are negatively constructed are regularly set up for punishing policies. Welfare reform built the mechanisms for punishment in poverty governance through the "stick and carrot" approach to behavioral management. People living in poverty who are negatively socially constructed and live in jurisdictions where their political mobilization is a potential threat to the status quo are more likely to be subject to sanctions. For example, states with large populations of people of color tended to opt for second-order devolution to manage people living in poverty at the county or regional level, and racial isolation in these states results in disparate sanctioning of people of color at that level.[15]

Because the wealthy are more likely to have large organizations lobbying on their behalf, they are much more likely to directly participate in the formulation of policy (Winters and Page 2009). While campaign contributions amplify the voice of the wealthy and both parties rely on affluent donors to finance their campaigns, legislative proposals and the analyses that are used to support them are most often produced by organizations controlled by the wealthy. Policy formulation, like all aspects of the policy process, is a fluid and ongoing course of negotiations that take place in multiple intergovernmental venues. Access to those conflict spaces is a fundamental aspect of "who gets what, when, and how." These negotiations shape the consideration of policy options, the causal framework for potential policy action, and the venue in which action might be taken. Successful negotiations result in policy adoption.

The formal adoption of a policy necessitates administrative action outlining the implementation structures and procedures. Despite an "inadvertent bipartisanship" characterizing the "national consensus" to reform "the poor" and the bureaucracy, states did not take a systematic approach to the adoption of welfare reform policy choices.[16] States in which blacks made up a larger percentage of the welfare caseload were significantly more likely to adopt more disciplinary program features (Soss, Fording, and Schram 2011a). Numerous studies indicate that state policy choices to restrict benefit levels and eligibility respond to the racial makeup of the caseload, tax revenues, overall caseloads, Republican control of the statehouse, and a more conservative citizenry (see R. Brown 1995; Hero 1998; Howard 1999; Orr 1976; Plotnick and Winters 1985; Soss, Fording, and Schram 2011a; Wright 1976). Additionally, the percentage of black residents and their relative dispersion across the state were a primary factor determining whether or not states adopted second-order devolution. Although devolution may serve conservative, progressive, and/or democratic purposes in general (Freeman and Rogers 2007; Fung 2004), state decisions to localize authority in poverty governance are most likely in states in which there is a larger black population unevenly dispersed in an effort to strengthen social control (Soss, Fording, and Schram 2011a). State choices in the adoption of first or second-order devolution as a governing structure are politically contingent. The adoption of second-order devolution represents a conscious effort by the state to use "flexibilities" to manage the "underclass," and racial disparities in sanctioning patterns likewise reflect local control over people of color (Soss, Fording, and Schram 2011a). States with higher percentages of racial minorities in the welfare caseload tend to adopt more disciplinary measures and are more likely to adopt second-order devolution (Soss, Fording, and Schram 2011a).

The implementation of public policy is highly responsive to the environment. In other words, poverty governance is an open system (Keiser and Soss 1998) in which portals of influence in implementation come from a variety of actors (Derthick 1990), the political orientations and cultural beliefs of agency personnel and the local community (Khademian 2002), the attitudes and beliefs about poverty held by those responsible for social service provision (Reingold and Liu 2009), organizational norms (March and Olsen 2006; J. Martin 1992; Weick 1995), as well as the "political and task environments" (Meier 1993). The street-level action of implementation imposes poverty governance. The everyday practices of social service providers enact policy, giving meaning to the law and interpreting the values represented in policy. Devolution and privatization were justified as strategies for making government more flexible, accountable, and responsive, and the findings regarding the implementation of these reforms are mixed. Some find that devolution mobilizes the citizenry and enhances volunteerism (Gonzales-Baker 1993; Marston 1993); while others find that the devolved public-private partnerships tend to lead to staff professionalization that distances volunteers and community ties, particularly as competition among nonprofits increases (Smith and Lipsky 1993). Studies also indicate that local control over implementation increases the influence of community employers and political actors (Katz 1996; Piven and Cloward 1993; Ward 2005).

Policy implementation makes policy through action and is therefore inherently political (Lineberry 1977). Consequently, the use of "sticks" and "carrots" to promote compliance are likely to vary in accordance with the ideological makeup of the region of authority (Ridzi 2009) and client characteristics (Hasenfeld, Ghose, and Larson 2004; Kalil, Seefeldt, and Wang 2002; Keiser, Mueser, and Choi 2004; Koralek 2000; Wu et al. 2006). The implementation of the punitive elements of welfare reform, such as sanctions, are products of governance, and the appropriate level of analysis for understanding patterns of punitiveness in poverty governance is determined by the level of devolution (Soss, Fording, and Schram 2011a). In fact, poverty governance that is most responsive to local control exhibits disciplinary practices that are more punitive in conservative counties, and risk disparities accumulate over time (Soss, Fording, and Schram 2011a). Marital status, age, family size, education level, work experience, and race are the factors that determine who is most likely to be subject to the punitive elements of TANF (Hasenfeld, Ghose, and Larson 2004; Kalil, Seefeldt, and Wang 2002; Koralek 2000; Pavetti, Derr, and Hesketh 2003; Wu et al. 2006). State-level aggregations of national sanctioning patterns also indicate that states with larger nonwhite caseloads sanction more frequently and that state sanction patterns respond to individual-level factors that are often contingent upon the order of devolution (Kim and Fording 2010; Soss, Fording, and Schram 2011a).

Managerial reforms and welfare privatization have substantially changed the implementation of social policy. The successful push to implement Osbourne and Gaebler's (1992) strategies for "reinventing government" through "innovative" consumer-oriented, cross-sector collaborations modified service provision in at least two broad ways: (1) managerial practices replaced the "helping relationships" model of service provision and (2) service provision shifted from government agencies to private for-profit and nonprofit organizations. The "welfare management gold rush" resulting from welfare outsourcing was typically framed in the media as opportunities for profitable investment in social capital and as a cost-saving efficiency

(Brophy-Baermann and Bloeser 2006; A. Cohen 1998; Ehrenreich 1997), but the real story was that billions of dollars in state and local service contracts were transferred to the private sector, primarily to for-profit corporations (Sanger 2003).

The evidence regarding the efficiency, effectiveness, fairness, or accountability of private implementation of welfare is mixed. Where there is adequate capacity and experience in contract management, policy expertise, political savvy, negotiation and mediation skills, oversight capabilities, and effective communication, welfare contracting performs at its peak (Kettl 1993). However, contractors regularly use information asymmetries to advance their own interests in a managerial context focused on performance measures that do not capture service quality and where competitive bidding is rarely the standard (DeParle 2004). Carol Miller (2001) demonstrates that the privatization of disability services resulted in fewer clients served and a decline in effectiveness. A 2006 audit of the privatized child protective services in Florida found increases in the incidence of abuse and a 70% increase in costs (*Tampa Tribune* 2006a). There have also been incidents in which audits reveal cases of fraud by private contractors (see L. Brown and Jacobs 2008; Caputo 2004a, 2004b). Privatization has not been shown to produce cost savings across very many contexts (Vestal 2006), and the limited competition for contracts undermines the assumed competitive market gains (Handler and Hasenfeld 2007). The efficiency, accountability, savings, and performance of welfare privatization depends on competitive pressures from multiple bidders, a situation that is less likely over time as public sector capacity diminishes and the costs of entry and exit become increasingly disparate (AFSCME 2006; Van Slyke 2003).

Research on the use of discretion in the implementation of welfare suggests that federal guidelines inhibit challenges to systemic practices (Lens and Vorsanger 2005; Soss 2000) and focus managerial attention on quantitative metrics to the exclusion of concerns regarding well-being (Brodkin 2006). The formal implementation procedures and informal patterns of practice among welfare service providers efficiently shed caseloads by imposing costs that have a pronounced effect on those vulnerable to information asymmetries and time constraints (Brodkin and Majmundar 2010). "Welfare leavers" are often discouraged from reapplying for welfare despite the temporary and contingent nature of their job market (Handler and Hasenfeld 2007). The exercise of discretion employs procedures that may make resources less accessible to those living in disadvantaged circumstances in which the presence of choice is increasingly limited as disadvantages accumulate (Cherlin, Bogen, Quane, and Burton 2002; Super 2004). In addition, case worker discretion interacts with race and ethnicity in a highly complex manner that varies at the state, local, organizational, and individual level

(Brodkin and Majmundar 2010; Fording, Soss, Schram 2011; Watkins-Hayes 2009). Welfare rights advocates were concerned about the abuse of discretionary power by caseworkers, particularly with respect to the discrimination against minorities in access and utilization. At the same time, there are some estimates that suggest that by 1973 16% of welfare payments were overpayments or payments made to ineligible families (Bane and Ellwood 1994), conflating the notion of the "undeserving other." Consternation regarding discretion by caseworkers resulting in discrimination and payment errors led to various efforts to limit discretionary power. The Department of Health, Education, and Welfare (HEW) issued an order separating income maintenance from social services. A series of Supreme Court decisions restricted states from enacting their own eligibility rules. The federal government also implemented measures intended to minimize payment errors. The restructuring and oversight by each of the three institutions of government was aimed at gaining compliance with the rules and procedures of the federal program and to compel impartial administration. Consequently, bureaucratization and eligibility determination based on means-testing characterized this state of being in welfare administration.

The organizational cultures and enactment practices of welfare agencies under AFDC were described as "fundamentally flawed" (see Winston et al. 2002) by "permissive" mentalities that failed to teach the "underclass" how to behave (Mead 1992). The concerns at the heart of the controversy about welfare were complex and further complicated by bureaucratic politics. The widespread perception that the vast, impersonal, and cumbersome welfare bureaucracy of AFDC was a failure was met with nuanced stories regarding the appropriate role of government. Scholars such as Teles (1998) and Mead (1992, 1997, 1998) argued that the unpopular federal welfare program hurts people in poverty more than it helps and suggested that government should instill a strong work ethic by leading through traditional social values. These arguments at the center-Right, though different in important ways, met with the fairly sophisticated communitarian notions of social justice from the center-Left, noting that citizenship requires responsibilities as well as rights (see, e.g., Etzioni 1994, 2000; Galston 1991) and producing a story line in which poverty governance supervises the work responsibilities of people living in poverty. Efforts to reform the bureaucracy, to restructure or dismantle the welfare state, the revolutionary turn to the right in American politics, and the glocalization of social policy are among the critical political factors that converged in the 1990s when the Clinton administration greatly expanded the number of waivers approved. The welfare policy experiments provided a forum for welfare stories told by researchers, politicians, bureaucrats, business leaders, lobbyists, and the media, but largely absent was the perspective of people living in poverty.[17]

The neoliberal paternalist ideology that dominates welfare case management under TANF replaces social work practices with the business model, reorganizing the casework experience for caseworkers, not just clients (Ridzi 2009). Recasting welfare service provision from the helping professions to production management disciplines agencies, case workers, and clients to the neoliberal logic of behavioral management and performance metrics (Schram, Soss, Houser, and Fording 2009). The emphasis on meeting legal obligations with performance metrics has been shown to distort incentives and create problematic working relationships between providers who need to cooperate to meet client objectives but who are expected to compete to maintain the organizational performance (Schram et al. 2010). One of the most noteworthy findings regarding enactment also indicates a persistent problem in the feedback loop. Poverty alleviation is more difficult where there is a pervasive failure to account for the client's perspective (Dias and Maynard-Moody 2006).

Evaluation is inherent throughout the process. Program evaluation in poverty governance is dominated by performance metrics. The objectives defined in the law and in contracting relationships specify the measurements and determine the outcomes assessed. Researchers, policy analysts, and other "experts" provide feedback that may differ in approach, depending upon whether the assumption is that policy causes politics or that politics cause policy. Yet by and large, performance metrics limit the extent to which learning is possible in the system (see Cohen and Levinthal 1990).

Persistent exclusion of the interests of any group is likely to demobilize and further marginalize that group over time (Schattschneider 1960; Solt 2008). Resources structure political advantages as wealthier people tend to have more information, time, and civic skills, which tends to lead to higher rates of registration, voting, lobbying, and campaign contributions (Verba, Schlozman, and Brady 2006; Winters and Page 2009). In fact, longitudinal evidence indicates that paternalist welfare governance regimes lower the likelihood of voting, political participation, civic participation, and civil engagement (Bruch, Ferree, and Soss 2010). And, empirical investigations of the interplay between economic and political inequality demonstrate strong differences in the responsiveness of policymakers to citizens from different income groups, with heightened attention to the affluent at the expense of lower income groups (Bartels 2008; Druckman and Jacobs 2011; Jacobs and Page 2005; Jacobs and Soss 2010; Rigby and Wright 2011, 2013). The governing mentality of compliance with the neoliberal logic and to paternalist behavioral expectations increases the civic and political marginality of people living in poverty (Soss, Fording, and Schram 2011a). Over time, the contracting relationships generate interdependence between the public agency and the private contractor (Smith and Lipsky 1993). Public and

private agencies develop long-term relationships in which the costs of exit
for either party increase over time, producing political regimes that affect
the character of service delivery and regulate the welfare contracting market
(Smith 2007). The weight of the evidence demonstrates that the pursuit
of discipline subjugates women and people of color, limits citizenship to
workers/consumers, and pushes people in poverty further to the margins (see
Bruch, Ferree, and Soss 2010; Collins and Mayer 2010; Soss 2000; Stone
2008; Soss, Fording, and Schram 2011a; Wacquant 2009; L. White 2002).
The escalating political and social marginalization of people living in poverty is likely to produce more degenerative effects as political opportunities
rely on expanding categories of deviance (see Schneider and Ingram 1999)
and as increasing social and political exclusion continue to decrease the
likelihood that the preferences of the marginalized might be considered for
the political agenda (Bachrach and Baratz 1962). Consequently, the feedback loop in the system of poverty governance appears to be spiraling toward
growing inequalities that may be fueled by some of the practices of poverty
governance, and program evaluations dependent on performance metrics are
not adequate for learning how these policies and practices compare.

There is a tremendous amount of welfare research testing causal
notions that are focused on particular aspects of the policy process. However, there is very little to link the findings in these discrete units to build
an understanding of the fluid and diffuse system of poverty governance as
it evolves. To date, a systemic framework for understanding the operation
of the structures, policies, and evolving practices of poverty governance
remains absent from the literature. Outlining the structure of devolution is
essential to selecting the appropriate level of analysis and making reasonable
comparisons across contexts. Locating the shifting sources of authority is
crucial for discerning the elements in the system that may alleviate poverty.
This book provides a thorough description of how state poverty governance
structures compare and examines the role state policy choices may play in
creating opportunities for people living in poverty through welfare programs
and enabling legislation that may foster social entrepreneurship. The systemic study of poverty governance centered on poverty alleviation as an
organizing principle provides a comprehensive understanding of how antipoverty policy might be designed to promote self-sufficiency with minimal
intervention. The purpose of this proposed framework is to offer a forum for
scholars interested in poverty alleviation to build knowledge from various
perspectives across the policy process on poverty governance.

The system of poverty governance is inherently political, fluid and
diffuse, subject to manipulation, and regularly the target of reform. The
set of interrelated concepts in the systemic analysis of poverty governance
includes the following:

- the networked, contractual, and interjurisdictional regulatory regime of policies and practices;

- the aggregate impact of policy choices on opportunities to move out of poverty;

- the perspectives and experiences of people living in poverty;

- the organizations enacting social service provision; and

- public consciousness about poverty and welfare.

The system of poverty governance is delimited by the networked, contractual, and interjurisdictional regulatory regime of policies and practices governing welfare in the United States. Policy choices across jurisdictions at multiple levels of analysis generate a considerable degree of variation within the system, but this fluidity maintains the system equilibrium over time. Change tends to be incremental and is framed within the boundaries of inclusion and exclusion that set the system parameters, defined by deeply held beliefs in moral individualism in the United States. Capturing the impact of policy adjustments requires 10 to 12 years of data.[18] This book utilizes 18 years of data to examine the role of state poverty governance structures and policies in fostering opportunities for individuals and private organizations. I show that while there is a tremendous amount of variation deserving of further attention at all levels of the interjurisdictional networks of governance, state structures and policies locate opportunities.

Theoretical Approach

Theories of impoverishment attempt to explain why people are poor. Broadly speaking, there are three ways to understand poverty: (1) poverty as pathology; (2) poverty as accident; or (3) poverty as structure. Theories of the sources of poverty from these perspectives overlap at times but generally tend to be antagonistic to each other. The belief that behavioral characteristics explain why people living in poverty are poor is a common explanation. The assumption is that people living in poverty have character deficits, psychological or cognitive weaknesses, and motivational inadequacies. People living in poverty are presumed to lack the ability to delay gratification, save money, control their sexuality, and avoid criminal activity. The location of pathology may vary from the individual, family, to the culture. Culture of poverty arguments contend that people living in poverty are trapped in an intergenerational pattern of insecurity, irrationality, marginality, low aspirations, and low expectations. The culture of poverty approach theorizes about an "underclass" characterized by weak community organization, dysfunctional families, political apathy, an incapacity or refusal to participate in legitimate labor markets, disengagement from law enforcement, and a lack of integration in mainstream institutions, such as banks. The policy prescription attempts to address the pathology. Proponents of this view contend that ending poverty requires demanding self-sufficiency, fostering self-motivation, and facilitating self-esteem among people living in poverty. Complicating matters, there are two cultural forces at play that are theorized to fuel poverty: (1) the broader beliefs and attitudes in society about people living in poverty, which perpetuate stereotypes; and (2) the shared outlooks, modes of behavior, traditions, belief systems, worldviews, values, skills, and preferences that emerge from patterns of isolated intragroup interaction that serve to limit access and/or utilization of opportunities. Within this perspective there are two opposing programmatic approaches: (1) some call for investments in social work and therapeutic solutions, and (2) others argue that restricting access to welfare benefits and associated programs that are presumed to make people "dependent" is the only solution. Critics of the notion of poverty as an individual, familial, or cultural pathology point out several limitations. First, there is no valid or reliable definition of character to base such assessments. Second, there is no evidence that people living in poverty are any more or less lazy, pathological, self-destructive, passive, aggressive, psychologically or cognitively deficient, or immoral than any other group. Third, the behaviors of people living in poverty can easily be understood as rational when the context is taken into account. For example, there are a number of rational responses to oppressive conditions that include but are not limited to working in the informal economy when discrimination limits access to legitimate opportunities. States influenced by paternalist beliefs that people living in poverty are pathological or in need of help set up TANF programs in which the government (by proxy) teaches people to save, treats perceived family dysfunction, etc. The extent to which these programs may help people move out of poverty are likely to be conditioned upon race, gender, and the level of analysis.

Explanations of poverty as an accident claim that poverty results from temporary weakness in the economy and not necessarily the result of pathological behavior. When economic growth slows, employees are laid off. The weak demand for labor makes people vulnerable to impoverishment based on their location in the market. Poverty is believed to be temporary, so short-term relief is the policy prescription proposed by this perspective. Unemployment insurance, job training, and public programs are strategies proponents contend are necessary to get people through when the economy is not providing enough jobs. However, political support for programs that might benefit people living in poverty is difficult to maintain. Yet, some critics of the theory of poverty as an accident contend that short-term relief is inadequate because the temporary natures of the programs and policies do not aim to eliminate poverty. On the other hand, proponents of the poverty as pathology view criticize even short-term relief for generating "dependency" among people living in poverty. Some scholars also point out that accidents that happen repeatedly may be patterned elsewhere in the market. This critique takes on distinct flavors. Those who focus on structural or institutional sources note that discrimination or patterned preferences make some people repeatedly (and perhaps increasingly) vulnerable to poverty, which might make an instance of poverty potentially accidental but not patterns of impoverishment. Culture of poverty proponents argue that these patterns are evidence of pathology. In any case, welfare reform made relief temporary, but the extent to which states limited access to relief under welfare reform reflects the belief that pathology should be addressed in state policy.

The theory that poverty is a function of the structure of the U.S. capitalist system contends that uneven and unreliable labor demand are fundamental aspects of capitalism. Essentially, the claim is that capitalist exploitation requires cheap labor for wealth accumulation. Proponents of this perspective point to the weakened industrial structure in the United States and the rise of business class political power that undermined labor protections and put downward pressure on wages. Policy prescriptions from this perspective call on government to enhance political engagement and economic integration. Structural theorists strategize cross-class collaborative policy designed to benefit workers and the unemployed, not just the wealthy. Strategies addressing the structural components of poverty also include creating government jobs for the unemployed. From this perspective, government intervention to facilitate a living wage is justified. Opponents attack the structural view of poverty from the left and the right. The modern version of laissez-faire doctrine that has dominated American thought on political economy since the 1970s makes structural claims highly controversial. The hope that the uninhibited and unregulated economic power to leverage wealth will eventually be the "tide the raises all ships" has become a taken-for-granted notion. Yet despite this opposition, strategies addressing the structural factors causing poverty are also evident in poverty governance.

The award-winning book *Separate Societies*, by William W. Goldsmith and Edward J. Blakely (2013) describes how each of these theories of impoverishment was capitalized on by various political forces during global economic restructuring, dividing and isolating people living in poverty. They demonstrate that race, gender, and class divisions separate assets and opportunities, locating assets and opportunities among the privileged and isolating people living in poverty in underemployed communities with depleted public services. The evidence they provide shows that poverty policies contribute to contemporary trends in growing inequalities rather than combating poverty. Jacob Hacker (2006) argues that corporate and political leaders could have responded to dramatic economic shifts by enhancing safety nets, but the "personal responsibility" crusade and "ownership society" ideal instead produced a society of empowered owners and shifted risk to the rest. He shows that the increasing economic insecurity resulting from policy choices that subsidize "mini-welfare states" in the private sector are spreading risk beyond the isolated "poor and uneducated" to "educated, upper-middle-class Americans" as public and private insulation from economic shifts erode.

POVERTY GOVERNANCE ACCORDING TO NEOLIBERAL PATERNALISM

The neoliberal economic theory of welfare supposes the welfare function is an aggregation of individual utility maximization. The primary contentions are that market rules, free trade, and private property rights govern and that public policy should contribute to conditions that enhance exchange. Market dynamics are presumed to enhance individual liberty, where individual liberty is defined as the unfettered pursuit of self-interest and the freedom from external coercion. Neoliberalism within the political rhetoric of "Reaganomics" or supply-side economics has dominated American political discourse and finds appeal among liberals and conservatives.

The progressive storyline about welfare devolution and privatization was that opportunities for integrating people living in poverty into economic and social systems are maximized by the "flexibilities" of devolution and the "choices" in market logic. The conservative storyline was that devolution afforded states greater flexibility in regulating people living in poverty so that institutional stability was not compromised. These intertwined storylines characterize the neoliberal paternalist logic of poverty governance that structures the implementation of welfare, and the paternalist stories of social order typify the enactment of welfare service provision. Although the dominance of neoliberal paternalism attempts to present this perspective as the only legitimate story of poverty governance, the evolving welfare story presented here allows for an understanding of poverty governance as a system in which there are numerous opportunities for improvement that can be identified with adequate perspective. Every story has a moral, and the moral of this story is that poverty alleviation is a worthwhile goal. The evidence in this study shows that circumstances in which the system of poverty governance is focused on regulation over poverty alleviation contribute to greater impoverishment overall. A systemic framework is essential because the level of analysis is highly variable and critically important in poverty governance.

Neoliberal poverty governance colored by the theme of moral individualism produces a welfare story that increasingly subjugates people living in poverty to narrowly defined market forces. The states of consciousness regarding welfare are increasingly influenced by private for-profit and non-profit organizations responsible for social service provision. This welfare privatization refers to three distinct mechanisms diffusing the government monopoly on services. First, vouchers are a common form of privatization utilized in many welfare programs for choices among training providers, methods of paying vendors in lieu of providing cash assistance to partici-pants, and assistance with education at two- or four-year colleges that part-ner with the state for certain job categories or professions that are in demand in the state. Second, the welfare transfers to the private sector are many and varied. Benefits like the Work Opportunity Tax Credit (WOTC) to subsidize hiring and the utilization of workforce development boards/commissions in some states to oversee the efficient regulation of the state's labor force are a few examples. Third, contracting out is an option that states have for all aspects of service provision. Welfare privatization also refers to the increas-ing privatization of the conflict space.

The new institutional arrangements of poverty governance serve critical regulating functions at multiple levels of authority throughout the devolved and increasingly privatized system. The structure and practices of these new institutional arrangements of poverty governance may generate opportunities or enforce the status quo. Perspective on the system of poverty governance and the outline of the component parts allows for further examination of how differences in the structures and practices of poverty governance may inform antipoverty policy. Poverty alleviation requires that current realities about poverty are known and realistic objectives and approaches to reduc-ing poverty must be identified. This book presents the aggregate reality of people living in poverty[19] based on 18 years of evidence across U.S. states and outlines the components of devolution and privatization so that the structures and practices that reduce poverty can be identified.

The regulating functions of poverty governance are based on two basic goals of social welfare that may not necessarily be mutually exclusive. They are poverty reduction and social control, and these goals may also be con-sidered in terms of the target of policy. In general, the progressive perspec-tive on social welfare includes the following themes: (1) humanitarianism, or an assumption that human nature is more or less beneficent; (2) a faith in progress through learning, or a belief that knowledge is incremental and can be cumulative; and (3) a commitment to social citizenship. The themes of the social control perspective on social welfare include the following: (1) the notion that social welfare policy represents one of many mechanisms by which the state supports the ruling class; (2) an inherent paradox in the implementation of social policy through professionalized, hierarchical "helping relationships"; (3) the control of deviance or incentives to conform; and (4) the contention that public relief functions serve to regulate the labor force. The tensions along these dimensions drive the evolution of the welfare story. Reform rhetoric acts as the catalyst for changing the substance of the welfare story by affecting the framing of administrative action, and restructuring is the impetus for enacting the new storyline. The system of poverty governance that exists currently is a function of the negotiated tensions along each of these dimensions over time.

Who or what is to blame for poverty and the perspective on social welfare determine the assumptions underlying policy. These assumptions affect the extent to which policy achieves its objectives (Stone 2002). Storytellers often call upon different explanations of poverty to lay claim to control over the people and/or conditions defined as impoverished. Consequently, welfare policy is often in a state of flux as the boundaries of inclusion and exclusion are negotiated and influence over the story and its meaning is contested. Judeo-Christian traditions dominated the story of the welfare state in the United States. The legacy of the tensions negotiated from those particular sets of assumptions produced an enduring theme as it interacted with American pluralist ideals.

The theme of moral individualism justified the evolution of devolution. Devolution refers to the process by which the power to design social policy within federal guidelines and the authority to manage social service provision has been transferred to subnational units of government. Managerial reforms associated with the implementation of devolution diffused social policy across dense networks of contracting relationships among the public, private, and nonprofit sectors. This evolution of the welfare story followed from negotiated storylines based on different assumptions about maximizing liberty for whom, to do what, that are shaded by the theme of moral individualism. Progressives arguing that humanitarian progress is possible through the economic liberty of individuals held a common point of agreement with conservatives capitalizing on behavioral economics to manipulate the choice architecture for labor regulation. While the different sides, perhaps, had different goals in mind, the shared assumption that individuals making "moral" choices can move up and out of poverty was a common theme. The progressive storyline was that devolution presented more opportunities for states within the federalist system to integrate people living in poverty into economic and social systems. The conservative storyline was that devolution afforded states greater flexibility in regulating people living in poverty so that institutional stability is not compromised. These storylines intertwined to make up the neoliberal paternalist perspective that characterizes poverty governance. The neoliberal logic of governance structures the implementation of welfare. The paternalist approaches to social order characterize the enactment of welfare service provision. And, neoliberal paternalism is the only perspective considered legitimate in stories of poverty governance. This book attempts to challenge the notion that neoliberal poverty governance is the only valid perspective on poverty and presents a framework for analyzing the realities of poverty governance.

The regulation of choice for maintaining the status quo or fostering incremental change was implemented through administrative reforms that favored stories of private sector superiority. This meant that those with a faith in progress through learning had something in common with those who argued for conformity. The standardization of performance metrics utilized the administrative hierarchy to shift the "helping relationships" of social work to the management of progress or conformity to economic or social objectives defined by the state within federal guidelines.

This neoliberal paternalist welfare regime is made up of contracting networks, intergovernmental grants, public and private sector loans and loan guarantees, and intricate interjurisdictional policies and practices that characterize the institutional mechanisms of poverty governance. The contracting relationships and enactment practices make up the informal processes of poverty governance. The conceptions of citizenship regulated through poverty governance reflect the points of agreement between neoliberals and paternalists who championed the rhetoric that employment is the only form of responsible citizenship. The current exercise of poverty governance in the United States employs the muscle of workfare regimes across jurisdictions to reduce caseloads, increase work rates, transfer commitments from public assistance to private services, and enforce the values of neoliberal paternalism through New Public Management (NPM) reforms.

SOCIAL CONSTRUCTIONS IN WELFARE REFORM

Paternalist strategies for "managing the poor" and neoliberal market rationality converged to construct a system of poverty governance designed to discipline political and economic participation according to social status managed by employment. The race, gender, and class biases that plague "operational definitions of citizenship" defined by paternalists as well as neoliberal market logic are a function of the history of policy targets and are perpetuated by implicit associations regarding social status and subsequent distribution of political power. The current realm of possibility in the United States is characterized by societal problems and policy responses that have become increasingly complex; where public officials have not enlightened citizens regarding policy alternatives nor facilitated discourse to increase understanding. Anne Schneider and Helen Ingram (2005) consider this context in terms of the social construction of target populations. They present a typology of targets characterized by their political power and social constructions. They describe four types of groups that might be targets of policy:

1. The *advantaged* have considerable political power, are positively constructed as meritorious and deserving, and are oversubscribed benefits.

2. The *contenders* are politically powerful but constructed as undeserving or greedy.

3. The *dependents* lack political power but are constructed as good people, although not as meritorious as those who are advantaged.

4. The *deviants* lack political power and are negatively constructed. The strong electoral incentives to punish deviants contribute to policies toward deviants becoming oversubscribed and constant searching for new targets that can be constructed as deviants for the electoral gain of politicians.

The targets of welfare policy have changed with the various states of welfare politics. In the colonial period through the western settlements, positive constructions of European Christians as hardworking, God-fearing people deserving of the blessings of freedom, contrasted by the negative constructions of the "other" as savages requiring control for their own good, served to justify the policies that endowed white, male property owners with the rights of individuals. Welfare benefits were assigned to the privileged as wealth was redistributed primarily to white males through the system of property rights in the United States. The expansion of participation through charitable endeavors, electoral politics, and protest movements continues to generate increasing complexities in the welfare conflict. The makeup of the advantaged, contenders, dependents, and deviants shifts as the stories of merit redefine the boundaries of the issue. Opportunities to represent the broad interests and diverse values in policy diminish as political incentives to increasingly target more deviants and redistribute wealth to the advantaged are exploited for individual gain.

The realm of possibility may be manipulated by exceptional storytellers. Stories that manipulate the dimensions of the debate for individual gain are opportunistic and are likely to be degenerative. Welfare stories that enhance organizing principles have the greatest likelihood of expanding the realm of possibility. Organizing principles are ways to solve independence and uncertainty problems by creating a logical approach to coordinating work and gathering, disseminating, and processing information. Organizing principles are enhanced when the stories that foster a willingness to accept vulnerability based on positive expectations about another's intentions or behaviors are widely considered plausible. When trust is widespread, decision making is considered more efficient. Widespread trust facilitates the acquisition and interpretation of information that guides action. Behavior patterns that maintain the viability of the trust in relationships are based on the expectation that vulnerability is not likely to be exploited. The plausibility of a story about poverty that enhances trust operates through two primary causal pathways: (1) by structuring the way activities are organized and coordinated, thereby shaping the relatively stable and enduring interaction patterns, and (2) by mobilizing action based on a logical reason to believe that combining and coordinating resources to collective endeavors will be worthwhile.[20]

The pervasiveness and efficacy of trust as an organizing principle requires that the actual and perceived intentions, motives, and competencies of the trustee are consistent more often than not. Trust in a degenerative context would be simply naive because trust is not sustainable without trustworthiness. The speed and degree of alignment between trust and trustworthiness affect how well trust may operate as an organizing principle (McEvily, Perrone, and Zaheer 2003). Increasing the alignment between trust and trustworthiness requires credibility, or the power to inspire belief. The extraordinary storyteller who might expand the realm of possibility must credibly align trust and trustworthiness in the story by resisting opportunism, demonstrating competence, and exhibiting trustworthiness; all of which require goodwill.

Current constructions of the state of welfare in the United States capitalize on perceptions of an "undeserving underclass" that amplify inequality and undermine trust. The degenerative nature of American political discourse on welfare produces policies that tend to increase social distance and undermine the trust promoted in democratic regimes in which opportunism is minimized (Brehm and Rahn 1997). There are innumerable stories perpetuating stereotypes of people living in poverty, but few perspectives examine the circumstances of poverty. Policies that attempt behavioral modification in a degenerative context are likely to affect behavior in ways that benefit those with advantages. Understanding the extent to which those policies may benefit people living in poverty by providing opportunities to move out of poverty is essential to determining the efficacy of welfare reforms as antipoverty measures and reveals a great deal about whether or not trust in welfare privatization is well placed.

Devolution

Devolution refers to the conferral of authority to design and manage social policy within federal guidelines to subnational units of government. Devolution diffuses responsibility for welfare across dense networks of contracting relationships connecting (and blurring the boundaries between) the public, private, and nonprofit sectors. The process of devolution in the United States began with the increasing use of welfare waivers.

The Family Support Act (FSA) was passed by Congress in 1988 by an overwhelming margin of 347–53 in the House and 96–1 in the Senate. The FSA was aimed at moving welfare recipients into the workforce by expanding work requirements and opportunities through the Job Opportunity and Basic Skills (JOBS) program. The federal JOBS program required recipients without young children to participate in education, job training, or some other work-related activity. Before the FSA, states were allowed to extend eligibility to two-parent families but were not required to do so. The FSA made two-parent families universally eligible for AFDC under somewhat more restrictive criteria than single-parent families. The stories told about the changes made under the FSA did not change the common perception that welfare was "something for nothing" and that the system was not working. Since FSA, states have been granted waivers from the federal requirements of welfare policy and allowed to experiment with potential welfare policy reforms.

The issue of federal or state control over welfare policy has shifted in accordance with party control and has always been complicated by Confederate calls for "states' rights." Likewise, welfare waivers have a complicated history that, as Hugh Heclo points out, culminated in an "inadvertent bipartisanship" (Heclo 2001, 183). Prior to Reagan's election and the corresponding gains by Republicans in Congress, waivers were the tool primarily used by Republicans to shift the locus of control. The story for reform told by Republicans was that the federal welfare state was too large, too expensive, inefficient, and even out of control. Once Republicans gained a foothold on federal authority, they attempted to use federal authority to manage eligibility requirements, and Democrats began considering waivers to counter Republican efforts. The story Democrats told to defend the use of waivers against the memories of racism that "states' rights" stories evoke was that this sort of policy experimentation would turn states into the "laboratories of democracy." Under the conditions of shifting partisan control, waivers became a mechanism of compromise, and their use grew throughout the 1980s. "Republican Revolution" strategies to increase their representation at the state and local level focused campaign funding efforts at those levels.

They were increasingly successful at achieving both electoral gains and, subsequently, appointments to the Electoral College. The welfare waivers that were sometimes referred to as Presidential Waivers were encouraged by the George H. W. Bush administration. The story of waivers as a presidential tool also presented an opportunity for politicians in both parties to make electoral gains based on arguments for bureaucratic reform. The story of waivers as policy experimentation afforded the opportunity for ideologically driven analysis to justify the work-first strategies of welfare reform on which there was generally bipartisan agreement prior to experimentation.

Efforts to reform the bureaucracy, to restructure or dismantle the welfare state, the revolutionary turn to the right in American politics, and the glocalization of social policy are among the critical political factors that converged in the 1990s when the Clinton administration greatly expanded the number of waivers approved. The welfare policy experiments provided a forum for welfare stories told by researchers, politicians, bureaucrats, business leaders, lobbyists, and the media, but largely absent was the perspective of people living in poverty.[21] Conspicuously, they were unable to affect perceptions and practices in the social policy waivers. The Department of Health and Human Services approved 43 waivers between January 1993 and August 1996 and provided modest support for what were called demonstration projects that may be considered the first of several waves of welfare reform that ultimately devolved authority, privatized provision, and implemented program evaluation. States had to show that the projects would not cost the federal government any additional money. The random assignment of recipients to experimental and control groups permitted the evaluation of the extent to which various reforms affected welfare caseloads.

The customary story from the welfare demonstration projects was that work-first strategies reduced caseloads. Work was presumed to be good for the client, and a main argument was that caseload reductions suggested success for everyone. Those who believed the story that the welfare system was broken succeeded at ending welfare as we knew it. Those who found the story that reducing caseloads indicated successful antipoverty measures were comforted by the lessons drawn from the demonstration projects. Those who wanted the story of welfare in any state to be over saw an opportunity to tell a different tale. It was assumed by many that work was a success for the clients who gained access to education and/or employment opportunities. The expectation of successful employment for all made time-limited welfare a possibility. Those who enjoyed the demonstration stories for various reasons found alternative arguments implausible. The disarticulation of the structure of the welfare state and the articulation of "government innovations" such as New Public Management muted alternative welfare stories. Several claims that do not fit the neoliberal paternalist story line were marginalized in the welfare policy process. The notions that time-limited welfare might not lead to success during a recession, that compelling work might not lead to success for some people, or that the Natural Rate of Unemployment (NRU) in a capitalist economy might make a welfare state necessary were considered irrelevant or naive stories.

WELFARE PRIVATIZATION

Welfare privatization refers to the use of vouchers to reimburse private organizations or households for engaging in activities authorized as welfare purposes, the practice of contracting out services to private and nonprofit organizations, and the transfer of functions and assets from the public sector to the private sector. The feedback loop established by the welfare policy experiments attempts to close the neoliberal poverty governance system. "Innovative" efforts to "reinvent government" exercised a customary political strategy to gain advantage by blaming the bureaucracy and to reorganize executive authority with reform stories. Democrats heard the stories of innovative governance as opportunities for changing the perceptions and practices of governance depicted as failure. Republicans heard the stories of innovative governance as a means for deregulating business. Paternalists on both sides seized the opportunity to capitalize on managerial strategies for enforcing the status quo. Policy options that do not fit into the neoliberal paternalist paradigm are not considered, and the assumption that the private management of social problems is superior pervades the entire system. Vouchers, contracts, and welfare transfers from the public sector to the private sector are increasingly the mode of social service provision, and market-oriented managerial reforms focus welfare efforts on quantifiable gains. Consequently, the incentives, subsidies, and payments to private organizations that serve as reimbursements for activities deemed public purposes are efficiently shifting influence to those who are already advantaged in the market context. The private motives, development theories, and strategies of the advantaged thus matter considerably in terms of understanding the impact of welfare privatization on people living in poverty in the United States.

Recent attention has turned to how to best conceptualize and implement philanthropy in the public interest. Defining who deserves assistance, what kind, and how much is influenced by the charitable. The capacity to differentiate a public and direct the corresponding interest has tremendous potential to affect the opportunities available and shape the access to those opportunities. Social entrepreneurship has become the primary vehicle for driving social investments, and venture philanthropy is quickly becoming the dominant tool for financing social endeavors. Social entrepreneurship encompasses "the activities and processes undertaken to discover, define, and exploit opportunities in order to enhance social wealth by creating new ventures or managing existing organizations in an innovative manner" (Zahra et al. 2009, 522), whereas venture philanthropy refers to the financing of innovative social investments. Venture philanthropy is a form of social entrepreneurship in itself. Alternatively, social entrepreneurs may be funded by foundations using the venture philanthropy model.

The perspective on development defines the type of social entrepreneur. Social entrepreneurs operating from different perspectives utilize different strategies for divergent purposes. Zahra et al. (2010) outline a typology of social entrepreneurship, focusing on identifying different types of social entrepreneurs. They propose the following three categories: (1) the social bricoleur; (2) the social constructionist; and (3) the social engineer. Each of these types employs distinct repertoires of strategies.

Bricolage is an idea developed by Lévi-Strauss (1967) that refers to the process of combining and transforming existing resources to innovate and add value. Baker and Nelson (2005) refine this concept by specifying the following conditions: (1) focus on resources at hand; (2) utilization of existing resources for new purposes; and (3) recombining existing resources for the creation of new economic and social value. The processes, relationships, and interconnections among these networks are the focus of evaluation and the genesis of solution-focused intervention. Bricolage assumes that path creation is possible for rational individuals or firms in interaction with the environment or context in which the individual or firm operates. Generating novel solutions and targeting underserved markets is a part of the process of innovation sometimes referred to as intrapreneurship (see Mair and Martí 2006). Intrapreneurship patterns are theorized to occur in episodes that Corner and Ho (2010) characterize in the following manner: (1) opportunity development; (2) collective action; (3) experience corridors; and (4) spark. These innovative episodes are the critical components of entrepreneurship broadly defined.

Capitalizing on local markets with minimal or depleted resources that may be accessed at low cost by what is referred to as knowledge spillovers, economic regeneration, and proximity designs describes how bricolage functions (see Fayolle and Matlay 2010). Knowledge spillover occurs when a nonrival mechanism for distributing facts, information, and/or skills that have not previously been accounted for is picked up, stimulating broader improvements (Arrow 1962). Economic regeneration is distinct from economic development in that economic regeneration refers to the reinvestment in industrial or business areas that have suffered decline (Stöhr 1990), and proximity designs group related items to maximize gain (Lagendijk and Oinas 2005).

Social constructionists attempt to create social wealth by identifying the inadequacies in existing institutions or organizations and launching ventures to better address those social issues. Constructionists operate at the regional, national, or global level, and they design systemic solutions to address the perceived cause of a broader social problem. Constructionists may fund bricoleurs to build the infrastructure and/or code the operations for the systemic reform. The strategies that characterize the social constructionist are knowledge transfer and scalable solutions.

Social engineers find fundamental and irreparable flaws in the existing system and seek to undermine, deconstruct, and replace present practices in existing institutions. Social engineers require political capital to legitimize their projects. The strategies that characterize social engineers involve education and advocacy in addition to influencing the policy process through lobbying, resistance/protest, and the media. While all social entrepreneurs are likely to engage in these activities to some degree, social engineers rely on them to build the political capital necessary for collective, collaborative, or voluntary action.

Social entrepreneurship and venture philanthropy are potentially constructive approaches to poverty alleviation, although they remain somewhat controversial because the perspectives and strategies of social entrepreneurs shape progress for whom to do what. It is also worth noting that the assumptions of neoliberal paternalism are inherent in the strategies employed by bricoleurs, social constructionists, and social engineers. More importantly, little is known about the potential impact of increasingly placing public authority in the hands of entrepreneurs, who might be working at cross purposes or on different priorities.

Methodological Approach

In many ways, the study of politics is a science that can draw on lessons from the physical sciences; yet at the same time, the rhetorical nature of politics presents opportunities for self-interest to pose as scientific rigor. This is not to imply that political dynamics are mystical or deterministic. There may be mysteries that we do not understand in political behavior, and we may feel that political decision making seems like a foregone conclusion in some instances. However, these puzzles are significantly more manageable with the disciplined application of both the scientific method and the critical reflection on political discourse. A discipline that fails to engage in insightful self-reflection simply engages in putting together the same puzzles over and over again.

For example, the scientific investigations that helped us understand the 2004 Indian Ocean tsunami relied on various methods of data collection and analysis. Sediment samples provided evidence of the speed of the waves. Computer models and inundation maps helped determine the source of the tsunami and the progression of the waves. The statistical analysis of seismic and demographic data allowed for a greater understanding of the threat of offshore faults to human populations that are increasingly concentrated along the coasts. The firsthand accounts of survivors of the tsunami permitted researchers to learn new lessons. For example, video evidence showed that the velocity of water increased after a slower first wave created a smoother surface, which pushed subsequent waves much faster down the narrow passages of city streets. The observations of survivors supported evidence of waves of unheard-of heights, and the local knowledge passed down through oral traditions led some people to safety, while others were drawn into danger by their curiosity regarding the exposed seabed. There are significant lessons in the devastation and the sociopolitical response to it that yield important information about the potential for cooperation, and the development of the Global Earth Observation System of Systems (GEOSS) and the Deep-ocean Assessment and Reporting of Tsunamis (DART) provide organizational mechanisms for preventative measures. The scientific community has used this tragedy as an opportunity to learn, and these lessons can be applied to the physical and social world. Pulling together various perspectives on the social world and mapping them on the institutional landscape allows for a kind of three-dimensional view of the effects various policy choices have on people who live on the margins of society.

A reasonable and multifaceted approach to understanding policy presents significant challenges but also provides considerably greater wisdom. Deborah Stone's (2002) critique of the rational model of policy reasoning highlights the inherently subjective practices within the policy process. The systematic method of policy evaluation is as follows: (1) identify objectives; (2) identify alternatives; (3) predict possible consequences of each alternative; (4) evaluate the possible consequences of each alternative; (5) select the alternative that maximizes the attainment of objectives. Stone demonstrates that there are five goals that govern the policy process as they serve as the logical warrant or justification for policy: (1) equity, (2) efficiency, (3) security, (4) liberty, and (5) accountability.

Paradoxically, the policy process is a means by which values are articulated, as problems are defined, goals identified, and solutions outlined in the act of representation, while various interpretations and strategies compete in the conflict space. The emphasis on discovering the "correct," objective solution through the systematic application of the rational model and the negative connotation of the term *conflict* inhibit opportunities to resolve conflict through political reason. Stone's model of society provides perspective on the process of representing values in conflict by acknowledging the interpretive elements, recognizing the various interests at stake, and suggesting that policy decisions require reasons that make politicians accountable to the broadest interests in society. Consequently, this book reviews the various stories presented about welfare over time and assesses how well the reasons that have served as justifications for welfare reforms produce results that may or may not be in the interest of the broad public. This does not preclude logical argumentation; rather, it explains the ways in which logic and passion are mechanisms for leveraging influence through storytelling. Some stories are better told by passionate storytellers, while some people only find stories that suggest "rational" solutions to social problems convincing. However, building knowledge from multiple perspectives and comparing the relative merits of the approaches and weight of the evidence are essential to piecing together a coherent view of the system of poverty governance.

Welfare policy is a process of negotiation that requires attention to the various interests at stake, as well as critical reflection on the impact welfare policies have from multiple perspectives in order to gain an understanding of the system of poverty governance. But, that does not mean that every story is equally valid. Stories that provide a clear understanding of the way activities are organized and coordinated to shape relatively stable and enduring interaction patterns, and provide logical reasons to believe that combining and coordinating resources to collective endeavors will be worthwhile, offer realistic opportunities to alleviate poverty.

Stone's argument focuses on the value of accountability as an organizing principle in policy. However, one might reasonably conclude that each of the five goals or values identified by Stone (equity, liberty, efficiency, security, and accountability) serves the purpose of promoting versions of welfare. Equity, liberty, efficiency, security, and accountability are valued goals because they reflect the ways in which people understand the state of welfare. The objective of this study is not to promote any one value or goal over another but to argue that welfare matters, and welfare policies that function as antipoverty measures are a valid basis for comparing welfare stories across the states. And, comparing welfare stories according to how well they align trust and trustworthiness is essential to antipoverty policy. The purpose of this study is to explore the conflict space that serves as the context for welfare policy in the United States, and to examine the impact of welfare devolution and privatization on the least well off. Understanding the conflict space within the systemic framework presented in this book and estimating the aggregate effects of welfare reforms on opportunities to move out of poverty provides a baseline for evaluating how well trust and trustworthiness align in neoliberal poverty governance. The analysis presented here also highlights how trust and trustworthiness might be better aligned through policy choices.

Analytical Strategies

Impact assessments attempt to estimate the extent to which interventions produce their intended effects (Rossi and Freeman 1993). The basic aim is to estimate the plausible net effects of policy by comparing the existing conditions against the situation prior to the intervention and examining what has happened in relation to the specified goals or targets of policy. Critical reflection on the objectives and intervention strategies then allows for some estimation of likely future directions but may also inspire more resourceful approaches to fostering welfare policies that serve a broad democratic public. The promises of welfare reforms are that work should produce self-sufficiency, that devolution offers flexibilities to better address local circumstances, and that privatization extends choice and generates community economic solutions. This study assesses the impact of welfare reforms on people living in poverty, to determine the extent to which policy choices across states might provide opportunities to move out of poverty. Additionally, the framework for understanding the devolved and privatized structure of poverty governance maps the conflict space so that research from various levels of analysis within the system can be used to build knowledge on poverty alleviation.

Poverty alleviation represents an opportunity to enhance trust and reverse degenerative trends in American politics. Inequality is growing rapidly worldwide, but wealth and opportunity gaps are widest and expanding at the fastest rate in the United States (Neckerman 2004; Soss, Hacker, Mettler 2007). Understanding the accumulation of benefits and burdens is essential to establishing knowledge regarding welfare systems. Moreover, calculating the effects of state welfare policy choices on opportunities to move out of poverty and maintain self-sufficiency assists in the identification of investments that are most likely to provide the most value for the money. The net effects of workfare policies across U.S. states are analyzed using data from each state over 18 years, representing more than a full cycle of the policy process. The time-series analysis of the effects of different state welfare policy choices on impoverishment illustrate the reality for people living in poverty across U.S. states over time. It also provides an opportunity to examine some of the variations in state policy choices that might perform better as antipoverty strategies than other policy choices. The aggregate assessment of the impact of welfare reforms on impoverishment allows for an appraisal of the extent to which welfare reform rhetoric measures up to reality.

Workfare rhetoric promised opportunities to move out of poverty through work. If work pays, access to consistent work can decrease the intensity of poverty. If poverty governance efficiently minimizes transaction costs, corresponding increases in exchange may allow more people to secure a place in the financial and social mainstream and out of poverty. Estimating the net effects of welfare reforms on impoverishment provides a broad, fuzzy picture of the current state of welfare in the United States that is lacking. And, the contours of the devolved and privatized system of poverty governance offer fertile ground to understand how different public and private responses to economic adjustments compare as poverty alleviation strategies.

2

The Evolution of Devolution

.•————•.

Devolution evolved from the convergence of the New Right and the New Left regarding the individual responsibilities to work, which came to define civic affairs. On the right, devolution served as a means to enhance supervisory and accountability practices. On the left, devolution offered flexible, local community solutions to the complex economic, social, and political factors that affect poverty. Devolution evolved from the simultaneous focus on social justice and economic growth. Stories justifying devolution have primarily been told through the lenses of people who subscribe to the traditional, paternalistic values associated with rights-based belief systems. Waves of reforms restructured implementation, adjusted perceptions of poverty, and enacted practices that regulate opportunities and discipline participants. This chapter describes the process by which the welfare policy experiments diffused welfare policy to state governments and the extent to which welfare reform led to further devolution of authority in poverty governance. Welfare devolution distributed access points across states, and those perceived to have legitimate claim to individual, private intervention strategies colonized the conflict space.

The quasi-markets of the diffuse welfare states produce tremendous variation across space and time. This chapter outlines the variation in state policy choices that address the objectives of welfare reform and also describes changes in related welfare programs. Because welfare reform led to such an incredible amount of variation, it is impossible to cover every element of welfare devolution. However, the map of welfare devolution across U.S. states presented herein does provide a thorough overview of the current state of workfare. This chapter includes an accounting of state policy choices based on the most recent state plans, state policy manuals, and legislation. Differences in eligibility standards, employment strategies, sanctioning rules, flexibility and discretionary practices, family policies, labor regulation policies, public health standards imposed within welfare, funding streams, program structure, and related benefits are among the variations summarized by state. The purposes of this chapter are twofold: (1) to map the range of variation in poverty governance and provide a frame of reference for putting the pieces of the welfare puzzle together, and (2) to describe the components of the devolved policies and practices that make up the current American welfare state. Understanding how neoliberal paternalist stories shaped devolution is essential to gaining perspective on the current state of impoverishment and for future analysis of viable antipoverty policies.

Welfare Devolution

Devolution in the United States refers to the process by which the power to design social policy within federal guidelines and the authority to manage social service provision has been transferred to subnational units of government. In addition, the responsibility for social well-being is diffused across dense networks of contracting relationships among the public, private, and nonprofit sectors. Due to the complexities of funding and sovereignty as well as the standard level of analysis required for the comparative method, this study examines the variation in state policy choices resulting from devolution and explores state-level aspects of privatization.

The process of devolution has occurred to varying degrees across all aspects of social policy in the United States. Federal TANF guidelines constitute first-order devolution, transferring authority from the federal to state level. Some states are characterized by second-order devolution, in which state policies further decentralize, giving discretion to regional, county, or local units within the governance structure. A substantial amount of social service provision is currently delivered by private for-profit and nonprofit organizations; a practice that is referred to as "contracting-out" (DeHoog 1985), "government by proxy" (Kettl 1988), "networked governance" (Milward and Provan 2003), "shadow government" (Light 2003), and "third order devolution" (Wilson and Dilulio 2007).

The rhetoric of devolution disguises the extent to which mandates, regulatory actions, and grant procedures define the scope of action from the top down. Consequently, mapping the devolved orders is a critical component of understanding poverty governance implemented through New Public Management (NPM). Theoretically, NPM is a story of government efficiency achieved by managing government so that it "runs like a business" and evaluating outcomes for technical evaluation or incremental adjustment. Devolution extends the reach of governance, expands the influence of private enterprise, and limits the feedback to contractual objectives. The waves of reform that devolved authority and implemented the new regulatory contracts of TANF and the managerial practices of NPM restrict the "legitimate" welfare stories in a manner that inhibits challenges to the neoliberal paternalist paradigm.

The capacity to assume responsibility for social policy is conditioned upon historical and geographical differences in governance. Consequently, there is a great deal of variation across states in terms of the policy choices made to address the statutory mandates of welfare reform. Although the networks of social service provision are different across states, its enactment by service providers in the private and nonprofit sectors, with administration through contract management at the level of devolution defined by the state government, is the standard.

The design of welfare policies is determined by individual state governments within the broader objectives defined in the Personal Responsibility and Work Opportunity Reconciliation Act of 1996 (PRWORA). PRWORA replaced AFDC, the Job Opportunities and Basic Skills Training (JOBS) program, and the Emergency Assistance (EA) program with the Temporary Assistance for Needy Families (TANF) Block Grant, which is allotted to each state on a competitive basis. TANF includes a lifetime limit of five years on the amount of time a family with an adult can receive federally funded assistance.

The TANF block grant is a competitive grant to the 50 states and the District of Columbia that is capped at approximately $16.5 billion per year, which is basically equivalent to the 1995 federal expenditure on the four component programs.[1] U.S. territories compete for an additional $0.1 billion in federal welfare funding. Puerto Rico, Guam, and the Virgin Islands currently operate TANF programs, but American Samoa has not opted to operate one. Federally recognized Indian tribes may choose to operate Tribal TANF programs that serve "carded members" of the tribe. Allocations for Tribal TANF are made to the state in which the tribe offers services and derive from the basic TANF block grant. Due to the complexities of Tribal welfare, I have not included it in this study.

There are also Supplemental Grants that can be used in any manner that a state reasonably calculates will meet a TANF objective, including applying them to Child Care and Development services and/or Social Services Block Grant (SSBG) programs. The additional funding that states disadvantaged by the TANF funding formula might access has been available since the enactment of PRWORA, and from fiscal years 2001–10, $319 million was set aside for states experiencing high population growth and/

or low welfare spending per person in poverty. The Supplemental Grants were extended through September 30, 2010, by the American Recovery and Reinvestment Act (ARRA or Recovery Act), and $211 million was utilized for this purpose during the 2011 fiscal year. The Supplemental Grants were intended to give states that were considered to be disadvantaged by the block grant formula the opportunity to achieve the objectives of TANF.[2] Although the Supplemental Grants had consistently been renewed since 1996, this funding stream dried up as of July 1, 2011. Supplemental grants are a part of a trend in diversified, limited, and contingent funding sources for specific objectives that are competitively administered, making the scope of poverty governance difficult to assess.

A $2 billion contingency fund was also established as a part of the 1996 welfare reform law to assist states in economic downturns. In order to access contingency funds, states must establish economic need by meeting at least one of the following tests:

1. A state must demonstrate that its seasonally adjusted unemployment rate averaged over a three-month period exceeds 6.5% and is at least 10% higher than its corresponding rate in the previous two years.

2. A state may otherwise show that its Supplemental Nutrition Assistance Program (SNAP) caseload over the most recent three-month period is at least 10% higher than the adjusted caseload in the corresponding three months for fiscal year 1994 or 1995.

States are required to increase spending from their own funds above what they spent on AFDC programs in 1994 in order to qualify for contingency funding. The annual cap on contingency funds is 20% of the state's basic block grant. However, the $2 billion contingency fund established in 1996 was depleted early in the 2010 fiscal year. During the 2009 and 2010 fiscal years, a temporary emergency contingency fund was established in response to widespread economic need by states. Congress appropriated $506 million to continue contingency funding for the 2011 fiscal year, to cover only the existing obligations to states and $612 million for fiscal year 2012.

Prior to the Deficit Reduction Act (DRA) of 2005, TANF included two bonus funds. A $1 billion (over five years) appropriation to incentivize states through performance bonuses, and a $100 million annual appropriation to provide state bonuses for programs that reduce the number of out-of-wedlock births and abortions. Both were repealed by the DRA and were discontinued as of the fiscal year 2006 to allow for the appropriations made in the TANF Emergency Response and Recovery Act (2005) to assist states affected by Hurricane Katrina. In addition, the $1.7 billion federal loan fund to states for supplemental spending was repealed in the 2005 TANF Reauthorization. However, the Recovery Act of 2009 established a $5 billion TANF Emergency Fund to assist states experiencing increasing numbers of families seeking assistance during the economic downturn. The TANF Emergency Fund was not extended past the September 2010 expiration, but states with demonstrable caseload increases, increased expenditures on nonrecurrent, short-term benefits, or expenditures for subsidized employment that applied for and were approved for TANF Emergency Funds were allowed to use the funding to subsidize employment, education, job training, or even pregnancy prevention during fiscal years 2009 and 2010.

In addition, states must meet a Maintenance of Effort (MOE) requirement by spending at least 75% of the amount of state funds used on these programs in 1994 (80% if they fail to meet the work rate requirements), to prevent a "race to the bottom." The MOE requirement is not intended to slow caseload reductions. At the same time, states are strongly incentivized to reduce caseloads. The MOE requirement is intended to prevent states from depending on federal welfare funding and lowering their own contributions to welfare efforts. The MOE is an effort to control federal costs without reducing overall welfare efforts, but is based on the expectation that alternative funding is accessible in all states. Both federal TANF dollars and state dollars must be spent on families that include a child or expectant mother in order to count toward the MOE requirement. Consequently, states are not encouraged by the MOE requirement to contribute to assistance for less than employable or difficult to employ families and are limited in their ability to assist individuals without children through TANF. The Administration for Children and Families (ACF) approves the use of third party spending such as partnerships with local governments, school districts, foundations, nonprofits, corporate partnerships, or other sponsors in accounting for the MOE. In fact, some states have been counting third party spending in the calculation of the state MOE, such as nonprofit afterschool program spending and district-funded preschool programs, to increase caseload reduction credits, to claim additional TANF contingency funds, and/or to receive reimbursements from the TANF Emergency Fund.

PRWORA also includes modifications to child care, the Child Support Enforcement Program, benefits for legal immigrants, the Food Stamp Program, and SSI for children as well as adjustments to the child nutrition program and reductions in the Social Services Block Grant (SSBG). Because the law involves such far-reaching changes, states are also allowed to transfer up to 30% of their TANF funds (except contingency funds) to the Child Care and Development Block (CCDB) grant and/or the SSBG to afford flexibility according to the state needs assessment. Federal funds transferred to SSBG cannot exceed 10% and must be used to assist the most impoverished families. States are also now allowed to use federal TANF dollars to match reverse commuter grants that fund local governments and nonprofit organizations that provide transportation and support services to assist welfare clients and people with low incomes in accessing jobs. However, matching reverse commuter grants count against the 30% total transfer limit.

The use of federal funds for TANF is subject to the following restrictions:

1. Families that have received assistance for a cumulative total of 60 months cannot be provided federally funded assistance. However, up to 20% of the state caseload in any one year can be exempted from the five-year limit applying to federal dollars.

2. Families receiving assistance that include unmarried teen parents require the teen parents to stay in school and live at home in an adult-supervised setting.

3. Any person ever convicted of a drug-related felony is subject to a lifetime ban from TANF and the Food Stamp Program; states may choose to opt out of the ban or limit the ban.

4. Failure to cooperate with child support enforcement requirements, including establishing paternity, subjects recipients to benefit reductions or loss of benefits entirely. States are not allowed to use state dollars to fund those who do not cooperate with the child support enforcement requirements.

5. States are not allowed to spend more than 15% of their TANF grants on administrative costs.

These restrictions apply only to the use of federal dollars from the TANF block grant. Although states can use federal TANF dollars for activities that they were engaging in prior to welfare reform that are not considered as facilitating the goals of TANF, these "grandfathered" activities cannot be counted toward the MOE requirement. Also, any state welfare program that is funded apart from the TANF block grant is not subject to these restrictions.

In addition to the restrictions on the use of federal TANF funds, states must comply with the following work requirements established under TANF:

1. Unless a state opts out of the community service option, all nonexempt adult recipients who are not working are required to participate in community service within two months after they start receiving benefits.

2. All adults receiving federally funded support must participate in work activities two years after they start receiving assistance.

3. States may choose to exempt parents with children under the age of one from work requirements and can disregard them in the calculation of work participation rates.

4. Parents with children under the age of six may not be penalized for failing to meet the work requirements if childcare is unavailable.

HHS evaluates state performance according to the work participation rates. Each state was expected to have a minimum of 75% of the two-parent families on the caseload working at least 35 hours per week in the first year of TANF implementation (FY 1997) and a minimum of 25% of all families working at least 20 hours per week. By 1999, states had to have a minimum of 90% of the two-parent families on the caseload working at least 35 hours per week and a minimum of 35% of all families working at least 25 hours per week or risk being penalized for failing to meet the performance requirements for federal funding. States were expected to gradually increase the work participation rates of all families so that a minimum of 50% of all families were working at least 30 hours per week. Each state submits case-level data on participation in work activities and the requisite information to calculate caseload reduction credits, and HHS calculates the participation rate for each state. Once states are notified of the participation rate, any state that fails to meet the participation rate must submit a request for reasonable cause exception or submit a corrective compliance plan within 60 days as an accountability measure. General reasonable cause for exceptions can be filed when a state has not met the work participation rate because of a natural disaster, federal guidance provided incorrect information, and/or due to isolated problems of minimal impact. States may also file specific reasonable cause exceptions for failing to meet the work participation rates for the percentage of cases that meet the federally recognized good cause exemptions given to recipients who cannot work due to domestic violence and for the alternative services provided to certain refugees. If a state cannot demonstrate reasonable cause approved by HHS, the state may enter into a corrective compliance plan, and no penalties are imposed on the state if it achieves compliance with the plan.

The TANF regulations include a formula for calculating the penalty according to the degree of the state's noncompliance if the state continues to fail to meet the required performance indicator. Compliance with the work requirements of TANF are included in the annual report to Congress submitted by HHS and serve as feedback to the system of poverty governance. However, compliance with neoliberal paternalism is not likely to measure poverty alleviation, so figuring out what the work requirements mean for people living in poverty is essential to understanding poverty governance. If neoliberal paternalist stories offer a system of poverty governance that generates opportunities, impoverishment is likely to decrease overall. But because policy feedback is often limited to compliance evaluation, the overall performance of poverty governance as a system of poverty alleviation lacks perspective. Research beyond outcomes assessment and program evaluation are necessary feedback to inform antipoverty policy.

Within the federal restrictions defined by TANF, states are afforded considerable discretion in policy design and spending decisions. States are only restricted in that they must show how the program supports one of the four statutory purposes of TANF: (1) provide assistance to needy families so that children can be cared for at home; (2) end welfare dependence by promoting job preparation, work, and marriage; (3) prevent and reduce the incidence of out-of-wedlock pregnancies; and (4) encourage the formation and maintenance of two-parent families. States are required to demonstrate that the policy choices in the use of TANF funds are made in a manner "reasonably calculated to accomplish the purposes of TANF." PRWORA stipulates that states consult with local governments and private organizations over a 45-day comment period before submitting their TANF plans to HHS to be reviewed for completeness.

The intergovernmental relationships that make up the devolved welfare system are highly variable across states but relatively stable over time. First-Order Devolution (FOD) refers to the transfer of governmental authority from the federal government to the state. Second-Order Devolution (SOD) refers to the further decentralization to county administrative units, regional authorities, or localities. Third-Order Devolution (TOD) refers to service provision contracted out to public, private, and/or nonprofit organizations. Administrative devolution describes the authority to use discretion in program administration, and substantive devolution is the transfer of responsibility for outcomes to a lower unit of governance.

Table 1.1 in Appendix A illustrates the devolved and disarticulated nature of TANF. The administrative authority reflects the unit defining eligibility and establishing the rules and procedures for implementing the opportunity structure. Case management shows the substantive responsibility for managing outcomes. Defining eligibility is one form of discretion, but there is also a considerable degree of discretion in the management of outcomes that may occur within the rules and procedures for administering incentives and sanctions. Provider contract management is a form of administrative devolution in which the authority to define the terms of the contract, procedures for engaging partners, and rules for monitoring contracts may be a separate sphere of influence in some states. Work verification plans are required to be submitted to HHS in accordance with the DRA. The substantive responsibility for managing work rates conducted in the work verification process is another potential point of devolution. Across all states, service provision is contracted out to third-party providers (TOD) in the private and nonprofit sectors. However, the amount of administrative discretion afforded to providers varies across states and can vary within states by the type of service contract. TOD of service provision uniformly involves substantive devolution as the responsibility for performance outcomes is defined in the contract. However, this sort of discretion is constricted by each previous order of devolution. In other words, policy authority is restricted by each order of devolution, and contracts specify the nature of discretion authorized through managerial oversight.

The devolved and restructured system of workfare makes some differences in state choices evident. Some states repositioned work programs to be managed by departments other than the human/social services offices that implemented AFDC. The management of workfare through departments of labor, economic development, workforce services, or economic opportunity reveals the intention of state governments to direct the labor force and shift influence away from agencies established to provide assistance. States also established different networks of collaboration or oversight. Future research may explore the political conditions that produced these arrangements and the nature of these distinct collaborative networks on governance.

State Incentive Schemes

As any state is only required to show that its program meets at least one of the four statutory purposes of TANF, there is considerable variation across states with respect to antipoverty policy. The specific provisions of each of the state programs are outlined in the state plan. The state plans detail how the program is to be conducted in all political subdivisions, although it is not expected that the implementation necessarily be uniform. Each state program represents different strategies for compelling work, and each state is obligated to meet the federal performance standards, the most critical being the work rates. Behavioral contracts are used by states to define personal responsibility and activate labor, and the state plans are the mechanisms of accountability that are intended to enforce the federal guidelines. Each of the state incentive schemes reflects the assumptions of policymakers regarding the target population as well as the interpretation of welfare priorities within the context of the fiscal demands for caseload reductions and the state's economic opportunity horizon.

ASSETS AND ELIGIBILITY

States now have the authority to determine benefit levels, set eligibility standards, and establish means tests, or to engage in second-order devolution. In addition, states have the flexibility to establish separate state funds and establish time limits that are more or less restrictive. Each state establishes the terms of contracts with clients and requires that participants sign a personal responsibility contract.[3] In some states, third-party providers may also require that clients sign contracts that impose terms within and in addition to the contract established by the state. The language of the contract reveals the assumptions about the market, the participants, and the role of government in social and economic exchange. In addition, some states also provide a "customer's bill of rights" or a "clients' rights" document informing participants of their rights in the welfare administration process. Referring to citizens as customers reflects the internalization of the language of management reforms and suggests that those states enact welfare policy with an emphasis on business standards over professional social work standards. Those states that refer to participants as clients and provide them with written information about their rights signal to welfare agencies that enactment focuses on professional social work standards. States that do not provide any documentation regarding the rights of participants are likely to impose the welfare administration process without much regard for the relationship between the state and its citizenry.

It is also important to note that the HHS Office for Civil Rights (OCR) issued detailed explanations of the application of federal civil rights laws to certain aspects of welfare reform in 1999. "The Prohibition against Discrimination on the Basis of Disability in the Administration of TANF" is a policy memo that clarifies the obligations state and local governments must follow to ensure meaningful access to TANF programs by people with disabilities based on the Americans with Disabilities Act (ADA) and Section 504 of the Rehabilitation Act of 1973. It also outlines "promising practices" to ensure that adequate steps are taken to identify applicants and/or participants with disabilities. State and local governments are required to provide program modifications and support services, adequate screening and assessment, and exemptions from work requirements, and conduct all operations in a manner and facility accessible to people with disabilities. These regulatory efforts define the boundaries of discretion in the context of welfare devolution as it relates to the protected classes of disabilities.

States have considerable flexibility in the determination of eligibility. The formulas for calculating benefits are tremendously complex and variable.[4] However, all states disregard some of the earned income of recipients in order to afford individuals the opportunity to transition from welfare to work. In addition, welfare reform allows states to extend the time limits on eligibility using state funds. Table 1.2 in Appendix A outlines the time and asset limits for each state program as of 2012. This table illustrates the considerable degree of variation across states with respect to eligibility standards. States tend to adopt more or less restrictive eligibility and time limit requirements consistent with the ideological disposition of the state, conditioned upon the sub-population of expected or perceived targets (Schram 2006b; Schram, Soss, and Fording 2006; Soss 2000). However, these eligibility criteria and time limits are subject to further restrictions when demand increases in a manner that is primarily attributed to budget constraints (Schott and Pavetti 2011). It is worth noting that California, Indiana, and Rhode Island continue to provide benefits to children after parents have reached the lifetime limit. In addition, a few states have created a secondary safety net for those who have exhausted their lifetime limit and do not meet the requirement for an exemption. New Jersey's Supportive Assistance to Individuals and Families (SAIF) Program began providing intensive case management and continuation of services in 2004. The program uses federal TANF dollars and separate state funds to allow up to 24 additional months of cash benefits for clients who continue in a work activity. Support services such as child care, transportation, and mental health services may also be available in some cases. Eligibility for SAIF is reserved for those who are not eligible for an exemption but meet the following conditions: cooperated with the Work First New Jersey (WFNJ) requirements; experienced domestic violence but find it difficult to establish the documentation required for an exemption; suffered an illness for 12 months or longer that deferred participation in WFNJ or are currently deferred for such reason; are six or more months pregnant; or experienced recent job loss due to uncontrollable circumstances.

Table 1.3 in Appendix A shows how states use language to signal the emphasis of their Cash Assistance (CA) and work programs. While some programs simply refer to their programs as TANF, others choose names that emphasize the family in the name of their program. Still other state programs are known by names that stress work or work-first; while others focus on the temporary or transitional nature of the program. And, there are also those that highlight family investment, independence, or empowerment. These choices reveal the state's story about what work can do for them or signals a reverence for the story of welfare dependence.[5] For example, Alabama's Family Assistance (FA or FAP) focuses its mission on the traditional nuclear and extended family networks of social support. The Virginia Initiative for Employment, Not Welfare (VIEW) program identifies the goal of reducing welfare rolls through "personal responsibility, work in exchange for benefits, and time-limited assistance." Alternatively, Vermont's Aid to Needy Families with Children (ANFC) program maintains the language of need for assistance, and the Reach Up work program utilizing federal TANF dollars, along with the separate state program, Reach Ahead, focuses on moves out of poverty through stable employment and offers extended assistance.

States also use eligibility standards to shape individual choices that impact public health. The fraudulent autism study by the discredited British doctor Andrew Wakefield, published in The Lancet in 1998, marks the beginning of what has become a long period of increasing public health risk for diseases once well under control. A substantial percentage of parents refusing or delaying vaccinations due to false information has affected the herd immunity. Vaccination scares, increasing rates of home schooling, and declining levels of insurance coverage have contributed to public health risks that threaten communities where 20% or more of the population have not been vaccinated against preventable diseases. Some states have attempted to address this public health concern by linking eligibility for TANF to childhood immunizations. Figure 1A in Appendix A identifies those states that require immunization to access benefits.

Federal restrictions on the eligibility of immigrants for the range of federally funded welfare programs are specified in the following pieces of legislation: amendments to PRWORA based on the Illegal Immigration Reform and Immigrant Responsibility Act (PL 104-208), the Balanced Budget Act of 1997 (PL 105-33), the Agricultural Research, Extension, and Education Reform Act of 1998 (PL 105-185), the Noncitizen Benefit Clarification and Other Technical Amendments Act of 1998 (PL 105-306), the Trafficking Victims Protection Act of 2000 (PL 106-386), the Food Stamp Reauthorization Act of 2002 (PL 107-171), the SSI Extension for Elderly and Disabled Refugees Act (PL 110-328), and the Children's Health Insurance Program Reauthorization Act of 2009 (PL 111-3). Lawful Permanent Residents (LPRs) are generally ineligible for federal funds for SNAP, SSI, TANF, SSBG, Medicaid, and the Children's Health Insurance Program (CHIP) for five years from their date of entry into the United States. Refugees and U.S. veterans (and their families) are for the most part exempted from this ban. Immigrants are a group with low political power and low social status in the United States. As a result, their access to anything perceived as a benefit is likely to be heavily restricted. The language and regularity of these regulations reflects the degenerative nature of welfare politics. Rather than engaging in discourse that addresses the complexities of immigration in a global economy, politicians capitalize on stereotypes for political gain. The welfare policy process thus becomes increasingly dominated by trends that exacerbate social cleavages. Yet, the nature of the welfare policy process is also affected by the state context.

States have the authority to determine TANF and Medicaid eligibility for LPRs who arrived prior to August 22, 1996, and states can opt out of the eligibility restrictions on SSBG funds for LPRs regardless of the date of entry. Additionally, states set their own eligibility standards for access to state funds during the five-year ban from federal funding for LPRs. Table 1.4 in Appendix A denotes state choices regarding the eligibility of LPRs for state-funded TANF CA during the five-year period of ineligibility for federal TANF CA funding. States are also authorized to attribute the income of the family-based or employment-based sponsor to the LPR in a process referred to as deeming. Since 1997, sponsors are required to sign an affidavit of support stating that the sponsor will "maintain the immigrant at an annual income of at least 125% of the FPL." Consequently, states that allow access to state-funded TANF but may subject the applicant to the process of deeming deter potential applicants who might not meet the eligibility requirements for state-funded support with a sponsor's income and/or resources attributed to household eligibility or who might lose their sponsor if the affidavit is enforced.

North Carolina utilizes federal funding only for TANF CA, and 30 states do not extend eligibility to LPRs for state-funded assistance during the five-year ban on federally funded assistance. Ohio goes farther, restricting eligibility for state-funded TANF CA even after the five-year period of ineligibility for federal assistance. Alternatively, New York established the Safety Net Assistance (SNA) program to provide assistance to single adults, childless couples, children living apart from any adult relative, individuals who have exceeded the 60-month time limit, and the families of individuals with substance use disorders even if that individual refuses treatment. New York's SNA program extends eligibility to LPRs during the five-year bar from federally funded assistance. Differences across U.S. states with respect to immigrant eligibility reflect the history of immigration patterns, population demographics, state government and citizen ideology, and the broader economic conditions in the state. These factors condition welfare discourse by affecting the extent to which political gain may be leveraged by constructing and regulating a "deviant" group. Ultimately, these differences are likely to affect the ability of states with degenerative political contexts to attract an adequate workforce when population demographics change dramatically as the Baby Boomers leave the American workforce.

Restrictions for drug-related offenses present a similar challenge in poverty governance. Section 115(a) of PRWORA prohibits anyone con-victed of a drug-related felony from receiving federally funded assistance through TANF and federally funded food supplements unless states opt out of the ban or modify the ban. The lifetime ban against those convicted of state or federal felony offenses involving the use or sale of drugs has been maintained by 13 states. Twenty states have modified the ban by limiting the circumstances for permanent disqualification, requiring drug testing and/ or treatment, or imposing a period of disqualification rather than lifetime prohibition. Seventeen states opt out of the ban but do tend to retain discretion to allow case managers to refer individuals to treatment in any case in which addiction is identified as an issue. Figure 2A in Appendix A illustrates the various state policy choices regarding drug disqualification. For example, New York implements welfare through commingled and separate state funding. This affords the state the discretion to provide assistance to people with drug convictions and families of those with substance use disorders with separate state funds.

Vermont utilizes segregated and/or separate state funds to opt out of the ban. Alternatively, Arizona maintains the lifetime ban, and the state Drug Abuse and Gangs Bill (ARS 13-3418 allows the courts to render individuals ineligible for state public assistance. Additionally, Arizona HB 2678 (2008) denies assistance for 12 months to those who test positive for illegal drugs when a caseworker requires a drug test based on "reason-able cause." The Arizona Department of Economic Security (DES) manages the commingled and segregated state funds, which are used to pay for the drug testing. The Jobs DES caseworkers refer individuals to the Families In Recovery Succeeding Together (Families FIRST), a collaborative program with the Department of Health Services, when substance use is identified upon intake as a barrier to employment. Drug testing may be used when the issue is not identified as a barrier to employment at intake or may be used for caseload reductions at the discretion of caseworkers. Interestingly, testing positive for illegal drugs does not qualify an individual for treatment through Families First in Arizona because that program is accessed by referral from Child Protective Services to keep the family together or from DES to eliminate barriers to the work program. Since a positive drug test disqualifies a person for 12 months, those individuals with a positive drug test based on "reasonable cause" would not be referred to treatment in Arizona.

The policy choices described in these examples reflect differences in the degenerative political contexts across states. States that use drug disqual-ification to increase "deviant" targets for political and economic gain run the risk of excluding so many people from "legitimate" forms of social, political, and economic participation that it may begin to impact institutional credibility. "Get tough" criminal justice policies have resulted in a population under corrections supervision made up of approximately 80% drug-related offenses and reflecting monstrous racial disparities (Wacquant 2009). Some states have implemented policies that perpetuate perverse incentives to increasingly incarcerate drug offenders in private prisons, which fuel economic growth in the state. For example, the heavy enforcement of marijuana infractions in New York feeds the prison-industrial complex in upstate New York, largely with young men of color from New York City with low political power and low social status. Although the social and economic costs of sustaining a system that increasingly alienates a growing group of "deviants" mount exponentially, reversing the degenerative trend becomes increasingly difficult because those who gain economically and politically leverage greater political and social influence. When welfare policy also targets "deviants" by restricting access to institutions that might offer opportunities for drug offenders to reintegrate into legitimate economic activities, there is likely to be a growing trend toward heavy social control and increasing impoverishment. States that restrict access to assistance and do not refer to treatment are likely to increasingly rely on the carceral hand of the state and vastly increase inequality. Reversing trends toward degenerative poverty governance that threaten to increase impoverishment requires political discourse about the complexities of addiction, forms of adequate treatment, and what states can actually afford in terms of the costs of addiction and treatment.

State funds accounted for 46% of the total welfare expenditures for a given state under AFDC. PRWORA introduced myriad differences in funding streams and spending choices across states. The TANF block grant is conditioned upon the state continuing to contribute 75 to 80% of what the state had been spending on AFDC prior to PRWORA. States now have considerable flexibility in choosing funding streams and coupling them in ways that afford opportunities for extensions and exemptions from the time limits and work requirements linked to federal dollars. States may restrict TANF cash assistance to federal dollars only, and use state MOE funds to assist families in programs other than TANF. States may commingle state MOE funds with federal funds to provide TANF cash assistance. Commingled funds in a single TANF program render the entire program subject to the federal guidelines.

States may segregate federal and state funding streams, accounting for state MOE apart from federal funds used on its TANF program. Segregated state spending allows the state to distribute the caseload such that some families receive federally funded assistance and some families receive state-funded TANF; accordingly, states are held to the performance standards relevant to the funding source. States can assign funding to cases in a manner that allows the state to maximize compliance and/or maintain discretion without undermining federal guidelines. States may also establish separate state programs to fund programs that target people who do not meet the federal eligibility requirement or otherwise provide assistance that does not target a TANF objective. Non-TANF state programs may count toward the MOE requirement only if the program is linked to an allowable purpose, targets eligible families, meets the new spending test, is not funding a non-TANF program receiving other federal funding (exceptions for the CCDBG matching funds), and is not double-counted toward state matching of Welfare-to-Work or Medicaid programs. Separate state funding allows states to provide assistance that is not subject to the federal requirements.

Coupling funding streams maximizes state discretion. However, states may also maximize discretion and expedite caseload reductions by using federal dollars for programs other than cash assistance. For example, Florida funds TANF CA exclusively through segregated and separated funds, limiting cash assistance to 48 months and using federal dollars for other forms of assistance. Figure 3A in Appendix A illustrates the various choices states make in funding TANF CA. State choices regarding funding streams show how states manage discretion and demonstrate the importance of adequate perspective in research. Because states utilize numerous funding sources to achieve diverse objectives in poverty governance, a clear picture of the components of the policy process requires pulling together knowledge about the system from multiple levels of analysis.

FAMILY POLICIES

Several reform movements have affected the makeup of the family policies and approaches to addressing the TANF imperative for promoting and maintaining two-parent families. Scholars such as William Julius Wilson (1987), described a "culture of poverty" based on very clever research that demonstrated that some people have the advantage of living in communities that foster trust and that this tends to be absent in impoverished communities. There are two ways that one could read this story. On the one hand, a storyteller may explain the circumstances that inhibit constructive social norms. On the other hand, a storyteller may depict impoverished communities as disorderly and dysfunctional. Paternalists took the story of disorder and dysfunction and attempted to create opportunities to enforce patterns of behavior that serve traditional values. The use of behavioral incentives and sanctions to compel "right" behavior and gain compliance coalesced with neoliberal governance in a manner that rationalizes market discipline and justifies a high degree of social control. In addition, the devolution revolution affords new access points. Devolution modifies the conflict space, shifting influence to private providers that address welfare objectives defined within the contractual logic of poverty governance.

The feminization of poverty refers to three distinct poverty trends (see Heymann 2000; McLanahan, Sorenson, and Watson 1989; Pearce 1978):

1. the higher incidence of poverty among women;

2. that women are more likely to experience more severe poverty; and

3. that poverty among women is more persistent as women are at greater risk of being long-term poor.

The unequal state of men's and women's poverty rates and the processes by which the women's risk of poverty increasingly exceeds the poverty risk of men is also reflected in the gender poverty gap, which is the difference in current dollars necessary to move out of poverty. The feminization of poverty could be applied to almost any period in history except for major depressions, when large numbers of men also found themselves out of work. However, the prominence of poverty among women as a social issue results from the interaction of women's real poverty with modern feminism and public policy. The feminization of poverty largely results from low pay and discrimination in the labor market. In addition, undervaluing caregiving roles when traditionally held by women and a lack of child support enforcement contribute to poverty among women. However, the welfare system was blamed by paternalists for the rise of single-parent families.[6] Single-parent families, particularly households headed by women, were considered problematic by paternalists because they do not conform to traditional gender roles. Neoliberals also framed single-parent families as the problem. The problem for neoliberals was that single-parent households are less economically viable. Consequently, the neoliberal paternalist discourse on the feminization of poverty focused on making it society's goal to restore the traditional family.

The rhetoric of traditional family values and the complexities of the feminization of poverty were used to manipulate the dimensions of the debate over welfare reform. The complaints by some New Right theorists that antipoverty programs sap the authority of the male breadwinner and encourage feminism, leading to the moral corruption of society, are part of the fundamentally flawed rhetoric that remains a central element motivating family policies in some states. Alternatively, evidence regarding the feminization of poverty has been used to attempt to advance the social status of women in some cases, and to blame single mothers for the conditions of poverty in other instances. Consequently, the emphasis on the nuclear family as a means for fostering economic stability became an integral aspect of TANF. However, states vary considerably in their approaches to restoring good faith in the institution of marriage.

Able-bodied two-parent families were not eligible for TANF until the AFDC-Unemployed Parent (AFDC-UP) program was established in 1961. AFDC-UP benefits were required in all states beginning in 1988; although some states chose to time-limit those benefits. Eligibility for AFDC-UP upheld three means tests in addition to the standard AFDC rules: (1) the work history test required that the primary wage earner had worked at least six of the previous 13 quarters; (2) the 100 hour rule meant that applicants had to establish that the primary wage earner worked less than 100 hours per month; and (3) at least 30 days had passed since the loss of a job. Because TANF allows states to determine eligibility requirements and specifies the formation and maintenance of two-parent families as an objective, many states eliminated the work history test and/or the 100 hour rule through modifying the TANF program rules or by utilizing a separate state program. Alaska, Maine, Montana, North Dakota, Oklahoma, South Dakota, and Tennessee were the only states to maintain all three means tests for two-parent families. Some states made eligibility for two-parent families more restrictive. For example, North Dakota's eligibility requirements for two-parent families are highly restrictive. In order to avoid work rate penalties, North Dakota places two-parent families in a separate state program. However, access to workfare is generally less restrictive than AFDC-UP was for two-parent families in 43 states.

There are several states that provide what are referred to as marriage incentives. Marriage incentives signal a reliance on family and market solutions to welfare. Most of the states providing marriage incentives or bonuses are in the South. Alabama disregards new and reconciling spouse's income for three months, and Oklahoma disregards new spouse's income for three months for the purposes of determining eligibility. Mississippi and Texas disregard new spousal income for six months, and North Dakota disregards new step-parent's income for 6 months in determining eligibility. Tennessee disregards the income of a new spouse if the household falls below 185% of the need standard. New Jersey disregards the income of stepparents in cases in which the household income is at or worse than 150% of the federal poverty level. West Virginia provides a $100 monthly marriage bonus to parents eligible for TANF benefits with children in common if they marry.

TANF affords states flexibility regarding whether or not to increase cash assistance after the birth of an additional child in a family already receiving TANF benefits. In those states that do increase assistance when recipients have additional children, the state determines the amount of that increase. States that do not increase cash assistance to families that have

additional children while receiving cash assistance have what is referred
to as a family cap. Table 1.5 in Appendix A outlines variations in family
policies across states, including family caps. Family caps are a cost control
measure, and in some cases, they are intended to discourage people living
in poverty from having additional children.

Table 1.5 in Appendix A also lists healthy marriages and fatherhood
initiatives. H.R. 4737 altered the language of the welfare reform mandates
related to the nuclear family to read: "encourage the formation and maintenance of two-parent *married* families, and *encourage responsible fatherhood*."
This legislation also established annual performance metrics,[7] including
measures assessing "healthy marriages," and provided supplemental grants
to promote the definition of "healthy marriage" adopted by the state.[8] Arizona, Florida, Louisiana, Michigan, Oklahoma, Utah, and Virginia are highly
active in this area of family policy.

The DRA (2005) created new TANF funding of $150 million per year
over five years to promote healthy marriages (a minimum of $98 million per
year on demonstration projects), Indian child welfare ($2 million per year
to test the effectiveness of tribal governments' ability to protect children
from abuse and neglect), and responsible fatherhood initiatives ($50 million
per year). Congress extended healthy marriage and responsible fatherhood
funding through the 2011 fiscal year and altered the split to $75 million for
each. Any funds used for Indian child welfare is subtracted from the healthy
marriage and responsible fatherhood funds equally. The nuclear family policies and initiatives listed in Table 1.5 in Appendix A include currently
active marriage and fatherhood programs, activities, and services sponsored
by the state but does not include military marriage-related programs. Because
the funding for the various marriage initiatives that exist across states comes
from multiple sources, including initiatives and campaigns entirely distinct
from TANF, and may be led by state cooperatives, Community-Based Organizations (CBOs), or research institutions, state efforts to strengthen marriage vary considerably.[9]

The National Campaign to Prevent Teen and Unplanned Pregnancy
administers the Pathways to Responsible Fatherhood Grants and the Com-
munity-Centered Healthy Marriage and Relationship Grants. Most of these
grants are provided to local organizations and research universities, but some
are awarded to state Health and Human Services agencies. There are also
sources of funding for fatherhood initiatives beyond federal TANF grants,
including Child Support funded programs, state-funded efforts, statewide
commissions funded exclusively through donations, and community-based
efforts supported by components of the Administration for Children and
Families (ACF). The Office of Child Support Enforcement administers
the $10–12 million Access and Visitation State formula grant to facilitate

access and visitation between noncustodial parents and their children as well as the smaller programs the office funds to strengthen compliance. Additionally, President Obama's 2011 budget priorities included $500 million for a new Fatherhood, Marriage, and Families Innovation Fund for federal grants to states to evaluate state-initiated fatherhood programs and research family well-being. In many respects, these efforts are deserving of separate analysis, as a variety of sources of funding suggest variation in the criteria for understanding the health of marriages. In addition, the conflict space regarding the issue of marriage appears to have devolved. States and local governments have issued policies attempting to define marriage, and private providers within those jurisdictions influence the enactment of family initiatives. Future research is necessary to understand the governance of marriage, particularly as it relates to income, race, gender, and sexuality.

The "formation and maintenance of two-parent families" TANF objective produces a degree of variation across states with respect to the emphasis that states place on traditional family units that serve economic ends rather than an emphasis on safe, stable homes. States that attempt to maintain a professional social work standard utilize contracts that offer services (often combined with SSBG funds) to assist parents in providing a safe, stable home environment. States motivated by neoliberal paternalist stories of traditional family economic units tend to implement this objective through top-down managerial oversight. The constraints of NPM compel program evaluation that produces quantifiable outcomes. Therefore, states with stronger social work norms have to cleverly define objectives and establish the quality of services within the managerial logic. Resisting the dominance of managerialism over "helping relationships" requires more work and the skillful execution of program evaluation. Furthermore, the internalization of the morals of the neoliberal paternalist stories increases the pressure on social work norms in the welfare administration process.

There are a number of family policies that illustrate the differences across states with respect to good faith in the institution of marriage. Some states aim to transfer social obligations to the family unit. Other states attempt to foster good faith in the institution of marriage by focusing on co-parenting arrangements and addressing family violence. Family policies that treat marriage as primarily an economic contract fail to address the volatility that domestic violence introduces. Several states have established standards and procedures to screen and identify people with a history of domestic violence, refer cases in which there is a history of family violence to counseling and support services (sometimes even compelling participation in TANF self-sufficiency plans), and in some cases waive program requirements to facilitate safety. States that have chosen to certify their Family Violence policies can waive the requirements for those attempting to leave a violent relationship without negatively impacting the state's performance metrics. Table 1.5 in Appendix A also outlines the states' choices with respect to fostering good faith in marriage that places a premium on non-violence. Future research is essential to understanding the impact of welfare reform on the feminization of poverty. The risk to personal safety increases in relationships with a history of violence when a subverted partner attempts to gain self-sufficiency, so the choices states make with regard to domestic violence have a tremendous potential to impact both family violence and TANF objectives in complex ways that require knowledge of empirically based practices in family therapy and an understanding of the role institutions play in structuring alternatives and mediating violence.

Those states that recognize the threat violence poses to personal and economic stability, as well as the increased risk to those attempting to leave a violent relationship, tend to provide extensions and exemptions to assist those individuals. However, those states that do not offer exemptions or extensions in cases of domestic violence tend to make self-sufficiency more difficult for women and their children living in violent relationships. For example, Oklahoma has no exemptions or extensions for cases involving domestic violence.

The Oklahoma Marriage Initiative (OMI) is a public-private partnership to prevent divorce; although the statewide steering committee includes representatives who are involved in the treatment of family violence. The OMI programs are not counseling and are not meant to address the more serious relationship issues related to domestic violence. They are workshops provided by local community organizations and faith-based organizations to "maintain commitment." The OMI is part of a series of social goals designed to reduce the state's divorce and out-of-wedlock birth rates, which include reducing the marriage license fee from $25 to $5 for couples who participate in premarital counseling. In addition, private foundation and discretionary state dollars were used to take the plans of the steering committee and entertain competitive bids for contracts to coordinate, review, and develop the curriculum for marriage education for adults and high school students.

The Oklahoma State Cooperative Extension also offers marriage-related services in partnership with OMI, and the Army's Building Strong and Ready Families program is implemented at Fort Sill. The Army's program includes screening and referrals for substance abuse and domestic violence, but the state's marriage-related services and educational programs aim to commit people to marriage as a mechanism for addressing child poverty. Yet, it is domestic violence that has the most damaging impact on the quality and stability of marriage. For example, the Oklahoma Statewide Survey on Marriage and Divorce found that 30% of the divorced respondents who do not receive government assistance cited domestic violence as the reason for divorce. The same study also found that domestic violence was cited as the reason for divorce by 47% of the divorced respondents who receive government assistance. Additionally, findings from the Minnesota Family Investment Program evaluation show that women with more stable incomes and higher earnings may be less vulnerable to abuse. Oklahoma's strategy for investing in marriage depends upon increasing the good faith of potential abusers and requires economic conditions that do not enhance the vulnerability of women who are more often the target of abuse. Perhaps more importantly, there are currently no empirically based treatments with demonstrated success at rehabilitating perpetrators of domestic violence, so strategies that attempt to commit women to marriages despite the threat to safety may undermine both social and economic goals. Future research may utilize the Domestic Violence and Sexual Assault Data Resource Center, available through the Justice Research and Statistical Association, to examine the extent to which these initiatives serve as effective prevention and intervention measures that reduce the incidence of domestic violence over time.

EMPLOYMENT STRATEGIES

The conditions of the TANF block grant require that states have a set share of families participating in a minimum number of work hours each week prescribed by the family structure. The Workforce Investment Act (WIA) of 1998 increased the pressure on states to intensify work rates, and the Social Security Act now requires that every work-eligible individual must be participating in an approved work activity after receiving cash assistance for 24 months. These demands are increasingly met through unpaid work experiences, community service, and subsidies to the private, nonprofit, and public sector for work experiences and training. Federal law requires efforts to prevent unpaid work experiences, subsidized work, community service, and On-the-Job Training (OJT) from contributing to worker displacement.[10] TANF funds may be paid to employers to reimburse some or all of the employer's costs for providing the worker's wages instead of being distributed to clients as assistance. A third-party contractor can be considered the employer of record (often a temporary staffing agency) and paid a fee to secure the requisite work hours. An evaluation of a transitional jobs program in New York City recommends the following guidelines to maintain compliance: keep the wages of transitional workers at the same level as those performing similar work, utilize numerous worksites so that no one employer can replace the whole workforce with subsidized workers, and consult with unions in the development of job placements.[11] The use of unpaid work experiences, subsidized work, community service, and OJT to regulate economic transitions has the potential to provide participants with economic opportunities and/or expand the labor pool. Therefore, research that goes beyond the evaluation of contracts is essential to understanding who gets what, when, and how under the evolving conditions of poverty governance.

State and local workforce investment boards are led by regional and/ or local employers who manage the efficient training and placement efforts that meet what they perceive to be the existing labor market demands. Basic labor standards and protections are maintained in the WIA, and organized labor is not prohibited from participating in the planning and operations of workforce development boards. However, the extent to which labor is involved or consulted varies considerably.[12] Some states have reorganized their workfare programs to fall within the state's workforce development program, state offices of economic opportunity, or state department of labor. In Florida, for example, the Welfare Transition (WT) program operates under the authority of regionally organized Workforce Development Boards established by the Workforce Investment Act (WIA) of 1998. Florida's 24 Regional Workforce Boards (RWBs) are public-private partnerships made up of local business, labor, and nonprofit representatives but are legally required to maintain a majority membership of local employers responsible for defining workforce priorities. Statewide implementation guidelines are set by the public-private corporation Workforce Florida, Inc. The contracts established by RWBs are overseen by Workforce Florida, Inc. and administered in partnership with the Agency for Workforce Innovation (AWI), which is responsible for coordination. Florida's system is a highly decentralized and privatized and has been described by federal officials as an "innovative" model for integrating control over low-skilled labor (Austin 2005).[13]

The social status and political participation of organized labor within a state affects the likelihood of policies related to the eligibility of strikers. The relationship between organized labor in the state and workforce investment boards, as well as the differential and shifting influence of an assortment of trade groups across the state, results in a great deal of variation. Many states have no specific policy targeting strikers, which in some cases may result in increased caseworker discretion to that end. Some states restrict TANF eligibility so that strikers are disqualified, as it would be considered voluntary separation from employment. Some states deem strikers ineligible or disqualify the entire household unit. Federal regulations disqualify workers on a voluntary strike from nutrition assistance funded through federal dollars, but state-funded programs define their own policies. Table 1.6 in Appendix A outlines state policies that specifically address strikers in the eligibility or benefit calculations for TANF and/or state food assistance in the state policy manuals. Sixty-four percent of the states with striker restrictions are Right To Work (RTW) states.[14] Nine of the RTW states have no policy specific to strikers, which may mean that there are no restrictions or that it is an administrative or discretionary matter.

Restrictions on the eligibility of strikers suggest an emphasis on labor regulation in the welfare administration process. These restrictions are also likely to subsequently affect the political participation and possibly social status of organized labor in the state. In states that penalize the entire family under strike conditions, the strike can become the threat to the economic circumstances of the family rather than a means for securing benefits for labor. The more labor regulations a state imposes the greater the risk that the low-wage labor pool may become subject to the interests of business. Businesses consistently seek to lower labor costs and transfer costs to consumers. States that serve the interests of business to the exclusion of labor and consumers may experience lower wages, unstable employment, and increasing costs.

The organizational structures of state TANF programs also vary widely. To some extent, the organizational structure is conditioned by the funding streams, but the structure is also related to tasks and oriented around contract management. All states implement employment strategies through contracts with the household or assistance unit. These contracts are referred to in various ways across states, including but not limited to Personal Responsibility Contracts (PRCs), Personal Responsibility Agreements (PRAs), Individual Employment Plans (IEPs), Individual Responsibility Plan (IRP), Family Responsibility Plan (FRP), Mutual Responsibility Plan (MRP), and Family Self-Sufficiency Plans. In some cases, the responsibility plan and the work participation agreement are separate records. The contracts are "agreements" between the clients and the case manager, acting on behalf of the state in accordance with the state's TANF policy manual, which constitutes a plan to attach the clients to the labor market. Vermont is an interesting exception in that it is clearly communicated to eligible clients that "[y]ou and your case manager will create a family development plan that maps out your work goals and the steps you will take to achieve them. As you make progress, you will update the plan together." The Vermont Family Development Plan (FDP) utilizes the language of economic development but emphasizes the mutuality in the exchange in a manner distinct from most states. It is important to note that participation in TANF requires that applicants agree to the terms of the contract as a condition of eligibility. The work rates and compliance with child support enforcement are nonnegotiable. In addition, some states consider labor regulation, public health policies, and participation in nuclear family initiatives to be nonnegotiable as well. The type of work activities and the supports available are usually offered at the discretion of the caseworker. The client is made aware of and required to submit to the TANF rules, and the case manager uses the assessments and available resources to incentivize and sanction clients according to the clients' perceived compliance.

Access to information about available services and eligibility for the various programs that any given state may have is regulated in large part by the case manager. The discretion of case managers is influenced by perceptions of "compliance." The enactment of most of the services available to TANF clients is performed in the private and nonprofit sectors, often requiring compliance with varied contract objectives. This means that the patterns of interaction between case managers, caseworkers, and clients order access. This sorting may occur at multiple levels in the governance network. Thus, the potential influence of stereotype bias in the enactment of policy may regulate who gets access to what kinds of opportunities. Further analysis of these relationships across the governance network is essential.[15] When opportunities are sorted according to arbitrary stereotypes, social cleavages are enhanced and economic gains are not likely maximized. As Bachrach and Baratz (1962) note, power is not simply influence or agenda control. Power is also about who and how people and issues are marginalized and excluded. Power is expressed in observable behavior, the determination of the agenda, and through the forces that shape needs, demands and self-view (what Foucault refers to as the governmentality). Where the least powerful are marginalized and excluded, critical issues are at risk of being unheard or ignored. In addition, cognitive research suggests that proactive strategies for affecting bias at the first phase of the stereotyping process can effectively limit this type of cognitive error (see Moskowitz and Li 2011; Moskowitz and Stone 2011). Therefore, learning more about the enactment of poverty governance offers opportunities to provide professional training with the potential to minimize bias and reduce unstable power gaps.

In addition, the tools that states use vary considerably and often vary within the state across contracted service providers to the extent that the state may or may not define evidence-based practice and performance measures within the contracting relationship. An example of some of the tools used to facilitate employment can be found in the job readiness portfolio that some states utilize during orientation.[16] Generally, job readiness and skills training tends to focus on developing "soft skills," which is a management concept referring to "people skills," "emotional intelligence," personal habits, social graces, communication skills, and even optimism. Some states contract out job readiness, search, and skills training as well as placement services; while this may be a part of the eligibility determination process conducted by the local social service agency in other states. Figure 4A in Appendix A identifies states' requirements regarding immediate participation in job searches or job search programs as a condition of eligibility along with the corresponding changes in poverty among working families prior to the recession (2007–08). Eight of the states that require immediate participation in job search or job search programs saw poverty among working families decline during this period. Four of the states that do not require immediate participation in job searches or job programs as a condition of eligibility had reductions in poverty among working families during this period. Without controlling for the other factors that impact the economic outlook of each state, it is impossible to draw definitive conclusions. However, there appears to be at least some indication that states may effectively minimize transaction costs by connecting people with open jobs efficiently with this policy. However, a look at the implementation procedures within each jurisdiction specifically would be necessary to understand the extent to which this policy might be used to manage or restrict eligibility.

State TANF plans and policy manuals detail the opportunity structures that make up the workfare employment services.[17] Strategies range from subsidies to employers in the private, public, and nonprofit sectors to support services for participants that facilitate employment. Some states leverage various forms of federal supports to encourage microenterprise. Temporary Assistance for Needy Families (TANF), Workforce Investment Act, and Community Development Block Grants (CDBGs) are potential sources of support for job creation through microenterprise development, as well as training and services for entrepreneurs. Eighteen states chose not to use any form of federal assistance to support small businesses or allow self-employment or entrepreneurship training to count toward work requirements in 2012. Thirty-two states leveraged one or a combination of federal supports to facilitate microenterprise. Figure 5A in Appendix A illustrates the variation across states in the utilization of TANF, WIA, and/or CDBG funds to encourage small business development. However, employing federal block grants for this purpose can vary in any given state from year to year and is most often implemented through private for-profit or nonprofit contractors. For example, Oregon's support for microenterprise is organized through the state's business development department, Business Oregon. Oregon has consistently increased its support for microenterprise development since 2007, including providing support for the Oregon Microenterprise Network (OMEN). The Oregon Microenterprise Network (OMEN) operates programs and conducts analyses that are used to ease market entry, identify and assist in filling gaps in local markets, and provide consulting services to entrepreneurs that would otherwise be cost prohibitive. The research and advocacy of OMEN has contributed to the increasing investment in microenterprise as a job creation strategy in Oregon.

Iowa is another example of a state that offers considerable support for microenterprise as a job creation strategy. In fact, Iowa is considered a leader in supporting microenterprise as a poverty alleviation strategy because it was the first state to design a welfare-to-work strategy intended to foster microenterprise development through the PROMISE Jobs program in the 1980s. However, access to capital for small business startups has consistently been problematic in Iowa. State support for microenterprise has varied over time in Iowa, primarily due to broader economic constraints, and in 2012, Iowa did not employ any federal supports for microenterprise development. Currently, there are disparate outcomes assessments evaluating the performance of contractors or programs in meeting contract requirements or objectives, and there are advocacy groups that engage in research to promote the expansion of microenterprise investments. But, a thorough analysis of the broader economic impact of these investments across space and time is generally lacking.

Work subsidies refers to the use of public funds to offset some or all of the costs of employing an individual, and are another workfare strategy. Subsidies for private, public, and nonprofit employers for employment, work experiences, and OJT may come from a variety of sources, including but not limited to federal WIA funds, state departments of labor and economic opportunity, and public-private partnerships. Table 1.7 in Appendix A illustrates the TANF dollars spent by each state on work subsidies from 2004 to 2009. The TANF dollars spent on subsidized work may reflect the state's priorities with respect to spending on welfare that targets people living in poverty. However, without an accounting of subsidies to the private sector from various sources along the range of priorities, it is impossible to understand whether and how work subsidies may benefit people living in poverty and/or the private sector. The current state of performance metrics makes it incredibly difficult to assess the true size and scope of poverty governance. It also makes determining the extent to which subsidies might have shifted to the private sector problematic. These challenges have to be overcome before one can even begin to assess whether or not these subsidies might be beneficial and to whom.

There are a few states that do not provide direct subsidies to private, public, and/or nonprofit organizations to facilitate employment. All states have various programs or stages in the employability process that TANF participants are subject to in which assistance is provided to private, public, and/or nonprofit organizations. Since TANF client benefits are distributed as wages from the subsidized employer, income and payroll taxes are collected on them. In an effort to ease the transition to the work force, the Earned Income Tax Credit (EITC) was established to provide incentives for work, and the Work Opportunity Tax Credit (WOTC) was established to provide incentives for employers to hire TANF participants by offsetting the costs of payroll tax increases that would otherwise result. The EITC and the WOTC are federal programs that have also been adopted by some states to apply to state income and payroll taxes.[18]

TANF requires parents or caretakers receiving cash assistance to participate in community service if the individual's work activities do not meet the work rate requirement after two months. However, some states, such as Ohio, opt out of this requirement by immediately assigning participants to other allowable activities. Participants assigned to unpaid work experiences and community service are protected by the Fair Labor Standards Act (FLSA) of 1938. Discretion is often assigned to county agencies or local workforce boards responsible for examining which specific work experience and community service activities are subject to FLSA. Unpaid work experience and community service activities that are subject to the FLSA requirements limit the number of hours a cash and/or food assistance recipient can be required to participate in these activities. The idea is that participants are "working off the cost of their benefits" and "gaining experience" that might make them more attractive to employers. The FLSA sets the guidelines for the calculation of this exchange, including the maximum allowable hours for work experience and community service. Work experience may include assignments assisting in the refurbishing of publicly assisted housing or other activities deemed appropriate by the caseworker to assist in acquiring "the general skills, knowledge, and work habits necessary to obtain employment," according to the ACF.

Additional examples of supports that states may utilize to assist people living in poverty include job skills training, OJT, vocational education, and assistance with adult basic education, English as a Second Language (ESL), and GED classes. Job skills training may be conducted as a part of the job search and readiness program, or training may be a separate service in some states. However, structured job training is supervised by the state or the responsible contracting agency. Job training provided to an individual learning the knowledge and skills essential for adequate performance in a given job in the private or public sector is considered OJT and is generally partially or fully subsidized. Vocational education refers to preparation for employment in emerging occupations and is most often implemented through partnerships with local community colleges and technical schools. Teen parents are required to attend school and make adequate progress toward a high school diploma or obtain a GED in order to qualify for assistance. Consequently, priority for the money available to enhance educational opportunities is often given to teens. When states have made adequate funds available, there may also be GED and ESL classes available to participants for whom their absence represents a significant barrier to employment. Some states also fund workforce advancement grants for education that provide laptops, Internet access, textbooks, funding for courses not covered by financial aid, counseling, and possibly assistance with childcare and transportation. States, such as Connecticut, that have additional supports for educational opportunities, often target occupations that are likely to expand, and the grants are usually contingent upon remaining in the state for a given period of time.

The use of TANF efforts to mitigate educational gaps in the state workforce varies considerably, as does the focus on occupational categories.[19] Future research is required to assess the extent to which some states may mitigate transaction costs for growth sectors. The relative success of such efforts has to be understood within the context of the system of poverty governance because the economic outlook, demographic makeup, existing educational gaps, political climate, and institutional mechanisms for facilitating transaction costs are important differences between states that are likely to affect the types of investments and jobs created that TANF clients might access.

Some states also implement various forms of supplemental employment assistance to allow for a stable transition to employment with greater economic outcomes. Often these programs operate in combination. For example, Maine administers a TANF Worker Supplement (TWS) in combination with Parents as Scholars (PaS), and Alternative Aid, in addition to offering child care, extended medical, and transportation assistance for work-related activities and an emergency assistance program. TANF or PaS participants in Maine who become ineligible due to increased earnings may qualify for assistance with the purchase of food products when they are not able to access Alternative Aid. Parents in Maine who qualify for TANF may participate in PaS if the caseworker determines that they meet the following conditions: (1) enroll in a two or four-year college; (2) do not already possess a bachelor's degree in a field in which there are available jobs; (3) do not have the present ability to make at least 85% of Maine's median income for their family size; (4) have the requisite background to complete the degree they hope to pursue; and (5) pursue a degree that is likely to improve their financial future. PaS participants in Maine receive support for transportation, childcare, required books and supplies not covered by financial aid, and up to $300 per year for essential clothing. PaS students receive cash benefits equivalent to TANF CA, and tuition assistance up to $3,500 per academic year may be available for PaS participants who do not qualify for financial aid. PaS participants also participate in the ASPIRE job preparation program. Alternative Aid in Maine provides vouchers for up to three months of TANF benefits to assist qualified applicants obtain or retain employment, which does not count against the time limit on assistance. Alternative Aid in Maine is a diversion strategy, whereas the TWS program is a postemployment strategy. TWS is available to ASPIRE TANF or ASPIRE PaS participants in Maine who choose to terminate their benefits for those programs or become ineligible due to increased earnings, to ease the transition to better employment outcomes through assistance with the purchase of food products. Maine's emergency assistance program operates only to the extent that funds are available through annual state appropriations. Although the program does not cover all emergencies, families with children who are at risk of destitution or homelessness may qualify for a combination of payments or services for a 30-day period.

Table 1.8 in Appendix A details the share of TANF funding spent in 2009 on different aspects of each state's work program. TANF work-first strategies can be broadly categorized as transportation or support services, education and training, work subsidies, and other work-related expenses such as support services. These figures account for how TANF dollars are spent within the work programs. However, in order to understand the commitment to any given strategy, one would have to ascertain the totals from all of the various sources of funding for each category in each state and put that into the context of the total funding for all the services offered in each state.

There are two stories one could tell about how these systems of accounting simultaneously increase accountability for dollars spent from specific revenue streams and diminish the capacity to capture the full scale of effort on any given priority. On the one hand, the increased accountability for outcome metrics defined by the grant maker limits discretionary spending through the chain of devolution. On the other hand, the increased flexibility to structure and resource social services and hold contracting agents accountable to various, specific outcomes limits the transparency of governance. Because there are numerous sources of funding for any given objective and accounting is based on contractual obligations, ascertaining the total amount spent on a given objective may be possible at the agency level but is difficult to estimate across funding streams. Consequently, the scale of spending priorities is obscure. And while agencies are subject to oversight from multiple principals and expected to meet performance goals, more comprehensive analysis of the impact of various policies in the system of poverty governance is inhibited by the data collected. In this case, the data that are often excluded serve to marginalize any potential challenges to the neoliberal paternalist story line.

SANCTIONS

The neoliberal story of behavioral contracting promoted the notion that rational individuals respond to incentives and sanctions. The moral of the neoliberal welfare reform story was that manipulating incentives and sanctioning nonstandard behavior would increase efficiencies. The paternalist welfare reform story presented the "stick and carrot" approach as necessary for leading people to appropriate, responsible citizenship. Both neoliberals and paternalists sold the idea that work is responsible and requires management. Alternative approaches were silenced by claims that challenging behavioral contracting amounted to undermining work. Consequently, the neoliberal paternalist story line defined the contracting language and the implementation of poverty governance. Compliance by contracting agents, as measured by performance metrics, and the perceived cooperation of individual participants, discerned by case managers, became the expectation.

There are a number of administrative tools welfare agencies utilize to compel cooperation and produce caseload reductions, including procedural accessibility, withholding of benefits to punish rule violations, and discouraging of dissent through street-level practice.[20] Sanctions are financial penalties imposed on TANF clients for noncompliance with the program requirements that serve as one of the primary instruments for caseload reductions. The sanctioning language satisfies the neoliberal story of behavioral interventions facilitating market performance while it simultaneously calls upon paternalistic notions of punishment for deviant behavior.[21] The case manager's role is thus shifted to disciplining individuals perceived to be irresponsible and managing metrics to meet performance goals. The authority to identify deviant behavior and the power to punish noncompliance are present at all points at which opportunities to move out of poverty are not present. Sanctions are therefore one of the primary mechanisms for efficiently regulating the opportunity structures devised by the states within the federal guidelines.

TANF affords states the ability to develop sanctioning strategies that vary in structure and in stringency. States are required to sanction noncompliant behaviors but are allowed the authority to devise sanctioning rules and procedures that vary along several dimensions, including type, duration, remedies, and approaches to repeated noncompliance. States may adopt partial sanctions, gradual full-family sanctions, immediate full-family sanctions, or pay for performance incentives. Payfor-performance incentives are the carrot of the "stick and carrot" approach to behavioral contracting in poverty governance. The duration of sanction imposition varies across states from no minimum (meaning until compliance), to one month, or up to three months. Caseworkers are required to establish that a cure for noncompliance is evident, through documenting in the case file that either a willingness to comply is apparent or a period of compliance is recognized.[22] However, there remains a considerable degree of discretion in ascertaining the cure requirements for noncompliance in some states. Several states impose a longer minimum duration when sanctioning repeated noncompliance; whereas others impose stricter cure requirements. Others utilize still more stringent sanctions for repeated noncompliance or require reapplication for benefits. There are also a few states that impose lifetime bans on assistance for repeated noncompliance. Additionally, states may impose different sanctioning procedures for different types of violations, and may also institute procedures that afford caseworkers discretion in ascertaining the severity of the sanction applied. In some states, violations of personal responsibility may call for a greater degree of discretion, as the contract is interpreted by case management, which involves different procedures than more consistently interpreted sanctions for work noncompliance. Table 1.9 in Appendix A specifies the variation in the maximum sanction policies regarding personal responsibility and work noncompliance across states. States are required to sanction, allowed to devise their own sanction policies, and are under increasing pressure to use sanctions to increase work rates and reduce caseloads.

The DRA of 2005 changed the calculation of work participation rates. Each percentage point decline in average monthly caseloads can be credited to work participation rates. States must meet the statutory requirements for work participation for all families and for two-parent families to avoid financial penalties. The individual target rates for each state are calculated by the statutory rate minus credits for caseload reductions. The credits states might have received for caseload reductions occurring after 1995 were phased out. Beginning in the fiscal year of 2007, state eligibility for credits to work participation rates is based on caseload reductions that occurred after 2005. Additionally, the count of total families now includes families receiving TANF assistance as well as families receiving separate state assistance to account for the MOE requirements. Work participation rates are calculated by dividing the number of families engaged in federally acceptable work activities for the requisite hours by the currently calculated number of total families. Consequently, states are under pressure to reduce caseloads at a rate that upholds the MOE requirement and/or increase participation rates in order to reach the new compliance standard.

Sanctions are also linked to the receipt of other forms of assistance for people living in poverty, although the programs themselves are considered to be delinked. For families participating in more than one assistance program, overlap and inconsistency in the rules and procedures can confuse and intimidate participants. Moreover, the networks of communication linking these programs within the state affect the extent to which problematic errors or bureaucratic exclusion may influence the experiences of participants.[23]

Federal law prohibits full-family sanctions from applying to Medicaid eligibility, so when an adult family member is deemed noncompliant it should not result in the entire family's becoming ineligible for Medicaid. And as a general rule, the conduct requirements of the personal responsibility contracts have no bearing on Medicaid benefits. However, states have the option to eliminate Medicaid eligibility for an adult who is not pregnant, in addition to TANF CA, when that individual is not in compliance with the work requirements. Nineteen states terminate both Medicaid and TANF assistance for adults who are considered noncompliant with work requirements, although both federal and state policies provide for various good-cause exemptions.[24] All states, however, are prohibited from using work requirements as a basis for evaluating the eligibility of children, with the exception of teens who are the head of household and pregnant women, for whom there are separate program guidelines. All TANF and Medicaid programs across states have distinct child support cooperation requirements built into the programs. Those states that implement SCHIP through Medicaid expansion operate under those same Medicaid rules and procedures, and many states allow this type of sanctioning for those receiving assistance through separate state funds for medical support. Fourteen states have distinct child support cooperation requirements and/or comparable disqualification procedures in their food stamp programs, which result in an automatic sanction in the food stamp program for failing to perform a required action. Violations of child support cooperation agreements may also result in sanctions affecting childcare assistance in 14 states.

The punitive nature of state sanctioning schemes is highly contingent upon the definition of cooperation in each state's TANF policy. If cooperation is defined in a highly restrictive manner, obligations that are contradictory or difficult to meet may have consequences beyond a single program. The actual costs of sanctions imposed on families are difficult to estimate in the aggregate due to the variations in state policies, extent of devolution and dispersal of authority to issue sanctions, and variations in benefit amounts by family size, in addition to the contingencies within other programs. Furthermore, state sanctioning procedures interact with employment strategies. The state's preemployment requirements and approach to exemptions also impact the role sanctions play in welfare provision. The more a state enforces stringent preemployment requirements with fewer exemptions for circumstances such as caring for young children, disability, or family violence, the greater the likelihood of exclusion for those who tend to be the most disadvantaged on the market or have the greatest barriers to employment as they struggle to locate opportunities in their circumstances (Danziger and Seefeldt 2002; Wu, Cancian, Meyer, and Wallace 2006). They are also subsequently at a higher risk of suffering hunger, homelessness, utility shutoffs, material hardships, lack of medical care, and poor health as a result of the sanctions (Kalil, Seefeldt, and Wang 2002; Reichman, Teitler, and Curtis 2005).

Research consistently shows that the likelihood of being sanctioned and the experience of extreme hardship are significantly higher for black people living in poverty, who are subject to the most disciplinary regimes and pervasive discrimination in employment and incarceration practices (Fording, Soss, and Schram 2011; Soss, Fording, and Schram 2011a; Western and Petit 2005). This is also the case for people with lower levels of education or limited English proficiency who struggle with the complexities of the welfare system and face limited opportunities in the labor market (Kalil,

Seefeldt, and Wang 2002; Watkins-Hayes 2009). Recent research also shows that the severity, timing, and duration of sanctions have lagged effects on access to labor market opportunities. Sanctions that are more severe and of longer duration increase the risk of separation from assistance before positive employment outcomes are achieved (Wu 2008). Although the experience of race in welfare policy enactment plays out in subtle, complex, and contingent ways (Schram 2005), black people are likely to be subject to the most punitive regimes (Fording, Soss, and Schram 2011a). Concern regarding the extent to which these patterns may amplify opportunity gaps necessitates further study of how sanction schemes interact with client-caseworker relations within the organizational context.

Sanctioning cannot be untangled from the accumulation of disadvantages. Sanctions appear to function more as a punishment for perceived deviance than an instrument for regulating the orderly maximization of opportunities. Moreover, the logic of sanctioning requires that the intended message is communicated clearly, is interpreted appropriately, and affects the individual's rational calculus in a manner that results in behavioral change. However, the disparate circumstances and emphasis on market discipline over addressing transaction costs result in the heaviest sanctions often being imposed on the most marginalized. An individual may very well be made aware of the sanctioning rules and motivated to avoid a sanction but forced to choose between going to work and taking care of a sick child. That individual may know that failing to meet the work hours will result in a sanction but, without resources to care for a sick child, is forced to cut losses. The challenge from the client's perspective is that either choice is likely to result in being deemed irresponsible, and the family now faces a heavier burden as health issues and financial challenges accumulate. The emphasis on market discipline results in opportunity loss in each case in which participants face lose-lose choices. Sanctioning schemes and procedures that address the barriers to participation have a greater likelihood of enhancing opportunities for those with cumulative disadvantages (Danziger and Seefeldt 2002; Hasenfeld, Ghose, and Larson 2004; Wu et al. 2006). Moreover, disciplining parents has demonstrably negative effects on the school engagement (measured by disruptions in attendance and enrollment) of the children in TANF families (Larson, Singh, and Lewis 2011).

Sanctioning patterns are dynamic, and many of the unintended or perverse effects of sanctioning relationships can be masked if a researcher selects an inappropriate level of analysis or may be amplified if he/she fails to recognize the limits of autonomy or misinterprets the lines of authority in welfare provision. For example, Lael Keiser, Peter Mueser, and Seung-Whan Choic (2004) demonstrate that the complexities of discretion in sanctioning can be diluted in aggregate estimations of sanctioning rates. They show that while nonwhites are sanctioned at lower rates overall, nonwhites are sanctioned more than whites in every local area in their study. Their research suggests that in the Midwest, nonwhites tend to live in areas with lower sanction rates but are subject to more disciplinary authority until a population threshold is reached that affords nonwhites greater political power. Understanding the role of sanctions in poverty governance requires a schema for mapping the system and identifying the potential points at which participants might be directed to opportunities rather than disciplined for struggling in their participation. The current state of knowledge on sanctioning suggests that the severity of the sanctioning scheme increases the efficiency by which market discipline is imposed, activating a contingent labor force and excluding those on the margins. However, sanctioning schemes and their implementation vary considerably, and the different levels of devolution are problematic for the comparative method at this point. Assessing choices and practices that function most effectively as tools for realizing opportunities relies on piecing together research on sanctioning at different levels of analysis, evaluating their interaction with other parts of the system, and estimating how these networks compare as they relate to the state's economic opportunity horizon and strategic plan. For example, understanding how a state such as Florida, which structures welfare provision and the corresponding sanctions to serve the agriculture and tourism industries, compares to any other state requires more comprehensive studies of the disciplinary regimes within each state, such as the research conducted by Joe Soss, Richard Fording, and Sanford Schram in Florida. Replicating their research in other states will reveal whether or not states with less punitive structures and practices realize greater economic opportunities and for whom.

DIVERSION PROGRAMS

A state is allowed to use federal funds to assist up to 20% of its caseload beyond the 60-month federal time limit if hardship is established or domestic violence is confirmed. In addition, state MOE funds are not subject to federal time limit restrictions, and states may also use separate state funding to allow for time limit exemptions, extensions, and to develop diversion programs. A few states choose to identify groups for whom the TANF time clock does not run. Many states also establish criteria for which assistance may be extended or provided for through a separate state program that suspends the federal time clock on assistance (although there may still be a count against the limits on that state assistance).

State diversion programs operate in three forms. One form of diversion that some states provide offers lump-sum payment programs that assist those who are employed or who have a job offer with a one-time cash or voucher payment to meet immediate needs as their families transition or adjust to a transition, in lieu of utilizing TANF funds. A second form of diversion some states utilize waives the applicant work requirements during the 30 to 45-day certification period. A third form diverts participants from TANF time limits by providing separate support programs offering up to four months of assistance, which does not count toward federal time limits or work participation rates. However, the growing pressure that states are under to meet the increasing demands of the DRA of 2005 make diversion strategies more important to welfare provision across states. By 2008, all but three states had implemented at one time or another at least one diversion strategy, but a number of states also discontinued their diversion programs after the 2005 DRA. Table 1.10 in Appendix A outlines the diversion strategies across states based on each state's 2012 TANF plan. It should be noted that Hawaii, Massachusetts, Montana, Ohio, and Tennessee have exercised waivers for work-related activities to extend the time clock on assistance for all, select, or a subset of cases. However, the aspects of those waiver policies that were considered inconsistent with federal work requirements expired and were discontinued. The various diversion strategies are critical components of the poverty governance system. Diversion programs allow states to manage performance metrics. A diversion may extend assistance to some participants outside the standard restrictions on funding. It may afford some people the opportunity to avoid or delay TANF participation. Diversion programs may also be a strategy states employ to inhibit participation in TANF. Understanding how diversions are utilized and who may benefit (as well as which clients might be diverted altogether) is essential to determining the role diversion programs play in poverty governance.

Diversion programs may offer exemptions and/or extensions for various hardships. There are important differences between exemptions and extensions. Hardship exemptions stop the time clock from running on a family, based on particular, usually temporary, circumstances. Exemptions allow for assistance to families experiencing hardships that do not count toward the family's lifetime limit. For example, a mother attempting to leave a violent relationship, who has difficulty working because of the threat of violence, may be exempted from work requirements and/or may be exempted from the lifetime limits for a given period in some states in order to establish safety and stability. States with such policies recognize certain circumstances as out of the control of individuals, which necessitate additional time to establish stability and security. Hardship extensions refer to instances in which families reach a time limit but are provided ongoing aid if they meet certain criteria. Extensions may be based on hardships particular to a given family or on external circumstances, such as high unemployment in the area. Extensions generally consider current rather than past circumstances. However, some states utilize both types of policies to accommodate individual circumstances and the general economic conditions. States vary in terms of the administration of formal diversion strategies, and they also vary with respect to what might be considered "good cause" for an extension or exemption.

Diversion programs, much like sanctioning schemes, involve a degree of discretion in that caseworkers screen and present the program to those they deem eligible. In addition, caseworkers have an information asymmetry when it comes to evaluating job search and job readiness activities. Caseworkers are trained to have more knowledge of the demand for labor in the context. They may use that knowledge to afford some temporary support. Caseworkers may also use their authority (or may be required by the pressure of performance metrics) to claim that a participant is deviating from the standard. Patterns in the exercise of this authority reflect who gets what, when, and how.

The boundaries and placement of discretionary authority with respect to diversion vary by state policy and are often revised by states adjusting to changes in federal policy or fiscal demands. For example, Arizona expanded eligibility for its lump-sum diversion program in 2007 from only those who could prove employment to those who are likely to secure employment within 90 days. Eligibility caseworkers, case managers, and supervisors answering to the Arizona Department of Economic Security now judge the employability of applicants and direct them through the welfare process accordingly. A four-step approval process is implemented at the organizational level to minimize subjectivity and secure agency compliance. For applicants, the process begins with a three-day compliance exercise in which the rights and responsibilities are reviewed and assessments are completed. Two days of required activities are assigned based on the assessments and applicants' willingness to comply (as judged by the caseworkers). Referral to the Two-Parent Employment Program is contingent upon verification of the satisfactory completion of the assigned activities. All TANF applicants in Arizona complete an initial eligibility screening conducted by an intake financial worker in the same office as the grant diversion specialist. Applicants identified as work ready are referred to a grant diversion specialist. If the applicant is interested in diversion, they are referred to the TANF service coordinator who serves as the ongoing case manager. Employability is assessed by the case manager, and if the client is approved for the diversion program by the case manager and the TANF supervisor, a lump-sum cash payment equivalent to the amount of three months' TANF assistance, which the family would qualify for, and possibly emergency payments for transportation, shelter, and work-related clothing is issued. Participation in Arizona's TPEP disqualifies a family from receiving TANF for at least three months.

Some diversion programs issue cash grants to eligible participants. Some issue payments or vouchers for essential services in addition to or in lieu of payments to participants. Other diversion programs operate as no interest or low interest loans rather than grants. For example, Wisconsin's diversion program offers "job access loans" up to $1,600 available once every 12 months at no interest for those who have not defaulted on any prior loans through the program. Although LPRs are eligible for separate state assistance in Wisconsin, the diversion program excludes migrant workers. Participants are required to repay the loan within 12 months through cash payments and/or community service, although repayment may be extended by a case manager with supervisor's approval for up to 24 months. Wisconsin's diversion program is a revolving fund that relies on loan repayment for the extension of future loans up to a maximum of $2,500 per applicant, so the state is allowed to seize a portion of the client's state tax refund for failure to repay.

Understanding the role that diversion plays in the states' strategies for maximizing employment and managing caseloads requires mapping diversion programs in relation to employment strategies over time within each state. Assessing the extent to which diversion programs can assist families in transition and evaluating how different programs compare in terms of outcomes will reveal how well a given program might respond to the needs of people in vulnerable circumstances only when the programs are understood as a part of the state's system of welfare provision. Currently, there is no valid method for analyzing at the state level whether diversion programs serve a regulatory function that assists people living in poverty or caters to business interests. Future research is essential to understanding the role of diversion programs in the welfare system.

ASSETS FOR INDEPENDENCE

The dominant story of the state of welfare policy under AFDC was that it failed to reduce poverty. There is some disagreement as to whether or not income transfers through AFDC alleviated hardship, but most agree that it was widely unpopular. In an effort to shift thinking about the structure of welfare as merely income maintenance, Michael Sherraden (1991) outlined an alternative state of welfare based on asset accumulation and investment. His vision of asset-based policy for people living in poverty represents a very influential attempt to cultivate a story about welfare that goes beyond consumption to stakeholding. The basic premise is that people living in poverty might achieve greater economic stability by building assets (e.g., savings accounts, home ownership, education, and enterprise investments).

Many people find the asset-building approach to be a convincing long-term antipoverty strategy with the potential to connect people to the economy and society. In fact, his policy proposal for Individual Development ment Accounts (IDAs) provides the foundation for various federal and state welfare programs.[25] The purpose of IDA programs, according to Sherraden's proposal, is to use subsidized deposits matched by people living in poverty to promote long-term financial planning for the "achievement of life goals" (297). At the same time, asset-building approaches address a persistent problem in the American psyche—inhibited saving. Although American spending habits tend to fuel economic growth, the widespread lack of adequate savings reveals long-term economic insecurities.

These programs serve a number of objectives within the neoliberal story line. They hope to get people invested in economic and social institutions, afford more people the opportunity to build credit, and assist in building assets that may provide insurance from market shifts. These programs may also serve paternalist purposes as the accounts are managed by caseworkers, and the allowable expenses are determined by the state based on the story that the state has an obligation to "tell the poor what to do" (Mead 1998). The neoliberal interest in creating access to opportunities and fostering social wealth, coupled with socially conservative mechanisms to regulate access and the value of those opportunities, sound like good stories at first. Including people in economic and social institutions who have largely been excluded seems fair, and the notion that people might need some direction to orient themselves in new institutions seems reasonable. However, it does make one wonder how likely it is that the ideals of independence and inclusion will serve people living in poverty who have been excluded from these contract negotiations, as opposed to the rational interests of those with control over the terms of the contracts.

Although Sherraden very clearly distinguishes his approach from the disproven notions of welfare dependence, the fact that some states refer to their programs as Independent rather than Individual Development Accounts signals a reverence for the story that suggests the state has the charge to prevent welfare dependence. Some states justify their savings initiatives with direct reference to the federal objective "to end welfare dependence" in their state plans. For example, Pennsylvania links the Family Savings Account (FSA), administered by the Department of Community and Economic Development, for TANF participants whose earned income is not more than 200% of the Federal Poverty Income Guidelines (FPIG) at the time of enrollment as an initiative that meets "TANF purpose number two—end the dependence of needy parents." It is also the case that the story of asset accumulation itself places a lot of stock in individual bricolage. In any case, the success of asset-building approaches relies upon interest rates that keep up with inflation and financial partnerships that are mutually beneficial.

Asset-building approaches were motivated in large part by a sincere interest in minimizing wealth gaps and affording people with low incomes access to reasonable sources of credit. Although many small banks and credit unions provide low-cost loans and accounts to people who tend to be largely underserved and often alienated by the banking system, the most financially vulnerable people often have no checking or savings account. In fact, low-income households make up the vast majority of those who do not have a bank account. Blacks, Hispanics, and Native Americans are disproportionately represented among low-income and unbanked households. The banking system is acutely alienating in the South, where there is a long history of policies and practices designed to exclude people of color and inhibit the extension of credit to them. According to the FDIC's 2009 Report on the National Survey of Unbanked and Underbanked Households, approximately 51% of the unbanked households have had bank accounts in the past. Income poverty is inextricably linked to asset poverty, and 37.1% of the unbanked households reported that they did not have enough money to need an account. The lack of benefit relative to the cost, including an inability to meet minimum balance requirements, was cited by 30.6% of the unbanked respondents. Consequently, the extent to which people living in poverty will be "brought into the banking mainstream" depends largely upon the measures states take to facilitate the availability of bank accounts that are cost effective for people with low incomes and curtail predatory credit products.

Funding for asset building approaches comes from several different sources.[26] Under the authority of the Assets for Independence Act (AFI), HHS offers competitive grants to nonprofit organizations, Community Development Finance Institutions (CFDIs), and low-income credit unions administering IDA programs, sometimes in partnership with state or municipal governments. HHS also administers IDA funds for refugees or intermediary organizations through the Office of Refugee Relocation and distributes TANF funds to states that may decide to administer IDA programs through a combination of funding sources. Housing and Urban Development (HUD) administers CDBG funds to entitlement communities and states which may also be used in various ways to support IDA programs. HUD also administers the Home Investment Partnership (HOME) Program, which allocates grants to states and local governments for public, private, or partnership programs for affordable housing. The Federal Housing Finance Board administers the Affordable Housing Program, which provides resources to regional member banks to support home ownership. The Treasury Department awards competitive grants through the Bank Enterprise Awards that may be used for IDA programs. The federal program may serve as a point of entry, and the different access points have different restrictions on uses at different levels of government; although funding may move through an organization from a combination of sources. The programs are designed by the various public, private, and nonprofit organizations and partnerships across the United States that target specific populations for clear economic purposes, presumably for mutual gain. Consequently, IDA programs are linked across a number of different federal initiatives that utilize common organizational units that cross sector boundaries but mobilize funds according to rules that are linked to the funding source.

States may use federal TANF funds to initiate IDA programs, provide matching contributions, or apply to the administrative costs of the IDA program. Arkansas, Indiana, Louisiana, Michigan, New Hampshire, New Jersey, Ohio, Pennsylvania, South Carolina, and Virginia used TANF funds in 2012 to support IDA programs. IDA savings that utilize federal matching funds may be used for purchasing a first home, financing a business, or paying for postsecondary education. However, states are also allowed to expand the qualified expenditures in their asset-building programs to include any purpose that is reasonably calculated to accomplish one of the objectives of TANF. For the most part, states determine the allowable purposes for the savings, the match rate, and the conditions for matching savings. Participant contributions may only be derived from earned income. States are restricted from using TANF funds to meet the nonfederal funds match requirement of the Assets for Independence Act (AFI), which provides competitive grants from HHS to nonprofit organizations, state and/or municipal governments partnered with nonprofits, Community Development Finance Institutions, and low-income credit unions administering IDA programs.

Several states choose to utilize TANF dollars for IDA programs. The funding streams and account terms vary according to how the state intends to use asset-building mechanisms to secure economic and social institutions during the structural adjustments associated with globalization. Understanding how IDA programs fit into this larger strategy is beyond the scope of this study, but mapping the use of TANF dollars to gain an understanding of the extent to which people living in poverty may be helped to move out of poverty begins with an account of the variation in IDA programs' rules for TANF clients across states. There are several models for allowing people receiving TANF assistance to accumulate assets so that they may move out of poverty. States may structure their savings plan by setting contribution limits. States may impose account limits, restricting the amount of savings an individual can benefit from while participating in TANF. Some states may also choose to match contributions using various sources of funding.

Table 1.11 in Appendix A outlines the program model, permitted uses, match rates, and account limits for each state with an IDA program that TANF participants may access.

States vary considerably with respect to IDA programs that target TANF recipients. States with TANF plans that include IDAs are authorized by different authorities across states, vary considerably in terms of the rules, regulations, and tax treatment, sometimes operate at different levels of devolution within states, and are managed by an assortment of different contracting relationships that may also combine funding sources. For example, Chapter 541A of the Iowa code establishes the legal boundaries of the IDA program. The division of community action agencies of the department of human rights administers the Iowa IDA program that TANF recipients may access. The program targets those with household incomes equal to or less than 200% of the federal poverty level. The accounts may be established by an individual for the purposes of saving for postsecondary education or job training, buying a home or home improvement that increases the tax basis of the property, starting a small business, or medical expenses. An account holder may make a withdrawal from the account for emergency medical costs, purchasing an automobile, necessary assistive technology, or a purpose determined by the account manager to help move the client to self-sufficiency only with the prior approval of the account manager. Deposits and earnings from the accounts are not used in calculating benefit eligibility for any program administered by the Iowa DHS. The account is limited to $30,000 principal and $50,000 in total assets. IDA account administrators may approve a 15 to 25% savings match to be paid from the state savings match fund. Income earned in an IDA is not subject to state income tax. State match fund payments flow through the community action agency, which is required to spend 85% of those funds in matching and may use the remainder for administrative costs and services such as financial education and technical assistance contractors. The variation in asset-building policies, funding streams, and the enactment of IDA programs presents considerable challenges for studying the value of the social wealth potentially created. This study examines the aggregate role IDA programs directly related to TANF might play in helping people move out of poverty. However, this is only a small part of the story of asset building. Future research is necessary to understand the extent to which TANF participants might access asset-building programs through the varied access points in the network of community and individual development programs that make up the asset-building policy process.

Iowa does not use federal TANF dollars on the IDA program and does not have to include reference to it in the TANF state plan, although TANF clients can access the program through referral. Some states do utilize federal TANF dollars to operate IDA programs. Table 1.12 in Appendix A illustrates the use of federal TANF dollars for IDA programs across states from 2004 to 2009, along with the percent change in asset poverty from 2006 to 2009. This is not to suggest that federal TANF dollars may or may not have an effect on the asset poverty rate in any given state. Rather, it is intended to show another choice states have in utilizing federal TANF dollars relative to their changing needs.

The creation of a state IDA program may be funded by a variety of potential, usually discretionary block grant, funding sources, including but not limited to TANF, Assets for Independence, Community Development, Workforce Investment Act appropriations, and state student assistance commissions. The terms and conditions within which the unbanked are brought into the banking mainstream through IDAs is negotiated in the contractual arrangements between the grantee and the participating banking partners. Some states also negotiate contracts with subsidized employers to contribute funds to Individual Education Accounts for workfare participants. Cash assistance and child support collections are uniformly transacted electronically. However, some states charge collection and transaction fees when IDAs are linked to child support collections. These state charges are on top of the bank fees that are likely in areas in which banking options for people with low incomes are restricted.

In addition, asset-building approaches buy heavily into two pervasive American myths. First, the myth of the self-made man is omnipresent in the story of independence through individual efforts to achieve the "American Dream." Second, the myth about the *nature* of markets as neutral rather than sorting mechanisms underlies the hope that every individual can access assets of value and that these acquisitions will also retain their value if widely held.[27] Moreover, the assets for independence story is still captured by the idea that well-being is inextricably linked to acquiring things.

These stories are also obscured by common stereotypes about people living in poverty, particularly people of color. The widespread belief that people living in poverty fall short when it comes to investing their money wisely in assets that accrue value fails to account for the greater risk of experiencing multiple economic hardships that those who carry multiple burdens accrued from health, wealth, and social status inequalities must confront. This belief also fails to recognize the human tendency to invest in those things one can afford that reflect social status as a means to enhance economic viability.[28] For example, many people invest in a business wardrobe that they cannot afford in an effort to obtain a better job. When young people who graduate from college do this despite tremendous amounts of debt, it is considered rational and necessary. When people living in poverty invest in clothing to reflect status, it is perceived as irrational and irresponsible. These huge leaps in logic, stereotypes, and myths affect the implementation of IDA programs.

The success of IDA programs hinges on clear, consistent information regarding the rules and regulations (Emshoff, Courtenay-Quirk, Broomfield, and Jones 2002; J. Losby, Hein, Robinson, and Else 2002; M. Losby, Robinson, and Else 2004), and the restrictiveness of the program rules affects who is likely to benefit from the program.[29] Limiting savings strictly to home ownership, education, and enterprise fails to account for the asset-building needs of severely disadvantaged communities in which home and car repairs are major investments and where barriers to home ownership are exceedingly difficult to overcome due to debt burdens, credit constriction, and/or land trusts (Christner 2003; Dewees and Florio 2003). Financial emergencies such as job loss and medical emergencies also inhibit savings (Gorham, Quercia, Rohe, and Toppen 2002). While direct deposit may be an efficient tool for facilitating savings (Schreiner, Clancy, and Sherraden 2002), it may also be problematic for people experiencing a financial emergency. Such individuals require control over withdrawal decisions rather than giving bureaucrats decision-making power over the accounts.

CHILD SUPPORT ENFORCEMENT

The Child Support Enforcement Act became a new component of Part D of Title IV of the Social Security Act in 1975, commonly referred to as IV-D. The act was amended by the Child Support Enforcement Amendments of 1984 and again by the Family Support Act of 1988. It promised to locate absent parents and obtain support from them. The Child Support Enforcement program of the 1996 legislation increased the level of child support that could be required of absent parents. The program requires states to provide assistance in locating absent parents, establishing paternity, establishing and enforcing child support obligations, and collecting support payments. The Family Support Act also provides for immediate withholding of wages even in the absence of arrearage unless the court finds good cause. The Family Support Act under AFDC upheld a $50 disregard of child support payments in the calculation of benefits only if such payments were made on time.

Miller (1990) demonstrates that child support enforcement by states under AFDC yielded the following results: (1) states have been slow in establishing paternity and obtaining support orders; (2) states have not addressed the lack of parenting—"women appear to be as upset about fathers' lack of parenting as they are about their failure to pay support" (82); (3) collections did not exceed administrative costs as of 1985; and (4) a lack of adequate tracking and monitoring of interstate cases exists. During the welfare reform debates, the lack or failure of child support enforcement was referenced by many different storytellers to insist upon the necessity for bureaucratic reforms. The reforms attempt to establish a network of cooperation across states, compelling both parents to take responsibility for children. So, the reforms were designed to increase the efficiency of operations, diffuse costs, and develop a system for tracking and monitoring parents across the United States.

The Federal Office of Child Support Enforcement (OCSE) is the structural component of the ACF in HHS responsible for overseeing the standards and minimum organizational requirements for state programs. The OCSE reviews and approves state plans and provides technical assistance to states through the National Child Support Enforcement Reference Center. Welfare reform authorized the use of 1% of the federal share of retained child support collections for disseminating information and providing technical assistance, and an additional 2% of the federal share is set aside for the Federal Parent Locator Service (FPLS) operations. In 1997, the federal government allowed FPLS information to be released to noncustodial parents unless there is evidence of domestic violence or child abuse. The policy represents an effort to promote better relations between co-parents. In addition, welfare reform established approximately $10 million per year in grants to states for mediation, counseling, education, and supervised visitation to facilitate cooperation. The provision of these services is devolved at different levels across states. Providers may receive grants from various sources, and the order and enforcement procedures may be administrative or judicial and vary across states. Consequently, the contracts for different services are often managed by different agencies across states, but the services provided with those funds must follow the federal guidelines linked to the funding source for a specific service provided in a given case.

The Family Support Act under TANF is designed to establish the right of a child to support from both parents and to reduce and recover welfare costs. The Uniform Interstate Family Support Act (UIFSA) offers the following guiding principles (see National Conference of Commissioners on Uniform State Laws 1996):

1. It is the legal duty of both parents to support their children;

2. Residing in a single-parent home should not lower a child's standard of living;

3. Paternity is the first step in the process of establishing support;

4. Parental responsibility and family independence are keys to the long-term prosperity of children; and

5. The collection of court-ordered child support reduces the financial burden on the state.

Each state is required to have a child support enforcement agency with the authority to establish paternity, enforce child support court orders, and collect the court-awarded support. The state child support enforcement agency operates under the following guidelines of the IV-D program:

1. monitoring child support awards for compliance;

2. initiating court-based enforcement actions such as income withholdings and contempt applications;

3. reviewing financial support orders and initiating modifications when the order deviates substantially from the state guidelines;

4. serving as a clerk of the court in interstate child support actions; and

5. use of the program is not mandatory.

Services provided by state agencies include parent-locating services, genetic testing to establish paternity, child support order establishment and modification, medical support, wages withholding, computerized accounting and billing, and the interception of federal and state income tax refunds. An application fee may be charged and potentially waived at the discretion of the state. The state child support enforcement agency does not handle any problems related to divorce, property settlement, visitation, or custody. The agency generally will not take action unless the noncustodial parent is 30 days late in the payment of support. States retain ultimate authority over disregard policies, and states vary widely with respect to their treatment of child support disregards.

Under AFDC rules and regulations, $50 in child support collections was disregarded in the calculation of benefits. PRWORA allows states to choose whether or not to modify this policy. In addition, states now have a right to pre-assistance arrearages only while the family is on welfare. States can retain child support payments up to the cumulative amount of assistance to the family that is not reimbursed through work effort. Also, states that have pass-through policies issue the custodial parent a separate check, highlighting whether or not child support payments are collected. Twenty states disregard at least $50 each month in child support payments for the purposes of determining eligibility and benefits. Twenty-eight states do not disregard or pass-through child support payments. Texas and West Virginia retain all the support collected but increase the TANF grant by $50 per month when child support is collected.

The 2005 DRA mandates that a $25 annual service fee per child support case be imposed by each state in any year that at least $500 is disbursed in any case that does not involve a family that has received public assistance. Some states also impose various other fees for services but may place legal limitations on private collection agencies and/or implement debt compromise programs. Table 1.13 in Appendix A illustrates the fees, interest rates, limitations on private collections fees, the modifications and adjustments states may allow for incarcerated parents, and the kind of debt compromise program states may have.

The variation with regard to how states manage costs has important implications for the weight of child support debt, particularly as the imposition of interest by states and/or private collection agencies accounts for the bulk of the debt increase according to the ACF. TANF clients are automatically referred to the State OCSE and are not subject to the application fee or annual fee and may be exempted from the other service fees applied in any state. However, all clients are subject to the interest charges. Access to modifications and debt compromise programs varies considerably across states. For example, Alabama charges 12% interest on child support debt owed by the noncustodial parent to the state when the family utilizes public assistance, but the state implements a debt compromise program on a case-by-case basis. Incarcerated parents may apply for a reduced support order in Alabama, and the state forgives the interest on arrears adjustments for parents who obtain modified orders during periods of incarceration. There are no legal limitations on the collection of interest or fees by private collection agencies in Alabama.

According to the ACF, 92% of the child support collections that went through all the state OCSEs in 2007 went to families, and the combined state and federal cost for CSE was $5.6 billion to collect $25 billion in that year. The caseload in 2007 was approximately 15.8 million, with 1.7 million new paternities established through the program. Higher paternity establishment rates appear to decrease nonmarital births and have increased child support payments over the past 20 years (Case, Lin, and McLanahan 2003; Garfinkel, Gaylin, Huang, and McLanahan 2003). Evidence from the Fragile Families and Child Well-Being Study, which includes 3,700 in-depth interviews of unwed couples in 20 different cities across 15 states, indicates that child support enforcement and not increased resources contributes to declining births to vulnerable women and gains in the economic well-being of children over time (Aizer and McLanahan 2006).[30] These findings suggest that black, white, and Hispanic children are better off as a result of "stricter child support enforcement" but does not consider how differences in state policies may interact with race-gendered assumptions about who *deserves* to have children may impose differential costs depending on the subject population.[31] Furthermore, there are currently no studies that assess the extent to which the devolved and privatized implementation of child support enforcement takes a cut out of the support children actually receive across states. Perhaps more importantly, child support arrears exceed $100 billion dollars, and those holding the highest child support debt tend to have no or low reported income and multiple current support orders.[32] Since the primary reasons for the accumulation of child support debt are the interest charges imposed (sometimes by states and private collection agencies), it is important to examine the policies and practices of cost diffusion. Future research may look at the relationship between the costs imposed, the demographics of the target population, population dynamics, and well-being.

3

The States of PRWORA-Related Welfare Programs

This study focuses on welfare programs that target people living in poverty. A comprehensive examination of all the variations in social policy resulting from welfare reform affecting people living in poverty is beyond the scope of this book. However, there are several changes resulting from PRWORA that are not specific to TANF but need to be considered in order to understand the now-fragmented state of welfare for people living in poverty. This chapter details several PRWORA-related programs and outlines their relationship to the poverty reduction strategies of TANF, including the Earned Income Tax Credit (EITC), Work Opportunity Tax Credit (WOTC), Low Income Home Energy Assistance (LIHEAP) and State Emergency Assistance programs, Food and Nutrition Assistance, and Healthcare for low and middle-income families. It is important to consider each of these programs as a component of poverty reduction because they are intended to bridge the gaps between poverty and economic self-sufficiency. The degree of variation across states affords the opportunity for learning from state choices and investments in these programs.

Earned Income Tax Credit (EITC)

The Earned Income Tax Credit (EITC) is considered a work incentive that functions to ease the tax burden on low-income workers paying the Social Security tax in an effort to encourage labor force attachment by providing additional income to workers in low and moderate income tax brackets. The federal EITC, established in 1975, supplements the earnings of low-income workers through refundable tax credits that offset federal tax liabilities or provide funds credited for the amounts in excess of the federal income tax liability. The amount of the credit to any given family is contingent upon the level of earnings and family size, and the amounts and parameters are adjusted annually for inflation by the IRS. The federal EITC program was expanded in the late 1980s and 1990s, and in 1994 the credit was extended to include workers without dependent children at a substantially lower rate.

The 1993 Mickey-Leland Hunger Act prohibited counting the EITC within 12 months of receipt in the determination of eligibility for food stamps. Program rules allow participants to save refunds from the EITC without having those monies counted in the eligibility standards. Although states have discretion in deciding whether or not earnings from the federal EITC will count against eligibility, EITC payments are not generally used in the determination of eligibility for TANF, Medicaid, food stamps, low-income housing, or SSI.

Qualified applicants must file a tax return even if they did not earn enough money to be obligated to file. However, the IRS Volunteer Tax Assistance (VITA) program provides free help with tax preparation for people who make less than $50,000, and the Tax Counseling for the Elderly (TCE) program offers free help for all, with priority given to people who are 60 years of age or older. Alternatively, the 1997 budget bill stated that income from "community service" and "work experience" that are part of many states' employment strategies cannot be claimed by workers. Community service activities are considered services rendered to earn benefits, and work experience strategies subsidize employers who then pay employees' work benefits. Consequently, TANF participants in these programs cannot receive tax credits for what are considered TANF work benefits under the general welfare doctrine. Consequently, the more states subsidize employment through work experiences and community service the less EITCs serve as a ladder up and out of poverty.

The federal program has three distinct ranges: (1) the subsidy range; (2) the flat range; and (3) the phaseout range. The subsidy range phases in refundable tax credits that increase with earnings. The flat range targets those with moderate earnings with a credit that maintains a constant dollar value. The federal credit is gradually reduced in the phase out range, which targets workers earning minimum wage and working full time. The parameters of the federal EITC program for 2011 tax returns began at a threshold of $13,660 for individuals or $18,740 for married couples filing jointly, and the maximum credit was $464 with no qualifying dependent children. The thresholds increase with the number of qualifying children up to three dependent children. In 2011, the credit extended to individuals with three or more qualifying children making $43,998 annually or $49,078 for married couples filing jointly. They may receive up to $5,751 in refundable tax credits.

Wisconsin was the first state to adopt a state EITC, in 1983. Between 1989 and 2002, 15 states adopted state EITCs based on the federal credit. Additionally, Indiana adopted a state EITC from 1999–2002 that applied to families with children who had incomes below $12,000 in which earned income exceeded 80% of the family's total income. Unlike the other states primarily in the Midwest and Northeast that adopted EITCs during this period, Indiana's EITC was not designed to magnify the federal credit. As of 2009, 22 states offered state EITCs.[1] State EITCs vary considerably, and there are also a few cities that have implemented pilot programs for local EITCs.[2] However, the state (and local) policies are often contingent upon the availability of funds and are regularly suspended by some of the state and local governments that have enacted them.

The political story of EITCs is interesting in that limited relief is offered to policy targets dependent on wage work that is not keeping up with the high cost of living or inflation. As the targets may increasingly become contenders, assigning benefits becomes contentious and less straightforward. EITCs appeal to Republicans, who get themselves elected through expressing disdain for taxes and extolling the virtues of work. At the same time, EITCs have appeal among some Democrats because the policies suit the neoliberal paradigm in which individuals are offered opportunities in the market. Democrats can also argue that the policies moderate regressive taxes. However, disagreement increases as incomes increase because the neoclassical economic logic suggests that the phaseout may produce disincentives to work, and the neoliberal assessment is often contingent upon an institutional or transaction cost analysis. This issue is further exacerbated by the tensions along the tradeoffs between domestic and international market efficiency. Furthermore, both parties are left struggling to deal with the widening demographic gaps that pose long-term problems for Social Security.

There is a considerable amount of research on the effect of EITCs on labor supply.[3] However, the distinct roles that EITCs play in tax policy, regulating labor markets, and as an antipoverty measure require more clarification. Some studies show that the EITC increases the labor force participation of single women (Meyer 2002; Meyer and Rosenbaum 2001) and decreases the labor supply of low-skilled married women (Eissa and Hoynes 2004). The increases in exits from welfare have largely been a function of the broader economic circumstances and federal mandates to reduce caseloads. Decreases in welfare entries have primarily resulted from economic circumstances, the decline in the real value of wages, and the expansion of EITC (Grogger 2004). While the effects of EITCs on work effort are well documented, there is very little research on the extent to which EITCs achieve the other stated goal, which is income redistribution. Initial research suggests that there is a complex interaction between social and economic regulations in welfare policies, work effort, and wages that requires further clarification. The average EITC rate in the labor market tends to result in reduced wages. Low-skilled workers with lower levels of education are the most effected (Leigh 2010), indicating that the issue of whether the phaseout is a disincentive to work or a result of wage depression deserves further study.

It is unlikely that knowledge will move beyond partisan stories of need, entitlement, deservingness, and deviance without understanding how federal and state EITCs may interact with social regulations and how work effort may or may not be linked to wages.[4] It is also worth studying the qualitative effects on the least well-off. Increasing the labor supply is not likely to be the only downward pressure on wages. Social interaction theory explains how social decisions and economic practices have social consequences that are perpetuated by social distance (see Akerlof 1997). Under certain conditions, policy may function as feedback in ways that are limited and contingent but can be to some extent predicted (Soss and Schram 2007). These important findings contribute greatly to the understanding of how feedback may be internalized and are essential for adequate knowledge building regarding welfare systems. Future research is warranted to understand the role of social and political influence on aggregate wages in order to begin to put into perspective the efficacy of the EITC as an antipoverty measure.

Work Opportunity Tax Credit (WOTC)

Because employers are paying additional payroll taxes associated with subsidized employment, TANF recipients were included among the nine target groups with significant barriers to employment for which private sector businesses can qualify for the Work Opportunity Tax Credit (WOTC). The WOTC has its origins in the Small Business Protection Act of 1996, and the Welfare-to-Work (WtW) was initially a part of the Taxpayer Relief Act of 1997. The Tax-Relief and Health Care Act of 2006 reauthorized and expanded some of the parameters for the tax credits and combined the programs. The WOTC now refers to a combination of workforce programs, including the Welfare-to-Work (WtW) tax credit, to "help incentivize workplace diversity and facilitate access to good jobs for American workers."[5] It is intended to provide incentives for private businesses to hire TANF recipients, veterans, SNAP recipients, residents of Empowerment Zones (EZs), youth in the summer, people with disabilities, people with felony convictions, SSI recipients, and people receiving long-term family assistance by reducing the federal income tax liability. The tax credit to businesses is generally $2,400 for each new adult hire, $1,200 for each new youth hire for summer employment, $4,800 for each new disabled veteran hired in the tax year, and $9,000 for each new long-term TANF recipient hired over a two-year period. The current range extends to a maximum of $9,600 for each disabled veteran who has been unemployed for six months hired during the tax year. The WtW is claimed less frequently than the WOTC, primarily because the WOTC is more generous than the WtW in the first year and few workers continue to the second year.[6] Although the WtW targets generate a lower subsidy rate, the maximum WtW credit is higher when work effort is high.

Employer tax credits are also available in some states to cut the state tax liability for businesses employing citizens of the state with persistent barriers to employment. Information on each state's implementation of the WOTC can be obtained from the State Workforce Agency and the State WOTC Coordinator.[7] The variations in these policies across states are considerable given the complexity of tax policy, revenue generation strategies and tax capacities at various levels of government, competition among jurisdictions attempting to maintain stable tax bases, the politics of empowerment zones, and differences in state workforce development strategies. Mapping the landscape of WOTCs requires understanding the network of intergovernmental relations to identify the appropriate level of analysis for comparing policy choices.

In addition to the WOTC, 39 states implemented direct subsidy employment programs by accessing the TANF Emergency Fund during fiscal years 2009 and 2010. This part of the American Recovery and Reinvestment Act (2005) was distributed through the TANF block grant. States were allowed to use these funds to subsidize jobs for low-income families and youth who may or may not be TANF participants. Many of the direct subsidies provided though this funding stream covered 100% of employer hires from the target populations. States were also afforded the discretion to determine the employers and workers qualified to participate. Since the funding expired in 2010, some states have opted to utilize third-party spending to continue the employer subsidy programs initiated with this funding.

At present, the best available evidence comes from the administrative data maintained in Wisconsin, which allows for some understanding WOTC implementation in that state. Recent evidence indicates that while there are short-term improvements in employment levels and modest increases in wages in the short term, there are no improvements in long-term employment resulting from WOTCs (Hamersma 2005). Although it is important to note that there is no evidence of the negative effects associated with the Targeted Jobs Tax Credit, labor market outcomes for welfare and food stamp recipients suggest that labor market gains are limited and contingent

(Hamersma and Heinrich 2007). One might think that these findings are likely because the incentives for employers apply only to new hires and shorter job tenures inhibit wage increases that skilled workers would otherwise obtain. However, recent evidence suggests that fewer firms are participating in the program than are eligible, citing too few eligible workers and short job durations, thus making it such that the costs (although there is very little paperwork involved) exceed the benefits to the firm (Hamersma 2011). So, it is imperative that future research examine the employment decisions and eligibility standards that affect the implementation of this incentive. Research assessing the factors contributing to short job durations is necessary to understand the extent to which the policy may enhance "workplace diversity" and generate "good jobs" over the long term. There is some evidence that the occupational category may play a role in the separation rate (Gunderson and Hotchkiss 2007). Consequently, workplace diversity policies that do not produce new jobs at competitive wages for diverse groups are unlikely to do more than cycle different people through the few jobs reserved for the target groups, keeping them in competition with one another. Future research is required to evaluate the kinds of opportunities created for targeted groups compared to the average and compared across different targets.

Low Income Home Energy Assistance (LIHEAP) and State Emergency Assistance

In 1981, the federal government established the Low Income Home Energy Assistance Program (LIHEAP) to assist households with the lowest incomes that pay a high proportion of household budgets to home energy. LIHEAP is set up as a mandatory block grant of which states, territories, and Indian tribes compete for a portion annually based on the weather and low-income population. The statute includes the Leveraging Incentive Program that authorizes supplemental funds for nonfederal leveraged resources. The law also authorizes supplemental funding for the Residential Energy Assistance Challenge (REACH) Program, in which competitive grants fund innovative community-based implementation of plans to reduce household energy vulnerabilities. Additional contingency funds may be released by order of the president in the declaration of a disaster requiring emergency assistance. Under the law, recipients of TANF, SSI, Food Stamps, and some needs-tested recipients of veterans' benefits are categorically eligible for LIHEAP grants. In addition, some states authorize state funds for home energy assistance. The limited research on LIHEAP suggests that assistance tends to reach families with the highest social and medical risk and with more food insecurity, but funds deplete quickly (Frank et al. 2006).

In addition, some states have emergency assistance programs. The funding sources and types of emergencies defined vary across states, and references to Emergency Assistance (EA) or Energy Assistance (EA) do not appear to have a common point of comparison across states. EA programs may reference the state's energy assistance program and/or emergency assistance, which may include energy assistance among other types of assistance available to qualified families in emergencies. In fact, emergency assistance and energy assistance may reference the same thing in some states but not others. Emergency assistance can include temporary financial assistance with heat and utilities separate from the LIHEAP program. It may include food, home repairs, relocation assistance, burial assistance, emergency shelter, and services to prevent the loss of a home. The types of emergencies can vary from economic to natural disasters. Funds may come from state allocations, the Emergency Assistance Food Program, LIHEAP, HUD, the Home Energy Assistance Program, FEMA, SSBG, and/or supplemental grants. It is also the case that in some states emergency assistance is contracted to nonprofit organizations that may also supplement funding with donations, corporate sponsors, and partnerships with private organizations. However, it is always the case that restricted funds are managed by the funding source. In other words, clients have to qualify based on the requirements tied to the funding source unless the funds are unrestricted donations.

The stories about energy and emergency assistance reinforce the notion that temporary, contingent assistance is adequate antipoverty policy. The structure and implementation of energy and emergency assistance suggest acquiescence to the neoliberal paternalist myth of welfare dependence. Additionally, the increasing privatization of welfare is likely to place more and more control over funding restrictions in the hands of the energy companies, which have an interest in energy dependence. It also means increasing competition for funds for energy and emergency assistance as the likelihood of extreme weather increases.

Food and Nutrition Assistance

The Food and Nutrition Service of the United States Department of Agriculture administers the federal nutrition assistance programs, which include the SNAP, the Women, Infants, and Children (WIC), School Meals such as the National School Lunch Program and School Breakfast Program, the Summer Food Service Program, Child and Adult Care Food Program, Food Assistance for Disaster Relief, and Food Distribution Programs. PRWORA included major changes to the Federal Food Stamp Program (called SNAP since 2008). In an effort to "align food stamp rules with TANF rules," states were given greater flexibility to establish a "simplified food stamp program," although nutrition assistance remains one of the only federally administered entitlement programs. PRWORA also reduced benefits, eliminated benefits for most groups of legal immigrants, and increased work requirements for adults who are between 18 and 50 years old without dependents.

Since the official name of the Food Stamp Program was changed to SNAP by Congress in 2008, states have been allowed to refer to their state program by a name chosen by the state. Twenty-five states refer to their programs as SNAP. Eight states continue to refer to the program as Food Stamps or FSP, and three states call their programs Food Supplement or Supplemental Programs. Other names include Food Assistance, Nutrition Assistance, CalFresh, Food Support, Food & Nutrition Services, 3SquareVT, FoodShare, and the Basic Food Program. The limited devolution of food and nutrition assistance creates a network of food distribution that may be more responsive to local needs and may utilize more local foods. This may promote more sustainable (and more widespread) availability of healthy foods. However, the disarticulation of food and nutrition services also risks displacing responsibility for nutritional needs to levels of government or agencies without enough resources to address local needs. Future research is essential to understanding how welfare devolution and privatization affect food insecurity.

States began experimenting with changes in the delivery of nutrition program services before PRWORA, and at least 49 states began "re-engineering" their Food Stamp Programs by 2002. Thirty-four states implemented changes to improve access and utilization, bring TANF and Food Stamp rules in line, and increase program monitoring and evaluation. A total of 39 states implemented changes to improve accessibility, and 24 states focused on increasing program monitoring and evaluation. Thirty-four states made revisions to bring TANF and Food Stamp rules in line.

According to the USDA, there were approximately 49 million people in the United States who lacked access to enough nutritionally adequate food for an active, healthy lifestyle (including roughly 16 million children) in 2010. Although this food insecurity varies widely across counties, it exists in every county across the nation, and hunger is steadily increasing in communities with the highest rates of food insecurity.[8] States with consistently high rates of food insecurity also tend to have higher than average poverty rates and higher than average enrollments in food programs during the period of welfare reform (Nord, Jemison, and Bickel 1999). And, state policies continue to affect access and utilization after welfare reform. A study of the effect of food stamp policies, welfare policies, minimum wage policies, and the federal EITC on food program participation suggests that states with more lenient vehicle exemption policies, longer recertification periods, and expanded categorical eligibility increase access. The use of biometric technology may decrease utilization (Ratcliffe 2007). Future research is necessary to ascertain the extent to which state policies may be elastic and responsive to need, demand, ideological considerations, and/or capacity.

Research suggests that people tend to experience considerable hardship before seeking food assistance, and SNAP benefits may reduce the prevalence of severe food insecurity. Nader Kabbani and Myra Kmeid (2005) examine the risk of very low food security among those in the severe range of food insecurity using cross-sectional survey data from the Current Population Survey Food Security Supplement. The experience of very low food security in the 30 days prior to the survey did not differ between SNAP recipients and nonrecipients, but among SNAP recipients, households receiving higher SNAP benefits were more likely to have very high need in the 30 days prior to the survey. Households enrolled in SNAP tend to experience more persistent food insecurity than the average low-income household, and SNAP recipients tend to enroll after an extended period of deteriorating food security (Nord and Golla 2009). Consequently, estimating the effects of SNAP benefits on food security broadly are challenging due to this self-selection. Mark Nord and Anne Marie Golla's (2009) research attempts to account for the extent to which the fact that many SNAP recipients only enroll in the program after having experienced seven to eight months of very low food security weighs on the statistical averages. Evidence from their research indicates that SNAP benefits moderately improve food security among new entrants, and controlling for the subpopulation with the least access to food in the previous 12 months, SNAP appears to reduce the overall prevalence of very low food security.

Alternatives or supplements to SNAP are available through private or nonprofit community organizations called Emergency Food Providers (EFPs). The Emergency Food Assistance Program distributes USDA commodities to many of the EFPs such as food banks and emergency kitchens (soup kitchens) throughout the United States. However, the contribution of bonus commodities, entitlement commodities, and donations varies considerably, and EFPs consistently report increasing requests for assistance along with rising food prices.[9] Wage stagnation and improved access are cited by the Food Research and Action Center (FRAC) as the primary reasons that more and more working families are relying on various food assistance programs[10] and often in need of multiple types of food assistance (Mosley and Tiehen 2004).

Maureen Berner, Sharon Paynter, and Emily Anderson's (2009) work provides the most thorough research on client characteristics. Their analysis of 3,966 nonprofit food pantry visits reveals a number of important findings about the most vulnerable. The analysis shows that an increasing number of people who work but whose income is below the state median are having to rely on food pantries more often and for longer periods of time, whether or not they receive SNAP benefits. Their research also indicates that the capacity to respond to demand is lacking in most small towns. Continued research along these lines is essential for understanding how the various food assistance programs may best address hunger and the role food insecurity plays in entrenching poverty among the least well-off.

Healthcare for Low and Middle Income Families

The State Children's Health Insurance Program (SCHIP), a block grant to the states, was created by the Balanced Budget Act of 1997. The enactment of Title XXI of the Social Security Act implemented what are most often referred to now as CHIPs.[11] The purpose of SCHIP is to "provide funds to states to enable them to initiate and expand the provision of child health assistance to uninsured, low-income children in an effective and efficient manner that is coordinated with other sources of health benefits coverage for children."[12] In short, SCHIP was intended to reduce the number of uninsured children and improve the quality of healthcare provided to low-income children by expanding eligibility through federal-state cost sharing.

SCHIP is another aspect of the devolution of poverty governance. Neoliberal paternalism also dominates the healthcare discourse. Neoliberal stories focus on efficiencies in delivery systems. Paternalist stories emphasize the "right" kinds of care for "worthy" recipients. These stories impact how TANF participants may or may not access healthcare as devolution and privatization infiltrate the welfare administration process.

SCHIP operates under broad federal guidelines in which each state determines the design of its program, eligibility groups, benefit packages, payment levels for coverage, administrative rules, and operating procedures. States determine the implementation of SCHIP coverage by expanding their Medicaid program, creating or expanding a separate state program, or combining the two options. The federal government covers 65% or more of the costs of SCHIP, allocating funds to each state based on its share of the nation's uninsured children with family incomes below either 200% of the federal poverty level or 150% of the state's Medicaid eligibility, with adjustments for differences in healthcare costs (Bruen and Ullman 1999).

States with separate SCHIPs are afforded greater flexibility, whereas Medicaid expansions must follow the Medicaid eligibility process and follow the benefit and cost-sharing rules. States are free to act as an insurer and provide direct coverage, contract with managed care organizations, contract with a community-based delivery system, or offer coverage through employer plans. However, states are expected to involve the public in the design and implementation of their plans.

Research on the diffusion of SCHIP policies indicates that states respond to other states in the implementation of SCHIPs. States look to states that are ideologically similar (Grossback, Nicholson-Crotty, and Peterson 2004) and emulate states that show some evidence of policy success when making legislative changes to the nature of SCHIP implementation (Volden 2006). The administrative implementation of SCHIPs varies in important ways as well. Administrators in more comprehensive SCHIPs engage in more outreach and are more likely to increase enrollment (Nicholson-Crotty 2007). Perhaps more importantly, recent evidence demonstrates that CHIP implementation can increase public health coverage without crowding out employer coverage (Dubay and Kenny 2009).

The 2009 CHIP Reauthorization Act (CHIPRA) provides states with new funding and program options and includes various incentives for states to provide coverage for children through Medicaid or CHIP. CHIPRA includes a new Express Lane Eligibility option which allows states to enroll children in Medicaid or CHIP based on information processed through other programs or held in other databases, such as TANF and food assistance programs. At present, 43 states and D.C. have already integrated Medicaid and other assistance programs, and 24 states have the same eligibility system for Medicaid and CHIP. However, only six states implemented Express Lane Eligibility (ELE) by 2011, but the experimental implementation of ELEs in 13 states as of January 2014 suggests that ELEs may increase access, efficiency, and the effectiveness of utilization.[13] Grant funds are also available to fund state outreach and renewal strategies. CHIPRA also includes automatic eligibility for newborns whose mothers are covered through Medicaid and CHIP and performance bonuses for states. In 2010, then-HHS Secretary Kathleen Sebelius issued the Connecting Kids to Coverage initiative, which enlists stakeholders such as governors, pediatricians, faith organizations, school nurses, coaches, community organizations, etc. to assist in increasing enrollment, although recent evidence suggests that some increase in the rates of children who meet the standard of economic need qualifying them for eligibility but are uninsured may be attributable to CHIPRA requirements that link eligibility to citizenship documentation (Sommers 2009).

Coverage for childless adults under CHIPRA was terminated in 2009. CHIPRA prohibits new waivers to cover parents with the exception of pregnant women. Existing waivers for special populations of adults were not phased out, but funding is restricted. However, CHIPs are referenced in a number of initiatives of the Patient Protection and Affordable Care Act.

The Patient Protection and Affordable Care Act (P.L. 111-148), signed by President Barack Obama on March 23, 2010, and amended on March 30, 2010, when the Health Care and Education Reconciliation Act of 2010 was signed into law, includes provisions related to CHIPs. This new legislation funds CHIP through 2015 and extends authority for the program through 2019, mandating that states maintain eligibility standards through 2019. In addition, federal allotment caps that have inhibited the enrollment of CHIP eligible children are addressed by requiring screening for Medicaid eligibility. Children who cannot be funded by CHIP due to the allotment cap and do not qualify for Medicaid would receive CHIP comparable tax credits in the benefit exchange.[14]

Laura Katz Olson's (2010) insightful analysis in *The Politics of Medicaid* demonstrates that the Medicaid program broadly involves expansive costs that appear more closely connected to the demands of providers than the health needs of beneficiaries. Her research in the long-term care context is consistent with findings regarding the ideological adoption and implementation of SCHIP (Grossback, Nicholson-Crotty, and Peterson 2004). Although Medicaid and CHIP have made progress toward addressing healthcare needs, the political and economic tendency to shift costs to those perceived as the least "worthy" beneficiaries is a factor that has the potential to undermine the net gains in health. Evidence suggests that advances in the health of whole populations depend on reducing inequality (Brownson, Baker, Leet, and Gillespie 2003; Costa and Kahn 2006). Further, poverty accentuates racial disparities in health. The gap in health outcomes between blacks and whites is consistently evident in the literature and is strongly associated with wealth and income gaps (Cooper et al. 2001; Deaton and Lubotsky 2003; Holtgrave and Crosby 2003; Lobmayer and Wilkinson 2002; McLaughlin and Stokes 2002). Minimizing healthcare gaps offers the most promising gains for improvements in overall health, and shifting costs to those already disadvantaged threatens to increase health disparities. But, in the absence of critical reflection on the stories that perpetuate these disparities, new healthcare policies are likely to be more of the same—small gains at increasing cost to beneficiaries and continued struggle among providers for a bigger piece of the pie. Medicaid and CHIP are only pieces of the healthcare puzzle. The conflicts over whom the programs serve and decisions regarding what services are offered represent critical social, economic, and racial divisions that are the focal point of ideological storytelling. Future research has to engage the complexities and difficulties of healthcare.

4

The Privatization of Poverty Governance

.•——•.

The privatization of welfare may be considered a logical progression within a welfare state dominated by stories of moral individualism. However, the nature and extent of privatization in the welfare context must be understood in relation to the political rhetoric of reform that shifted blame for social problems onto government and insisted that "the business of government is business." The managerial prescriptions for social ills challenged government to compel individuals to be self-reliant and focus on production efficiency. Consequently, the privatization of welfare has come in three forms: (1) the use of vouchers to allow "citizen consumers" to shop around for things such as training services, for example; (2) contracting out services to private for-profit or nonprofit organizations; and (3) transferring functions and assets from the public sector to the private sector. The story of welfare privatization celebrates the efficiency of competitive services that are believed to allow individuals to choose their own adventure. Additionally, the paternalist story of private ownership of social issues is fed by a long history of racial oppression and gender bias in contractual arrangements. New Public Management by paternalists repackages the myth of the self-made man in "responsible citizenship" stories that capitalize on historical patterns of social, economic, and political exchange that advantage those privileged by a long history of property rights. As privatization has evolved in the context of the American welfare state, this dominant story line has increasingly eliminated competitors.

This chapter describes the privatization of poverty governance. Market-oriented managerial reforms utilized outcomes evaluation to justify increasing private provision of governance. "Innovative" efforts to "reinvent government" exercised a customary political strategy to gain advantage by blaming the bureaucracy and reorganize executive authority with reform stories. Democrats heard the stories of innovative governance as opportunities to change the perception of practices of governance that depicted them as failures. Republicans heard the stories of innovative governance as a means to deregulate business. Paternalists on both sides seized the opportunity to capitalize on managerial strategies for enforcing the status quo. Privatization has the potential to increase the efficiency of governance and the stability of authority. However, little is known about the costs, risks, and implications of privatizing poverty governance. The purpose of this chapter is to describe the extent of privatization across U.S. states in order to assess the aggregate effects of devolution and privatization over time.

Privatizing Welfare

Welfare privatization refers to three distinct mechanisms used to diffuse the government monopoly on services. First, vouchers are a common form of privatization utilized in many welfare programs to provide choices among training providers, methods of paying vendors in lieu of providing cash assistance to participants, and assistance with education at two or four-year colleges that partner with the state for certain job categories or professions that are in demand in the state. Second, the welfare transfers to the private sector are many and varied. Subsidies such as the WOTC and labor oversight through workforce development boards in some states are a couple of examples. Third, contracting out is an option that states may employ for all aspects of service provision. Evidence of the advantages of outsourcing may be found in circumstances in which tasks are straightforward, outcomes are measurable, and competition among vendors persists (Hodge 2000). However, human services operate in a domain in which problems are complex, the structure of service provision is diffuse, processes are varied, goals are contested, and outcomes are hard to evaluate.

PRWORA allows states to contract out any and all services, including eligibility determination. The extent of contracting, types of contracts, and forms of monitoring vary considerably across states and services. However, service provision is characterized by third-order devolution in every state with the exception of Vermont.[1] The utility of privatization in improving service quality, cutting costs, or reducing government monopoly is contingent upon the extent to which the types of services are conducive to market incentives, the maintenance of professional and highly competitive contracting, contract specificity, adequate evaluation, and the credible authority to enforce contracts (Johnston and Romzek 1999, 2000). The practices of contracting largely reinforce neoliberal justifications for individual ownership of social problems. The practices also appeal to paternalist stories that rely on contracts to impose their view of the behavioral conditions of "responsible citizenship." Contracting social service provision extends the reach of governance, heightens the oversight of those with influence on funding, and also has the potential to sell off public investments. The implications of contracting poverty governance may produce social wealth in the form of opportunities or may expand inequalities. In any case, questioning the influence of welfare privatization is deserving of extensive study.

VOUCHERS

Like many aspects of the evolving welfare states, vouchers are a confusing concept, because the term is used to describe a number of things. In a literal sense, vouchers are evidence of expenditures or authorizations for disbursing cash or credit for a proven expense. Vouchers have been used in early WtW experiments to provide subsidized housing in some jurisdictions, to place TANF recipients in homes so that they did not remain on the Section 8 housing waiting list while trying to transition to work. For the most part, these vouchers were awarded to metropolitan housing authorities but were applied specifically to TANF participants. The vouchers were intended to allow families to move closer or remain closer to jobs, to increase financial stability, and to improve job retention. It is important to note that some states do use TANF funds for housing programs, which varies across states but may include tenant-based rental assistance paid to landlords, Section 8 housing vouchers, home mortgage assistance, homeownership loans and grants, moving assistance, or direct cash assistance for rent and utilities. States that utilize TANF-funded vouchers for housing assistance may provide Section 8 housing vouchers (which means that TANF clients receive vouchers from the TANF program but remain in their place on the Section 8 waiting list) or offer vouchers to pay specific vendors.

The HUD-sponsored WtW voucher program experiment provided household-based rental vouchers for randomly assigned TANF participants from 2000 until 2004 and tracked the effects of the vouchers over five years as a sample test of the Housing Choice Voucher program. The study, contracted to Abt Associates by HUD with additional funding from the Rockefeller Foundation, the Annie E. Casey Foundation, and the Fannie Mae Foundation, found that vouchers reduced homelessness, crowding, the number of subsequent moves, and household size.[2] Vouchers improved mobility and produced some gains in neighborhood quality but had no effect on marriage or cohabitation. A study of the proximity to employment, by Scott Allard and Sheldon Danziger (2003), found that the probability of leaving welfare with work in three Detroit counties was affected by the employment opportunities available, suggesting that housing vouchers that allow people to live in neighborhoods where there is work may be critical factors in enhancing opportunities for TANF participants (Bania, Coulton, and Leete 2003).

In many cases, private for-profit and nonprofit organizations provide vouchers for basic needs assistance, which exist under welfare reform in lieu of cash assistance. For example, SW-WRAP is a nonprofit organization providing Wyoming's Recovery Access Programs (WRAPs) using the state's Basic Needs and Emergency Assistance (BNEA) funding that provides "wraparound" services.[3] BNEA is Wyoming's voucher program for basic needs assistance available to a handful of target groups, including TANF participating families with incomes at 185% of the Federal Poverty Level (FPL) who are attending school or training for self-sufficiency. This voucher program is funded with federal TANF dollars and was approved through 2012.

TANF participants may access vouchers from TANF funds and/or through other funding sources. And, there are a few states that offer TANF vouchers for services that are beyond basic needs. For example, the Child Care Development Fund (CCDF) is a solely voucher-based program. Some TANF participants may qualify for child care vouchers through CCDF. Qualified participants may also be eligible for vouchers for training or education in an occupational category considered by the state to be in demand, which may be funded through TANF (or a combination of sources). New Jersey, for example, is one of a handful of states that uses TANF funds to provide Career Advancement Vouchers to former TANF recipients who have been employed for at least four months. This particular voucher program is administered by the NJ Departments of Social Services and Labor and Workforce Development. The vouchers offer assistance with education or training for occupations in demand in the state for up to $4,000 per training program. The vouchers maybe renewed once for a maximum of $8,000 to assist a client. And, New Jersey's Career Advancement Vouchers are paid to the training facility.

It is often considered intuitively true that accounting for spending and maintaining compliance with funding restrictions may be more efficient with vouchers compared to direct cash assistance, particularly with the utilization of electronic voucher management systems. However, future research on the system design, error rate, and experiences of people from various perspectives in voucher programs may reveal how well this belief holds up in implementation. The ideal of privatization is based on competitive choice, so evaluating the extent to which different types of vouchers, and the relative extent of choice in voucher programs, may demonstrate how choice may be maximized and how well people utilize their choices.

WELFARE TRANSFERS TO PRIVATE COMPANIES

Vouchers themselves have been privatized to some extent. For example, the MAXIMUS[4] voucher management system is one example of a private company with ownership of the technical services such as electronic invoicing and vouchers for reimbursements in addition to providing training, outreach, and marketing services to governance organizations. For the most part, the service is contracted out, but the system technology is owned by the private company, MAXIMUS. Privatization in the form of transferring ownership of assets or tasks to private companies for things such as voucher management appears on its face to be a technology transfer that would likely be difficult to achieve within the traditional setting of bureaucratic politics. Politicians are unlikely to invest in new technologies that offer them little or no likely electoral gain, and civil servants have often resisted the implementation of new technologies. However, very little is known about how these innovations may impact people living in poverty. One thing that is fairly evident is that the transfer of this type of welfare service shifts the emphasis from the helping professions to production management (Schram, Soss, Houser, and Fording 2009). This is likely to lead to a few unique circumstances as investments and influence accrue to the private sector. For-profit companies require innovation and expansion to remain competitive. The profit motive is likely to result in firms with interests in capitalizing on new markets, which may contribute to a push for welfare expansion. Training, outreach, marketing, and other management services transferred to the private sector only remain less costly for as long as expansion is possible. When the limits of expansion are reached, costs are diffused. The expansion of production management to oversee work hours is likely to produce higher work rates from a growing group of people subject to hierarchical management. When those limits are reached, the costs are likely to increase.

The Workforce Investment Act of 1998 mandates the consolidation of employment services and job training programs into what is referred to as the One-Stop delivery system. The law allows for flexibility in the state and local implementation of these new workforce investment systems. In Florida, where TANF is administered by the Florida Department of Economic Opportunity and implemented through Florida's regional workforce boards, employment and service delivery systems are under the control of private organizations. Consequently, welfare policies in Florida have been privatized to a greater extent than in any other state.

In Florida, TANF is integrated into 24 incorporated Regional Workforce Boards (RWBs). The incorporation of these public-private partnerships endows the RWBs with the rights of an individual entity under the law, meaning that the local business, labor, and nonprofit representatives that make up the RWBs have governance authority. Local officials within each region control their respective boards. However, the U.S. Department of Labor investigation of Florida's RWBs in 2011 prompted the state to give the governor the power to remove board members and the executive director.[5] The private contracts that RWBs engage in are overseen by a hybrid corporation, Workforce Florida, Inc., authorized by the state to set implementation standards, and the Agency for Workforce Innovation within the Florida Department of Economic Opportunity coordinates the One-Stop delivery system across the regions.

Referring again to Table 1.1 in Appendix A, the continuum of welfare privatization across states is reflected by the extent to which case management, contract management, and work verification has been transferred to private interests. Consistent with the findings in the Florida case, devolution has shifted welfare from the helping professions to management across all states. Twenty-seven states have retained case, contract, and work verification management in human services. Collaborative governance characterizes case, contract, and work management in 16 states. Nine of those states collaborate with the private sector in poverty governance. Florida, Tennessee, and Texas have further transferred management authority to the private sector through regional workforce authorities made up primarily of private interests. States that maintain a traditional focus on helping professions retain more administrative authority in social service departments; whereas states that shift more emphasis onto neoliberal welfare analysis as a measure of well-being have moved more TANF administration to labor or economic departments. And, states that have transferred more authority to private interests use TANF as a tool for labor regulation. Heavy emphasis on labor regulation, along with immense pressure to meet performance metrics, makes it increasingly unlikely that caseworkers might reasonably be able to engage in the "helping relationships" that many were trained in. Shifting the influence away from the helping professions to management increases neoliberal paternalist controls by compelling discipline to the pursuit of social and economic outcomes. Alternatively, well-trained social workers leverage influence by developing relationships with clients that help the clients work toward goals mutually identified in the process of improving family functioning.

In addition to transferring services to private companies, welfare privatization transfers a good deal of wealth to the private sector in the form of subsidies. The WOTC is one example of this shift from the historical expansion of public employment to the use of public funds to attempt to incentivize hiring in the private sector. Funding for the WOTC does not come from appropriations. Subsidies to employers through the WOTC are determined by the number of certifications and tax credits requested by employers who hire qualified members of target groups. From 1997 until 2005, WOTC expenditures were fairly low but somewhat variable, but expenditures have steadily increased since the 2006 expansion of eligibility to young people 18 to 24 years old in families receiving SNAP. According to the U.S. Office of Management and Budget, WOTC subsidies to employers reached roughly $1.1 billion in 2010. Despite the escalating expenditures, there are still fewer employers requesting certification and filing for the tax credits than actually qualify due in part to the complexities caused by the split administration between state agencies and the IRS. While the program is intended to incentivize the hiring of target groups, it does not create new jobs. This transfer of assets to private companies diffuses the costs associated with low-wage, high-turnover jobs, but there is little evidence that it is an effective incentive for changing hiring practices.

Approximately, 37.6 million total TANF dollars were spent on subsidies to the private sector in 2009. This spending represents a significant change from AFDC, in which there were no work subsidies to the private sector.[6] Figure 4B in Appendix B illustrates the work subsidies to the private sector since welfare reform. The available data hint that the utilization of TANF money for private sector subsidies may be sensitive to executive administrations. At present, there are not enough data available to test the influence of executive policies on the total devolved use of TANF funds, but future research should endeavor to examine this question.

CONTRACTING OUT

The use of private for-profit and nonprofit organizations to provide publicly derived and funded services is an ancient practice with a long history in the United States that extends to the colonial period. The patterns in contracting service provision have varied over the years, but the managerial reforms of New Public Management (NPM) and welfare reform have resulted in substantial increases in contracting out public sector services that are monitored through performance-based, behaviorally focused contracts. Additionally, other varied and often multiple sources of funding that a given service provider may offer can result in an organization's being managed by public, private, and nonprofit sector benefactors for specific outcomes tied to the funding source. Therefore, implementation may be thought of as the managerial oversight; whereas service providers enact policy. The outcomes defined in the contract are by and large (although not exclusively) the only feedback. However, public managers can use evaluation to mobilize existing private for-profit and nonprofit organizations to implement innovations swiftly and broadly. Programs may also just as quickly be drawn back or cut without the traditional forms of resistance that have characterized bureaucratic politics.

The vastness and behavioral approach to contracting in poverty governance serves the neoliberal paternalist story line. The hierarchical control,
conditioned by funding sources that often define outcomes without accounting for the long history of oppression, imposes an order that is likely to
entrench poverty. Contracting out social service provision has the potential
to make government more accessible and responsive. However, contracting
social service provision also makes it possible for government to have a
number of agents to blame and revive the reform story. Understanding the
value and implications of contracting requires further study. The extent of
contracting has resulted in a widespread acquiescence to the notion. This
trend in suppressing challenges to the neoliberal paternalist story line inhibits a clear picture of poverty governance. Further research that pulls together
knowledge of the contracting networks is crucial to developing antipoverty
policy within the system of poverty governance.

Understanding the implementation of state TANF programs is essential to discerning the nature of contracting relationships. Welfare reform is
enacted at the organizational level, managed by administrative units of state
governments, and determined by the state policy process within the federal
guidelines. Whether the state or the counties oversee the administration of
TANF, most service delivery is provided through performance-based contracting. Service providers are held accountable for the deliverables defined
in the contracts by the county under the supervision of the state in the following states: Alabama, California, Colorado, Maryland, Minnesota, Montana, New Jersey, New York, North Dakota, Ohio, North Carolina, Virginia,
and Wisconsin. All other states administer TANF at the state level, so
service contracts are managed by the state exclusively.

Discretionary authority also varies somewhat across states. Most states
maintain control over eligibility, benefits, and the available services. However, there are some states that allow a degree of discretion across counties.
In North Carolina, the eligibility standards, benefit levels, and available
services vary by county. In Virginia, the state determines eligibility standards,
benefit levels, and available services, and in Wisconsin, the state determines
eligibility standards and benefit levels. Counties in Wisconsin determine the
available services except in Milwaukee, where the state provides direct contract approval for TANF service provision. Counties have discretion regarding benefit levels and eligibility standards in Colorado, South Carolina, and
in certain areas of North Carolina. In addition, the available services vary by
county in the following states: Colorado, Georgia, Iowa, Kansas, Maryland,
Minnesota, New York, North Carolina, Ohio, Oregon, Texas, Wisconsin
(excepting Milwaukee). As contract management devolves, the nature of
discretion is diffused. People living in poverty are subject to variation that
may make accessing services confusing. Perhaps more importantly, states

may devolve authority for contract management in a manner that heightens (and obscures) inequalities.

Traditionally, eligibility determination, intake, assessment, and case management were service functions performed by civil servants. PRWORA authorizes states to contract out any and all services. The state or the county (depending on the level of devolution specific to the type of discretion) retains authority for contract management and monitoring. The vast majority of employment-related services such as job placement are contracted out to the private sector across states. Most state welfare offices provide eligibility determination and case management as well. Some states contract out eligibility determination and case management. In states that contract out eligibility determination and case management, the state or county sets the standards. The service providers enact the contract provisions using the formula provided by the state or county along with the operations proposed by the organization (which must be consistent with federal, state, and local policies) and approved by the state or county.

Wisconsin is one example of a state that has contracted out eligibility determination and case management. However, Wisconsin's most recently amended TANF plan increases the public focus on eligibility determination and assessments by creating a W-2 Eligibility and Assessment Agency to provide countywide services in Milwaukee in the 2010–11 contracts. In Wisconsin, the state determines policy standards, and the counties manage the service contracts except in Milwaukee, where the state has direct control. In Milwaukee, private for-profit and nonprofit agencies provide case management services, and job placement services are contracted to private for-profit and nonprofit agencies by region. Additionally, the state contracts with a nonprofit organization in Milwaukee to provide SSI advocacy. The balance of the other counties in the state of Wisconsin are served by four nonprofit organizations, two private for-profit organizations, 32 county human service or employment agencies, and seven multicounty human service consortiums. The Wisconsin Department of Children and Families administers by county the W-2 Trial Jobs, Subsidized Private Sector Employment, and the Transitional Jobs Demonstration Project through contracts with private for-profit and nonprofit agencies, as well as a few county agencies across the state.

The state of Wisconsin mandates that service providers offer "strengths-based" and "family-centered" approaches to assistance in a "culturally and linguistically competent manner" throughout the state. Wisconsin requires that agencies contracting TANF services provide a one-page description of benefits and services to all individuals who ask for services. Wisconsin also defines the role of the Financial and Employment Planner (FEP). Contractors provide integrated case management in Wisconsin,[7] and the FEP is responsible for eligibility determination, employability plans,

employment placement, case management, child support enforcement referrals, and all other support services for assisting with self-sufficiency. FEPs may
also be Learnfare specialists who oversee the school engagement of minor
children, including minor parents. Learnfare specialists use discretion in
determining whether or not a parent has good cause for failing to cooperate
with Learnfare case management. Financial penalties can be imposed by the
Learnfare specialist in Wisconsin if children are not enrolled in school and
attending regularly or if parents are not participating in case management
cooperatively.

The Wisconsin Department of Children and Families describes its
administration of TANF as somewhat collaborative with the state's departments of Administration, Health Services, Public Instructions, and Revenue,
as many of the programs overlap. For example, the refundable portion of the
EITC established by the Wisconsin Department of Revenue (DOR) in 1999
counts toward the state's TANF MOE, and families in Wisconsin eligible for
the EITC are also eligible for the Homestead Tax Credit administered by
the DOR, which affords property tax relief that includes rent and may be a
refundable credit but are not available in any month that a family receives
W-2 assistance. Consequently, these agencies collaboratively share records
that account for proper qualifications.

Wisconsin is not unique in the shift toward welfare privatization. The
reallocation from civil service to private contractors in welfare administration happened across all states, but the types of contracts, extent of
contracting out, and contractual arrangements vary considerably across jurisdictions. There are three types of welfare contracts: (1) pay-for-performance
contracts; (2) cost-reimbursement contracts; and (3) fixed-price contracts.
Pay-for-performance contracts compensate contractors only when specific
performance goals are achieved. They are considered the least risky for
public agencies because the onus is on the agent to produce the federally
mandated outcomes. However, shifting risk entirely to service providers is
not often possible where risk-averse agencies that have little control over
client referrals may limit the pool of agencies competing for these types
of contracts. Cost-reimbursement contracts pay service providers for the
expenses incurred, but costs are generally restricted to the budget approved
in the procurement process. Payments are made regardless of the quality of
the services or outcomes, so public agencies carry the bulk of the risk in these
contracts; although the contracting agencies' actual cost-benefit ratio and
referral flow affect the utility of the contract as well. Fixed-price contracts
establish an agreed-upon fee regardless of performance or the actual cost
of provision. Cost increases are a risk to contractors, and the risk of poor
quality and low effectiveness is on the public agency. Most contracts across
states are considered hybrid contracts that attempt to balance performance

incentives with the viability of providers, particularly those that produce results. Over time, the contracting relationships produce an interdependence between the public agency and the private contractor (Smith 1993). Public and private agencies develop long-term relationships in which the costs of exit for either party increase over time, producing political regimes that affect the character of service delivery and regulate the welfare-contracting market (Smith 2007).

In addition to an absence of competition in welfare contracting, the capacity to manage contracts diminishes over time because public sector employment shrinks as contracting increases (Van Slyke 2003). Public managers act as sophisticated buyers of welfare services when there is adequate personnel capacity with experience in contract management, policy expertise, political savvy, negotiation and mediation skills, oversight capabilities, and effective communication (Kettl 1993). In the absence of "smart buyers" in welfare markets, accountability is reduced, and contractors often take actions to keep competition in local service markets low (Van Slyke 2003). However, evidence from case studies at the city level suggest that community organizations can serve a mediating function between competitive and collaborative pressures when those public-private partnerships enhance political voice and development capacity (Bennett and Giloth 2007).

The collaborative, interdependent context in which contracting relationships evolve and the constraints on management capacity contribute to goal alignment between public agencies and contractors such that opportunism and moral hazard may still be less likely despite low competition in welfare markets, because the contracting relationships come to rely on mutual exchange and reciprocity (Van Slyke 2006). However, the emphasis in enactment on meeting the legal obligations imposed through implementation structures that distort incentives can produce problematic working relationships between providers emphasizing outcomes management and those focusing on more traditional helping relationships in social work (Schram et al. 2010). Perhaps more importantly, neither approach takes into account the client's perspective, and the pervasive failure to account for the client's perspective makes poverty alleviation more difficult, particularly for long-term participants (Dias and Maynard-Moody 2006).

The private, nonprofit, and public sectors at the federal, state, and local levels are increasingly linked through grants, formal contracts, and informal partnerships that create network organizations with a common purpose. The clarity, pace, and credibility of the communication patterns that characterize the network reflect the extent to which competition or collaboration dominate the contracting relationships of governance. These somewhat fluid configurations of authority are like muscular hydrostats (used to manipulate). The more peripheral the distribution of discretion or devolu-

tion of authority, the more elaborate, innovative, or entrepreneurial managerial imperatives may be. Whether or not the tentacles of state welfare policy
direct people living in poverty to opportunities, assimilate, shuffle, or alienate depends upon the structure, culture, and craft of welfare management.
The management of competition and collaboration in welfare service provision is a delicate balance of risk shifting or risk sharing. The complexities
of these relationships have been studied much more extensively than the
experiences of people living in poverty. Understanding the perspectives of
people attempting to move out of poverty is crucial to learning more about
how to maximize opportunities. The web of authority that people living in
poverty are subject to may help them maneuver economic transitions in a
manner that allows at least some to move out of poverty, or it may trap
them in a relay of work cycles that do not alleviate poverty. The tackiness
of the web depends at least in part upon whether or not poverty alleviation is a policy objective but also upon the extent to which the presence
of legitimate choice exists for people attempting to move out of poverty.

Poverty Governance across States

Much American domestic policy is carried out through contracting networks, intergovernmental grants, public and private sector loans and loan
guarantees, and intricate interjurisdictional regulatory regimes (Kettl 1988;
Lynn, Heinrich, and Hill 2000; Mosher 1980; Salamon 1989). The current
exercise of poverty governance in the United States employs the muscle of
workfare regimes across jurisdictions to reduce caseloads, increase work rates,
transfer commitments from public assistance to private services, and enforce
the values of neoliberal paternalism through NPM reforms. State workfare
regimes serve a central role in the implementation of poverty governance.
Each state authorizes and manages the enactment of governmental power
through contractual arrangements intended to promote market productivity.
Consequently, the states of welfare in the United States presently mobilize
workfare regimes according to speculation in public-private partnerships
regarding the potential for economic growth. The extent to which economic
growth may be broadly beneficial is contingent upon the mutuality in the
contractual arrangements. Workfare regimes that conflate the interests of the
firm and the individual put downward pressure on wages and impose heavy
penalties to compel contracts that shift risk to individual agents, whereas
workfare regimes that maintain a higher degree of legitimate choice may be
more likely to function as antipoverty measures.

The structure of workfare administration and service delivery operates
at multiple levels in which there are not necessarily clear divisions between
task and function because the guidelines are defined in the authorization

for funding or in the contracts rather than the agency's charge or organization's mission. So, the objectives and the responsibility for the various parts of the process are outlined in law and negotiated through legal channels, but a good deal of discretion exists in the operations at each level. The boundaries between sectors are increasingly blurred, and lines of authority are linked to the funding source.

The federal government establishes target populations and performance standards for numerous sources of federal funding that people living in poverty might be subject to or benefit from across states. With TANF in particular, states are required to complete a state plan outlining the state's intended operations that has been subject to public review for at least 60 days prior to submission to HHS every three years. States have full control over the content, and the HHS secretary is responsible for ensuring that all the required components of the plan are included. The formats, contents, and details of the plans vary considerably by state, but the federal government must approve state plans in order for federal funding to be released. The federal government also measures accountability according to the work rates and caseload requirements outlined in the law, and states may receive incentives or be penalized for deviating from the standards. State policies set the lines of authority within the state, use discretionary authority to operationalize target groups, develop models to measure performance, track data, monitor operations at different levels of devolution defined by the state, and may establish specialized and separate programs to target specific social issues in a flexible manner. States also define the service delivery areas throughout the state and authorize authority to local administrative agencies, private industry councils, or public-private partnership organizations to manage contracts and/or deliver services. Contracted service providers develop program service plans specific to the funding source, which details the cost per client, delivers services, reports outcomes in the manner defined in the contract, and seeks reimbursement in the manner defined in the contract.

Consequently, governance bodies are simultaneously restrained yet given expansive authority within the boundaries of the authorizing legislation. The actions and expenditures are restricted by the funding source, and the degree of discretion is limited at each consecutive level of government through the legal authorizations. Although the use of funds is somewhat restricted by the source, the sources are quite varied, and the interjurisdictional negotiation of contractual relationships actually expands the systematic regulation of conduct considerably.

The flexibility of TANF implementation means that governance is enacted at multiple levels. While some states centralize administrative authority, others supervise the administration by counties. Discretion over eligibility, benefits, and available services may be devolved to the state or the county, and in some cases, large urban areas may operate under different authority than the other jurisdictions in the state. Case management, contract management, and work verification for TANF CA are managed by different organizational departments across states, and variation in managerial relationships may also exist within states in some cases. Additionally, discretion in service provision is devolved to the contracting agents across states. These variations in authority structures frame accountability for performance metrics, and each articulation allows for a degree of discretion connected to that line of authority. This also means that people living in poverty may be subject to an increasing governance authority that is complex, adaptable, perhaps inconsistent, often punitive, and all-encompassing.

The Workforce Investment Act (WIA) of 1998 established the structure for the workforce investment system comprised of state workforce investment boards. The WIA defines the composition of state workforce investment boards as being composed of the governor, two members of each chamber of the state legislature, and representatives appointed by the governor, for which a majority must represent the interests of business. Boards established prior to the WIA were grandfathered in, so states such as Texas that engaged in reforms prior to the federal legislation tended to secure an even greater degree of executive control as the state reforms were most often led by governors. States have combined workfare and workforce investment functions in different ways and to varying degrees. For example, Florida transferred workfare to the control of workforce development and privatized the operations across the state's workforce regions. In many states, however, workforce development and workfare functions overlap, and the agencies are expected to collaborate, most often through referrals to contractors. Because workfare and workforce investment functions and funds are often comingled in different ways, it is extremely difficult to estimate how the different configurations of governance affect poverty intensity where state policy choices and implementation strategies are not often comparable.

Because neoliberal paternalism defines the strategic game of workfare established through federal legislation, state policies reflect this form of reasoning in many respects. However, the paternalism of state welfare governance regimes varies and has important implications for autonomy. States that apply neoliberal paternalist rationality to serve business impose policies that restrict individuals and establish relatively rigid hierarchies in which the interests of governance authorities may tend to entrench poverty. States may also use normative policies minimizing deviance from economic or social standards to discipline hierarchies, reduce caseloads in a manner that unravels social obligations, and encourage conduct that promotes self-sufficiency. In fact, analysis of longitudinal data from the Fragile Families and Child Wellbeing Study by Bruch, Ferree, and Soss (2010) demonstrates that paternalist welfare governance regimes lower the likelihood of voting, political participation, civic participation, and civil engagement.

In states that emphasize discipline and harshly punish deviance, governance is a "culture of control" in which welfare and criminal justice policies regulate civic engagement.[8] The recent drug-screening policies in some states are examples of the variation in cultures of control or strategies of management that reflect the state's orientation toward social control. Table 1.14 in Appendix A outlines the status of drug-screening measures across states. Federal law dictates that no state is prohibited from testing for controlled substances or sanctioning those who test positive as long as statewide administrative funds and not federal funds are used for that purpose and appeal procedures are adequate. Some states have no drug-screening policy, but most states have debated or passed some form of drug screening. Many states conduct or require drug testing of recipients identified as at "high risk" of substance abuse, generally based on standardized screenings, and a number of states have passed laws requiring random drug testing of recipients. Some of the states that have opted out or modified the federal ban require a clean drug test for people attempting to restore benefits after a felony drug conviction. Michigan attempted to impose mandatory drug testing on all adult TANF recipients. However, the district court decision in *Marchwinski v. Howard* ruled in September 2000 that the policy violates the Fourth Amendment protections against unreasonable searches. The Sixth Circuit Court of Appeals initially reversed the decision but withdrew the reversal in 2003. Consequently, the case law as it stands currently requires individual suspicion, and receipt of cash assistance is not considered adequate basis for suspicion. Many state policies employ random testing, making the argument that it is in line with employment practices to defend the constitutionality of the state statute. Table 1.14 also identifies those state policies that include referral to treatment in circumstances in which recipients test positive for drugs in the implementation of the testing policy. A few states conduct a nontesting drug screen as a part of the intake process to identify substance use issues that may inhibit employment and require participants with substance use issues to participate in treatment as a condition of the TANF contract between the state and the client. Some states use the intake process to establish "reasonable suspicion" to require testing; while other states attempt to impose randomized testing of the segregated population of TANF clients. Other states consider it a violation of the TANF contract to refuse or fail a drug test required by an employer. A small number of states seek to use discretion at the county or case worker level in drug screening. States also vary with respect to the charges and results of drug screens. In some cases, the costs are deferred to the applicant, and in others, the state pays for drug testing (and sometimes even treatment). Some states refer to treatment, and other states disqualify those who test positive for illegal drugs for anywhere from six months to three years, or even indefinitely. In a few states, these policies apply to TANF, SNAP, and/or Medicaid as well. Mississippi is considering a proposal that would link welfare and criminal justice policies directly through drug screening by imposing criminal penalties for "willful violations" of the testing requirements.

The paternalist perspective on this state of affairs suggests that the logic of this governmentality whips into shape an orderly society, secure as shifts in the patterns and pace of exchange transform. The neoliberal story is that this state of affairs affords multiple access points and a malleable system for exploiting opportunities. An alternative perspective views the opportunistic harnessing of labor and attempts to use disciplinary practices to compel "the poor" to regulate themselves to be highly problematic for civic affairs. These are not simply different, equally valid perspectives. Some stories present a clearer picture based on the evidence. The weight of the evidence demonstrates that the pursuit of discipline subjugates women and people of color, limits citizenship to workers/consumers, and pushes people in poverty further to the margins (see Bruch, Ferree, and Soss 2010; Collins and Mayer 2010; Soss 2000; Soss, Fording, and Schram 2011a; Stone 2008; Wacquant 2009; L. White 2002).

The extent to which administrative rules and procedures may bind people in this process varies according to the order of devolution, the managerial attention to balancing metrics with well-being, and ideological orientations that shape perceptions regarding who might require discipline. Recent research suggests that the discretion in welfare delivery within federal guidelines tends to (1) inhibit challenges to systematic practices (Lens and Vorsanger 2005; Soss 2000); (2) focus managerial attention on quantitative metrics to the exclusion of concerns regarding well-being (Brodkin 2006); (3) employ procedures that may make resources less accessible to those living in circumstances in which disadvantages are cumulative and the presence of choice is limited (Cherlin, Bogen, Quane, and Burton 2002; Super 2004); and (4) interact with race and ethnicity in highly complex ways that may vary at the state, local, organizational, and individual level (Brodkin and Majmundar 2010; Fording, Soss, and Schram 2011; Watkins-Hayes 2009).

The formal standard operating procedures and the informal patterns of practice that welfare providers employ systematically impose costs that result in a kind of bureaucratic exclusion, which contributes to caseload decline, particularly among those who are more vulnerable to information asymmetries and time constraints (Brodkin and Majmundar 2010). Consequently, poverty governance efficiently sheds caseloads and inhibits resistances without imposing such policies directly. The rational calculus may indeed satisfy those who enjoy the story that new managerialism affords greater maximiza-

tion of opportunities as well as those who insist that the story of orderly
security is central to the current state of well-being. However, this requires
piecing together the knowledge gained from research at multiple levels of
analysis over time to understand poverty governance as a policy system.

ALIGNING THE WORKFORCE

Aligning the workforce with the economic objectives of the state's workfare
regime involves administrative reorganization, legal authorizations that shift
the emphasis from the administrative rules and procedures to contractual
authority linked to allocations, and attempts to use behavioral techniques
to impose market logic and oblige traditional family relationships. State
economic policy priorities arranged by those with access to the policy process
increasingly direct labor efficiently (without bargaining). The authority to
maintain the economic order pursued by the state is diffuse, and the myriad
partners in governance increasingly seek more influence. Those subject to
poverty governance face the progressive imposition of social controls that
serve business and/or shift responsibility for well-being to families and individuals.

Reorganization is often led by governors or legislators. In the cases of
Florida and Texas, restructuring the welfare programs began prior to devolution in anticipation of PRWORA, creating systems of work activation
dictated by the "needs of the state's employers." Select industries are targeted
for specialization based on what is estimated to give the state a competitive advantage, and opportunities for training are defined and regulated by
business interests. In Texas, for example, the Texas Workforce Commission (TWC) is the state agency charged with oversight of the provision
of workforce services. The commission is the governing body of the TWC
and is comprised of members representing the public, labor, and employers.
There are three full-time TWC commissioners appointed by the governor
for six-year terms with the potential for reappointment at the discretion of
the governor. The TWC administers state and federal workforce investment
grants and allocates the monies to the 28 Local Workforce Development
Boards (LWDBs) in Texas. LWDBs are local, collaborative organizations
accountable to the governor's Texas Workforce Investment Council, which
reviews the LWDBs strategic plans. The LWDBs, along with the TWC, are
referred to as Texas Workforce Solutions and implement the One-Stop delivery system through The Workforce Information System of Texas (TWIST),
the application designed to track benefit and training programs. Consequently, reorganization in this case brought welfare policy authority under more
direct executive control in both policymaking authority and allocations.
This restructuring of bureaucratic politics also shifted welfare policy from

social services to employment services. The emphasis on job placement in Texas policy is an executive-led regulation of the state's economic strategy, aligning the workforce for jobs that local officials determine are in order.

States utilize various tools for financing the alignment of the workforce and economic development priorities. For example, the Massachusetts Building Essential Skills through Training (BEST) program is implemented through a competitive grant process funding Regional Industry Teams made up of employers, education and training providers, and local workforce investment boards. Grantees are also required to involve employers in program design. Highly devolved and privatized governance strategies represent efforts to align the workforce with the economic development priorities of the state.

In Kansas, then-governor Kathleen Sebelius linked the "training needs of workers and employers" through an executive order combining the economic development and workforce development functions under the authority of the Kansas Department of Commerce. The state is one of only a few that also created cooperative networks between the Department of Commerce and community and technical colleges through the Workforce Development Trust Fund, diverting 10% of economic development appropriations for investments in human capital or infrastructure to "build the skills of the Kansas workforce" and "optimize resources" across the state's diverse economic interests. Where Kansas engaged stakeholders through "Prosperity Summits" across the state, the state of Washington utilizes what are referred to as Skill Panels, which are public-private partnerships between labor, education, and business representatives collaborating to generate career opportunities by providing support to industries considered vital to the region. Skill panels are coordinated across regions in Washington through Chambers of Commerce, local workforce boards, or community colleges. Generally, Skill Panels are made up of 15 to 20 business representatives clustered by industry to develop strategies for implementing innovative training to stock a pool of qualified job candidates in the state by leveraging Workforce Investment Act funds. Iowa's New Jobs Training Program uses bonds to finance basic skills training for new positions that are "highly responsive to employer needs" in order to attract corporations to locate in Iowa and is another example of state attempts to exercise control over labor force conditions in the state. Regulation of access to training is the responsibility of the Iowa Department of Economic Development, and the community college boards of trustees approve the agreements with employers for training subsidies. Missouri has a similar new jobs training program that utilizes bond financing, but the Missouri Department of Economic Development's Division of Workforce Development maintains a higher degree of control over industry targets and wage levels.

The utilization of bonds further complicates the web of welfare services. Government bonds are considered low-risk debt investments because the loan amount, loan period, and interest payments are fixed. Bonds that fund employment opportunities may be issued by the federal government through programs such as the Recovery Zone Economic Development Bonds authorized by the ARRA (2009) or may be municipal bonds issued by cities, counties, redevelopment agencies, special-purpose districts, school districts, public utility districts, publicly owned airports or seaports, and other governance entities. They may be general obligations accounted for in the budget of the issuer or secured by specified revenues. Interest income received by bondholders is usually exempt from federal income tax, and state income tax rules vary by state of residence and bond type. Government bonds might be referred to as "risk-free" because the government can raise taxes or (in the case of the federal government) create additional currency to redeem bond maturity. However, there are separate risks associated with increasing taxes and printing money to secure debt. Bonds to finance "employer needs" and economic development serve the neoliberal story line, but failed bonds and inflation pose higher risk of increasing costs to the least well-off in regressive tax structures. Bonds are also another example of how difficult it is to track the spending on particular policy objectives. Objectives are linked to funding sources, which makes agents accountable to principals for the outcomes specified, but because welfare policy is largely driven by the economic objectives of the state and is fueled by multiple funding streams, accounting for the total transfers to any policy target (individuals receiving public assistance or private companies receiving subsidies) is virtually impossible at this point.

THE LOGICAL ABACUS OF WELFARE GOVERNANCE

The logical machine that operates from the principles of welfare reform assumes that labor market participation is the means to independence and the supreme expression of responsibility. Establishing the validity of this formula for welfare relies on an accounting system in which meaning is assigned exclusively to the performance metrics inextricably linked to the objectives defined in PRWORA. The requisite metrics and their meaning are defined in policy to ensure that the interpretation validates the formula. Subsequent policies allow for exemptions of data that are likely inconsistent with this interpretation. However, maintaining voluntary compliance with or consent to welfare authority is contingent upon credible commitments, and the contract as a viable, mutually beneficial agreement depends upon the good faith of all parties involved. If or when the metrics tell stories that serve only to justify the policy but are inconsistent with the reality that many people experience, the interpretation is not seen as credible, and the commitments are likely to readjust.

The logical slate of the regulatory regime sets the boundaries for inter-pretation, implementation, and evaluation. These boundaries are evident in the determination of data, the methods of collection, and system of evalu-ation. Caseload counts, family characteristics, and individual information on recipients are required to be reported by states to HHS under TANF law. This includes basic demographic information, work activities and work hours of adult participants, and the financial circumstances of individu-als and families receiving assistance involving TANF funds. States are not required to include the caseload counts or participant characteristics for TANF-funded support services, such as job training, education, subsidized work, child care, and transportation assistance. It is interesting to note that states take account of how many and what kind of people receive cash assistance, but states are not required to account for how many people and from what kind of background they offer support services to through TANF. Consequently, states are not held accountable for the extent to which real choice exists, the kinds of opportunities offered, and the patterns of access to different types of opportunities. It also makes it difficult to assess the extent to which the state is subsidizing the private sector "to create opportunities" and to foster "new taxpayers" in their jurisdiction.

The reauthorization of the TANF block grant in 2010 included new data reporting requirements. The new supplemental TANF reports identify a broader range of work activity by counting cases having hours in countable activities that are over the federal limits or were otherwise not included in the regular TANF data report, cases with hours in noncountable activities that may help lead to self-sufficiency, and the reasons for nonparticipation relevant to those cases in which families are not involved in countable work or self-sufficiency activities. States have the option of reporting on their entire caseload or on a sample of 175 cases. States are also now required to provide a snapshot of program activity by describing in detail how fed-eral TANF and MOE funds were used in a supplementary narrative. The supplementary narrative has the potential to allow for the incorporation of qualitative measures in performance evaluation. It also has the potential to increase oversight and impose discipline in a more subjective manner.

In addition, $10 million is appropriated in accordance with TANF law each year to the U.S. Census Bureau for a longitudinal household survey. The Survey of Program Dynamics examines the effects of welfare reform. The longitudinal survey of a sample of people receiving welfare and other families with low incomes gives particular attention to "out-of-wedlock births, welfare dependency, the beginning and end of welfare spells, and the causes of repeat welfare spells."[9] There have also been appropriations to study welfare outcomes, including competitive grant programs, projects to improve data collection and capacity building, and other projects to evaluate welfare-related subjects including devolution, privatization, and special populations.[10]

Despite the superficial appearance of transparency and extensive efforts at evaluation, accountability remains elusive. Devolution allows for considerable flexibility to address the economic and social priorities defined by the state and enacted through cross-sector contractual partnerships. However, increasing variation in funding streams, emphasis on social imperatives, and deviation in operations responding to changing market demands, make it exceedingly difficult to map the scope of this evolving welfare regime. In addition, the utilization of wide-ranging sources of funding, which also tend to be competitive and time-limited, makes comparing policy choices challenging and results in tremendous difficulty in understanding the social value of these investments over time. Using performance metrics allows for evaluations of compliance with the law but does not provide much information about the impact these choices have on people living in poverty. Higher levels of devolution and broad disarticulation of service provision present a public image of "choices," but the presence and exercise of choice is exclusive to the economic and political interests that dominate contracting relationships

5

Workfare Policies and the State of Self-Sufficiency

.•———•.

Self-sufficiency refers to a state of autonomy in which aid and support are not necessary for survival. Neoliberal welfare reformers argued that self-sufficiency is a rational policy objective. According to the neoliberal story of welfare reform, self-sufficient individuals maximize individual liberty and social welfare. Paternalist welfare reformers seized on the notion that people living in poverty are not self-sufficient. They saw opportunities to direct TANF participants through managerial reforms. For neoliberals, autonomy is the purported goal. For paternalists, the perceived lack of autonomy justifies social control measures "for their own good."

The tensions in the neoliberal paternalist poverty governance rhetoric play out in interesting ways. Steps toward self-sufficiency are necessary to access TANF aid based on the expectation that need is temporary. This also means that people with the greatest barriers to self-sufficiency might have the most difficulty accessing support under these conditions. Additionally, managerial reforms increase oversight throughout the poverty governance process. So, agencies in the governance network are managed by contracts in which autonomy is restricted at each jurisdictional junction. Agencies in the private sector are often more autonomous than their government counterparts, but they are also now restricted by their contracts with government agencies. Therefore, the autonomy of individuals and agencies within the system of poverty governance is contingent upon their influence in contracting and perceived ability to achieve self-sufficiency. As long as demands outweigh resources at the agency or individual level, paternalists will have justification for intervention under this logic. As long as outcome metrics defined contractually remain an almost exclusive estimate of the "success" of welfare reforms, the neoliberal justification for labor regulations will be calculated as the only rational policies. Yet, the neoliberal paternalist picture of welfare reform may be far from the realities of people living in poverty.

In order for the welfare reforms outlined in the previous chapter to achieve the promise of individual self-sufficiency, workfare policies across states must make it easier for people to move out of poverty over time. Understanding the extent to which welfare reforms may or may not be a story in the interest of the public writ large may be assessed by estimating the net effects of workfare policies across U.S. states. This chapter presents the findings from the time-series analysis of the factors affecting impoverishment across states over time.[1] The analysis of data from each state over 18 years represents more than a full cycle of the policy process. The time-series analysis presented in this chapter provides the best available evidence regarding the extent to which welfare reforms implemented across U.S. states offer opportunities to move out of poverty in sufficient numbers. If the devolved and privatized system of poverty governance across states produces an overall state in which more people are self-sufficient, the ideal of individual welfare maximization is supported. If the net effects of workfare policies across states lead to increasing impoverishment, the policies are not functioning effectively as antipoverty measures. Estimating the realities for people living in poverty across U.S. states over time is critical to determining how welfare reforms might function as antipoverty policies. It also provides an opportunity to examine some of the variations in state policy choices that might perform better as antipoverty strategies than other policy choices. The aggregate assessment of the impact of welfare reforms on impoverishment presented in this chapter allows for an appraisal of the extent to which welfare reform rhetoric measures up to reality. The analysis in this chapter suggests that the implementation of workfare policies across states over time made it more difficult for people to move out of poverty in the aggregate. People in poverty are working more for less, and state EITCs and asset-building programs are not filling gaps between poverty and self-sufficiency in the aggregate. This does not mean that these programs are having no effect. It means that more research regarding the specific design choices is essential to understanding how to increase the aggregate gains.

Factors Affecting Impoverishment

The devolved and contractual nature of welfare reforms has led to increasing subsidies to the private sector and an expanding use of managerial controls regulating people living in poverty. PRWORA mandated caseload reductions and authorized the exercise of state authority to impose the federally defined notions of moral individualism. The WIA increased the efficiency of subsidies to the private sector, authorizing state authority to regulate workforce development with the counsel of business leaders, funding the training and placement of job candidates according to the needs defined by business leaders in the states, and implemented through one-stop delivery systems organized by state workforce investment boards and most often contracted to private providers. The DRA provided states with "flexibilities" to revise health benefit packages to mirror commercial insurance packages in order to slow the growth in spending on certain classes of beneficiaries and reauthorized TANF with provisions lowering the threshold for denying passports to individuals with child support arrearages.

Although many "welfare leavers" obtained some employment during the period of economic growth in the late 1990s, many subsequently became unemployed, and a substantial number of families remain in poverty with few permanent employment options. They are now discouraged from applying for welfare (Handler and Hasenfeld 2007). In addition, contractors use information asymmetries to advance their own interests in a context in which performance measures do not focus on the quality of services and competitive contracting is rarely the standard (DeParle 2004). This shift from income support for people living in poverty under AFDC to the expansion of subsidies to the private sector does not appear to have produced significant opportunities for people to move out of poverty.

In fact, the findings in this analysis demonstrate that each round of welfare reforms that inflate private interests actually make it increasingly more difficult for people to move out of poverty. Table 2.2 in Appendix B explains the estimation technique and details the results of the generalized least squares regression, and Figure 1B in Appendix B illustrates the model performance. The model is significant at the 0.001 level, and the predictions using the generalized least squares technique make feasible estimations accounting for heteroskedasticity in a manner that reduces the potential for the overestimation of the net effects of the independent variables over time. This analysis of the net effects over 18 years yields strong evidence regarding how welfare reforms have affected people living in poverty.

PRWORA mandated caseload reductions, and the WIA and the DRA increased pressures on states to reduce TANF caseloads. However, caseload reductions do not have a significant effect on impoverishment, but welfare privatization does contribute to increasing impoverishment. There is no evidence that caseload reductions extracted by welfare reforms function as an antipoverty measure. Reducing welfare caseloads has not made people living in poverty more self-sufficient, and the implementation of work-first strategies that privatize welfare across states actually contributes to increasing impoverishment.

Calculation of the marginal effects of welfare reform legislation indicates that each piece of legislation increased the intensity of poverty by a factor of 4.20 when all other variables are held at their averages, and Figure 2B in Appendix B illustrates the marginal impact of each piece of welfare legislation on impoverishment as it was implemented across states. The intensity of poverty increases as government serves private interests, in spite of the increasing work effort of people living in poverty.

Workfare marketization changes the decommodified space characterizing needs-based social protections under AFDC to a growing contingent of labor under increasing pressure to accept work under contract conditions that are increasingly managed by public-private collaborations organized around the needs of employers. The poverty governance market exercises networks of authority throughout the state to direct the labor force to the employment priorities of the state and local business leaders. Work participation rates are intended to quantify the extent to which families are engaged in work-related activities that are expected to lead to self-sufficiency.

States have broad flexibility to structure work-related activities within three principal constraints defined in the federal statute: (1) participation rates; (2) a 24-month work requirement; and (3) unless the state opts out in its annual plan submitted to the federal government for competitive block grant funding, a two-month community service requirement. There are no federal regulations on work rates in Separate State Programs (SSPs) in those states that operate state-funded, grant-funded, or those SSPs funded by some combination other than federal TANF dollars. Discretion regarding work-related activities is commonly delegated to county-level agencies that design and implement programs within the framework of state policy. However, most states specify exemptions or categories of adult recipients who are not required to participate in TANF work activities and place restrictions on the number of exemptions. Some states sequence the work activities in an employability plan. For example, an individual may be required to search for a job for no more than six weeks, then participate in an authorized work activity for up to 12 months, and be expected to do mandatory community service for 12 months afterward. Most states do not employ a fixed sequence of work activities, and those that do tend to utilize standardized sequences in the form of plans and backup plans. All states count the job search as an authorized work activity, and a majority of states authorize some form of subsidized employment as work activity. Virtually all states authorize Adult Basic Education (ABE) and English as a Second Language (ESL) as work activities meeting the work requirements, and some of those states require TANF recipients to demonstrate that they have met a given minimum standard, such as completing a GED. Education directly related to employment is considered an authorized work activity in most states, as is job skills training. Job readiness is typically defined as classroom training on completing job applications, resume writing, interview skills, life skills, career counseling, and workplace expectations. And, job readiness is often mandated by the state for some groups of individuals deemed less than employable at intake. These strategies structuring work activities have the stated purpose of moving people from welfare to work. However, evidence indicates that work may not be stable, and workfare contracts that are not negotiated by free and equal parties may not pay.

Ziliak (2005) shows that deep and persistent poverty rose while unemployment fell and working rates increased in the 1990s. Despite the fact that high work effort is characteristic of low-income families (Waldron, Roberts, and Reamer 2004), false notions about them continue unabated. These include claims that their low social status is due to a poor work ethic, limited skills and abilities, or poor decision making. False attributions about the causes of poverty based on these types of claims persist irrespective of work effort and circumstance. The false attributions include notions that poor work ethic, limited skills and abilities, or poor decision making results from individual characteristics (see Murray and Herrnstein 1994), the culture of the underclass (see Wilson 1987), or a "taste" for consumption over savings (see Lawrance 1991). These stories that do not match reality, and the false attributions that accompany them, persist despite extant evidence to the contrary. Waldron, Roberts, and Reamer (2004) show that the average low-income family put in 580 hours of work over the typical 40-hour work week every twelve months, but the work available is most often unlikely to pay enough to support a family (Blank 1995, 1997). More than 8% of workers spend more than five to ten years working in jobs paying less than minimum wage plus one dollar (Carrington and Fallick 2001). As a result, low-income workers are often unable to support a family working an average of 88 hours per week, and welfare leavers tended to obtain jobs that were of increasingly lower quality despite the strong economy from 1996–2000 (Coulton et al. 2003). Calculation of the marginal effects of the working rates of TANF participants shows that the intensity of poverty increases by a factor of 0.06 for each additional hour of work, when all other variables are held at their averages. Figure 3B in Appendix B illustrates this relationship as TANF work rates increase by 10 hours per week from 20 to 90 work hours. TANF participants who work a total of 80 hours per week (individual or combined effort) are more impoverished than participants working 20 hours per week.

Furthermore, people living in poverty make budgeting decisions from a position of greater risk and higher need with less advice and support (Gilliom 2001). Despite Nye's (2002) claim that the relative quality differential makes "the poor" better off than they have been in the past, people living in poverty are in fact much worse off relative to the average because living standards have increased dramatically while poverty thresholds still assume that total need is only three times the basic food needs. Consequently, the average family may be theoretically able to buy the shrimp in Nye's story as its increased quantity brings the price down. However, people living in poverty often cannot actually choose to buy the more "affordable" shrimp because the cost of housing, transportation, and child care continue to rise while their wages in real dollars do not. Table 2.3 in Appendix B illustrates the variation in family budgets for basic needs, the budget shortfalls faced by those making minimum wage, and the percentage of the population living without enough resources to meet basic needs across three randomly selected states in 2002 and 2007.[2] The patterns suggest that changes in the cost of living impact single-parent households considerably. It also appears as though increases in the cost of living have far outpaced growth in wages in some states, such as California, where minimum wages are higher than average; whereas right-to-work states such as Alabama show a pattern indicating that the least well off have seen budget gaps shrink or slow with minimum wage increases by comparison. However, a cursory examination of state patterns in poverty rates and inequality show that they have not increased much relative to poverty gaps, suggesting that the gaps between income and basic needs might account for differences in living standards for minimum wage earners (see also Bartels 2008; Massey 2007). In addition, the costs of work for individuals and families, such as transportation and unsubsidized child care, are heavier burdens on those earning the lowest wages, meaning that work may not pay for the least well off.

This time-series analysis shows that more densely populated areas, particularly with fewer high school graduates, experience more intense poverty. And, the increasing low-wage labor pool is not making enough money to move out of poverty despite increases in the working hours of TANF participants. Work effort may not pay off for TANF participants because higher rates of unemployment subsequently contribute to more intense poverty, particularly as the cost of living increases. So, more people are finding themselves in temporary contingent work, and wages remain low because the labor supply is high and mutable. The high cost of living, unstable work, and depressed wages make it increasingly difficult to move out of poverty. But, one cannot be more poor than deeply poor. At a certain point, the share of consumption by people living in poverty is so small by comparison to those with more money to spend that income transfers from the poor to the wealthy diminish and inequality decreases. This indicates that increasing impoverishment concerns more than those who are currently living in poverty. When work does not pay and/or is not steady, there is a limit to income transfers from the poor, and higher costs eventually impose more costs on those who have more resources.

State EITCs were intended to assist in moves out of poverty and serve a redistributive function. With the exception of Indiana's EITC program from 1999–2002, state EITCs are designed to magnify the federal EITC. While studies have shown that the federal EITC affects the labor supply and increases tax filings as people become more aware of the program,[3] state EITCs are not statistically significant in the time-series analysis presented in this study. State EITCs do not appear to serve the redistributive function, which some policymakers claim it was designed for, that is strong enough to affect impoverishment in the aggregate. Future research is necessary to understand the interaction between state and federal EITCs, as well as explore whether or not funding levels or spending decisions might impact the efficacy of EITCs.

IDAs are designed to incentivize people living in poverty "into the banking mainstream" (Stegman 1999). In many cases, IDA policies are designed to extend the reach of the banking system, lowering account limits without lowering the transaction costs for low-income account holders. IDAs received bipartisan support in the welfare reform rhetoric because the approach satisfies the neoliberal paternalist ideals. As the CATO Institute puts it, the poor will "internalize their new role as capitalists." The story of the ownership society mythologizes the ideal of moral individualism, but the contraindicating logic within the IDA approach is that the people targeted for this assistance often cannot determine for themselves *independently* their needs that are sufficient to necessitate a withdrawal from the account. Withdrawals most often require approval by the case manager. Future research is essential to understanding the extent to which case worker discretion affects the savings and well-being of people living in poverty.

The intuitive logic is that helping people improve their savings rate will allow people living in poverty to accrue assets that enhance wealth and provide long-term security as long as the interest rate on the account keeps up with inflation. There is some evidence of savings in IDA accounts (Sawyer 2010; Schreiner and Sherraden 2007), but findings regarding the savings rates and effects on net worth for people living in poverty are mixed (Grinstein-Weiss et al. 2008; Han, Grinstein-Weiss, and Sherraden 2007; McKernan, Ratcliffe, and Nam 2007). IDA programs with higher match rates and financial education tend to foster savings, but the average monthly net deposit is generally low (Schreiner and Sherraden 2007). Liberal scholars promoting IDAs hoped that such policies would assist in building the assets of people in poverty but have found that people who are poor are only able to save an average of ten dollars per month (Sherraden 2001) and more recently perhaps as much as $16.60 per month (Schreiner and Sherraden 2007). However, Hurst and Ziliak (2005) find that welfare policy changes regarding asset limits do not improve the savings of at-risk households. Some recent research shows a median savings of $117 without shuffling or $40 with shuffling between accounts; although the median savings effect is significantly smaller for blacks and nonwhite Hispanics (Stegman and Faris 2005). Demographic differences in savings are most likely attributable to the higher costs imposed on people of color (Shapiro 1995, 2004).

Differences in wealth accumulation reveal another flaw in the owner-ship ideal. Assets owned by people living in poverty may not accrue value as people engage in patterns of economic and social exchange that amplify social distance (Akerloff 1997). Additionally, Gittleman and Wolf (2000) show that savings rates are inextricably linked to income, and improving savings rates without a concurrent rise in permanent income is unlikely to benefit people who are poor. Moreover, financial emergencies can limit the ability to save, and control over IDA accounts by case managers may make some people living in poverty more impoverished by virtue of this lack of autonomy (Bax et al. 2005; Klawitter et al. 2006; Pinder et al. 2005; Sherraden et al. 2005). To the credit of Margaret Sherraden, Amanda McBride, and Sondra Beverly (2010), the perspectives of people living in poverty are taken into account with savings and survey data to facilitate policy approaches that genuinely help people *Striving to Save*. They show that people living in poverty are willing and able to save, but the financial pressures and pathways to building assets are much different for low-income families.

The results of the time-series analysis in this study indicate that the presence and structure of IDA programs for TANF participants do not afford people living in poverty opportunities to move out of poverty.[4] The net effects of IDA programs for TANF participants do not suggest a failure of asset-building programs, however. Some evidence indicates that income eligibility criteria may be too restrictive and savings goals may be too narrow (Bax et al. 2005; Finsel and Russ 2005; Pinder et al. 2006). Additionally, credit problems are often a barrier to savings (Bax et al. 2005; Klawitter et al. 2006; Pinder et al. 2006); although some participants have been able to use IDA savings to clear up debt (Grinstein-Weiss et al. 2008). The lack of significant improvements in the circumstances of poverty for TANF participants in various IDA programs does not discount the demonstrable gains that some have made in asset-building programs. There are many factors that might inhibit net gains, including higher than expected administrative costs (Bax et al. 2005; Pinder et al. 2006; Rowett 2006). The reality is that IDAs funded through TANF do not have a statistically significant impact on impoverishment in the aggregate. Yet, this does not mean that asset-building approaches have no potential as antipoverty policy. There is a great deal left to be learned about asset-building strategies as a component of the welfare system. Future research is necessary to understand who benefits from IDAs and how those gains might be extended to people who experience higher costs and greater risks in economic and social exchange.

Historically, racial threat has characterized the relationship between target groups and governing authorities. In other words, stories of welfare have been shaded by desires to control an "other" classified by the social construction of race in the United States. The long history of racial oppression in the United States has been, at least in part, implemented through welfare policies governing access. Consequently, the racial makeup of the state has to be accounted for in an analysis of impoverishment and is included as a control in the time-series analysis. However, findings regarding the influence of race have to be carefully interpreted because the level of analysis is particularly relevant in understanding the color of welfare reforms.

Racial hypersegregation is the trend in neighborhoods across the United States and increasingly concentrates the corrosive social issues that result from economic restructuring in areas where people of color are living in poverty (Massey and Denton 1993; Stoll 2010). This hypersegregation may wash out the aggregate significance of race at the state level in poverty governance. The significance of race may also be minimized by a broad and growing group of marginalized people living in poverty, as attempts by business interests to restructure the American political economy to allow "the rich to pull away from the rest" are increasingly gaining advantage (Bartels 2008). Alternatively, Soss, Fording, and Schram's (2011a) formulation of the Racial Classification Model (RCM) suggests that this test of the racial threat hypothesis may not achieve statistical significance due to the fact that those who govern poverty are racially diverse, making it more difficult to explain racialized policy outcomes with theories that frame racial minorities as out-groups. The racial threat hypothesis is based on notions of conscious prejudice and does not account for the extent to which racially patterned policy outcomes are positively associated with the extent to which implicit racial bias on the part of policy actors is expressed in the policy process. The salience of race varies across policy domains, time periods, and political jurisdictions, and the prevailing cultural stereotypes, pervasiveness of those stereotypes, and the presence of stereotype-consistent cues determine the likelihood of racially patterned policy outcomes.

The time-series analysis in this study does not contradict the persistent power of race in poverty governance. The reality is that the story is much more complex. Given strong evidence that race-gendered mobilization rose and fell in tandem with the racialization of welfare based on stereotypes of black people as lazy (Soss, Fording, and Schram 2011a), it is likely that claims of the declining significance of race fail to account for nuances in implicit racial cues. Future research is necessary to identify the contextual level of analysis appropriate for understanding the impact of racial stereotypes on the choice architecture. Patterns of devolution and privatization conceal racialized patterns of interaction and allow the illusion of choice to explain differences in the actualization of opportunities.

There are a number of dilemmas resulting from targeting gender in welfare reforms. The identification by paternalists of female-headed households as the source of the problem of poverty and the desire by some feminists to harness resources for disadvantaged women produce similar stories with different policy prescriptions told by paternalists and some feminists. The outcome of the gendered stories of poverty in the welfare reform discourse produced different strategies for affecting incomplete or underresourced households, including encouraging marriage and enhancing measures to enforce child support as well as targeted IDAs in some states. These strategies add a layer of complexity with respect to interpreting the findings regarding how female-headed households impact impoverishment.

Lone mothers run the highest risk of experiencing deep poverty when income is insufficient for child rearing (Chant 2009). Kelly (2005) finds that female-headed households are a significant factor in increasing inequality over the long term. Women are significantly more likely to be caring for both children and elderly parents, and a considerable portion of the pay gap between men and women is connected to the caregiving roles of women (Heymann 2000). Additionally, women deemed "deviants" by the social welfare system (the "welfare queens" who are perceived as resisting poverty governance, teen mothers, and unwed mothers) are subordinated and stigmatized by policies that enforce work and conformity to traditional gender roles (Abramovitz 1988, 2006). Service sector industries seek to increase the size of their labor force and decrease wages to increase profits, relying on a vast supply of workers involved in nonmarket institutions. As a result, poverty among women is central to retaining a large contingent labor force for the continued expansion of this sector of the economy (Katz 1989). Further, female-headed households are a heterogeneous category that may include relatively well-off women (Baden and Milward 2000). In fact, women may be significantly better off outside of the traditional household, depending on the division of goods and security within the family (see Abramovitz 1988, 2006; Brush 2006; Peck 2001). However, the lack of a statistically significant effect on impoverishment by female-headed households in this analysis may reflect differences in labor demands that spread poverty among men or may suggest that efforts to facilitate greater involvement of men in child rearing may counteract the feminization of poverty in some ways. The aggregate realities presented in this analysis provide a fuzzy picture of the factors that impact impoverishment and highlight areas where further research will provide a clearer picture. Future research is necessary to understand how various strategies compare as means to reducing poverty among women and figuring out how these changes may impact families overall.

The welfare reform rhetoric also promised that caseload reductions would reduce welfare dependency. Despite ample evidence disproving the welfare dependency thesis (Katz 1989, 1996, 2001; Schram 2006b; Schram, Soss, Fording 2006), storytellers continue to promote the idea that caseload reductions reduce impoverishment. The analysis in this study reveals no evidence that caseloads impact impoverishment. Future research is essential to assess whether this finding may be explained by shifting need in an increasingly contingent labor market or may be attributed to variations in implementation.

"On the front stage of organizational life, where governance is enacted, the business model is pursued as an aspirational ideal and deployed as a powerful regulatory norm. Like all cultures, however, it contains internal contradictions and counter-discourses that create tensions within its matrix of meanings and priorities" (Soss, Fording, and Schram 2011a, 205). The aggregation of these contradictions and counterdiscourses, playing out on a stage in which work-first prompts action, produces a complex story. Institutions matter less, or perhaps differently, under governance structures enacted through contracted networks of authority, and the extent to which individuals buy into the idea that business interests are their interests subverts the interests of people living in poverty. An ideologically liberal citizenry is comprised of people who resist efforts to control the "other" and find opportunities for individuals to make their own way in the market to be ideal for promoting liberty. However, ideology is divided by social and economic concerns. The economic and social dimensions of liberalism are points of tension in the neoliberal paternalist system of poverty governance. As paternalistic controls increase and market opportunities are managed, impoverishment increases. In the aggregate, citizens that promote high levels of social control and highly managed labor markets entrench poverty significantly.

Corruption is also a circumstance that varies across states and may affect impoverishment. Corruption across states is accounted for in this analysis to control for circumstances in the state that might entrench poverty. *Corruption* is a term that is used to refer to deviations from common interests to serve special interests in exchange for direct benefit to public officials, violations of the public trust, and the use of authority to maximize personal gain for dispensing public benefits to select recipients (Heidenheimer 1970). The misuse of public authority for private gain has to be distinguished from the use of public authority in governance that amounts to rent extraction. The illegal abuse of authority in governance may be political or bureaucratic, but the measures of corruption reflect either criminal prosecutions of violations of the public trust (Meier and Holbrooke 1992) or perceptions of corruption (Boylan and Long 2003). The federal prosecution of corruption used in this analysis of factors affecting impoverishment is limited in that the measure mingles corruption with prosecutorial effort and fails to account for state charges. However, the measure of the perception of corruption based on the priority of corruption in federal prosecutions according to the assessments of statehouse reporters is only available for 2002.[5] The analysis of the perception of corruption in a single year indicates that states in which prosecutorial discretion is not used to address corruption because it is not perceived to be a priority have higher rates of impoverishment. Over time, prosecutorial priorities change, and states with more federal prosecutions for corruption create conditions in the state prior to prosecution that contribute to impoverishment. When public officials use their authority for private gain, inequality grows prior to prosecution, and eventually corruption in the state draws federal prosecution. The states in which corruption convictions are high contribute to aggregate increases in impoverishment, as the inequality created by the corrupt conditions fuels a pattern that undermines public trust.

According to the World Bank, adequate institutions play a crucial role in economic performance, and social capital is essential for high-quality institutions. Miller and Whitford (2002) and Whitford et al. (2006) demonstrate the value of fostering a mutually beneficial relationship in which agents are entrusted with ample discretion and principals credibly commit to restraint in the use of power. Low levels of trust are associated with less efficient judiciaries, more corruption, and lower-quality bureaucratic administration (La Porta et al. 1997). High levels of trust are associated with economic growth (Easterly and Levine 1997; Knack and Keefer 1997) and financial development (Guiso et al. 2000). In addition, there is ample empirical evidence that income inequality reduces investments in social capital, undermining markets (Alesina and La Ferrara 2002). In general, corruption is thought to increase inequality by reducing economic growth, limiting the progressivity of the tax system, undermining the level and effectiveness of social spending, inhibiting the formation of human capital, and perpetuating an unequal distribution of asset ownership and unequal access to education.

Interestingly, this analysis highlights the complexities of these relationships. Corruption does indeed increase inequality, and when it begins to affect economic growth, even the wealthy are impacted, as the cost of living begins to have a greater effect on people with more consumption power. Investments in human capital are further inhibited when attempts to address regressive taxes are inadequate and a growing low-wage labor pool is compelled to work in temporary, contingent labor, keeping wages too low for self-sufficiency. Asset-building programs that are controlled by caseworkers rather than the individuals whose interests are at stake do not effectively mitigate inequities in asset distribution. At the same time, access to education plays a complex yet important role in this relationship. Increasing high school graduation rates lowers impoverishment, but inequality is increased as the access to higher education is restricted. Consequently, a highly unequal society with high dropout rates, high wealth inequality, regressive taxes, and low human capital correspond with high rates of corruption. Corruption subsequently fuels these patterns, and over time, the loosened restraints on political principals and lack of credible commitments in the exercise of institutional authority entrenches poverty.

Tax revenues to incentivize work and relieve wage pressures on employers increase labor participation among the poor (Grogger 2004; Meyer 2002) and contribute to reductions in wages for low-skilled labor (Rothstein 2010. Although economic returns on education have risen over the past several decades (Danziger and Gottschalk 1995), market shifts favor more educated workers (Marcotte 2000). The real value of wages has declined since the 1980s for all education levels with the exception of the top educational third of white males (see Neckerman 2004). Consequently, gains in high school graduation rates lower impoverishment, but increasing advantages to employers at the expense of low-wage workers widens poverty gaps. Another look at Table 2.3 in Appendix B shows that minimum wage deficits in the budgets of families in states where costs have outpaced gains in minimum wage standards increase the depth of poverty for minimum wage earners, even where minimum wage standards have increased at the state level. Additionally, family structure interacts with state policies in a manner that likely mediates the effect of minimum wage standards across states. While the analyses in this study show that minimum wage increases intensify poverty in the aggregate and that states with higher minimum wages experience more intense poverty, the mechanisms of action require further clarification. Future research is necessary to understand whether there is a tradeoff between minimum wage standards and employment stability in certain sectors and whether the expanding pool of low-wage labor drowns the most disadvantaged in the pool as tides rise.

Implications & Recommendations

Social constraints and active suppression by those who manage the poverty governance agenda can render the possibility for choice invisible or inaccessible (Bachrach and Baratz 1962; Hayward 2000). Neoliberal paternalism is characterized by the use of cognitive biases revealed in the study of behavioral economics to manipulate the "choice architecture" (Thaler and Sunstein

2008). The architects of choice manage behavioral contracts and regulate the labor force participation of people living in poverty through work-first strategies that subsidize costs for employers and maintain a low-wage labor pool. The rhetoric describes an opportunity structure that operates like a ladder up and out of poverty, but there appear to be too few ladders with enough rungs to function in accordance with the ideal. The storytellers that emphasize a belief in moral individualism tend to blame people living in poverty for not actualizing opportunities through work and savings. However, the evidence in this analysis suggests that while privatization offers opportunities for employers and contractors, TANF participants are working more for less. And while people living in poverty have a demonstrable ability to save, asset-building programs have not offered significant opportunities for people to move out of poverty.

The state has been reoriented to serve the needs of business leaders, and people living in poverty are directed to work more for less by contractual relationships in which entry and exit is managed through governance networks. The commercialization of welfare is characterized by increasing subsidies to the private sector and the expansion of managerial controls. Contractors and managers are the new primary beneficiaries; while people living in poverty are compelled to work. Yet, few permanent, stable, and adequate-paying employment opportunities are afforded the growing pool of low-wage, low-skill labor organized in the interest of business. The evidence suggests that this is not in the interests of people living in poverty. The use of the vast governance apparatus to inflate private interests makes the transfer of wealth to the wealthy more efficient. Furthermore, caseload reductions have no effect on poverty, and increasing the work rates of TANF participants raises aggregate impoverishment.

However, efforts to increase education rates have mutually beneficial gains. High school graduation rates contribute to increased work productivity and fuel economic growth (Aaronson and Sullivan 2001; Delong, Katz, and Goldin 2003). Additionally, those without a high school education face the greatest risks from economic instability and have the lowest median earnings of any other occupational group. According to the Bureau of Labor Statistics (BLS) in 2011, the unemployment rate for those without a high school diploma was 14.1%, which was 4.7% higher than those with a high school diploma. The BLS estimates that over the next 20 years jobs requiring a master's degree are expected to grow at the fastest rate, and those requiring a high school diploma have the slowest projected growth. The lowest growth projections are for occupational categories requiring less than a high school education. Although the construction trades in that category are expected to grow, construction jobs will not likely reach 2006 levels. Consequently, state efforts to increase graduation rates and attract employment opportunities may have tremendous implications for people living in poverty. It is essential that future research explore the potential tradeoff between minimum wage standards and employment stability in certain sectors and the extent to which the expanding pool of low-wage labor causes economic disadvantage to shift or accumulate. Understanding how educational attainment and wages may translate into economic stability for people living in poverty is crucial for designing effective antipoverty policies.

The federal EITC program fosters labor force participation and tax filings, but it remains unclear whether state EITCs are strong enough to magnify these effects or whether these effects do not afford opportunities to move out of poverty in the aggregate. Future research is necessary to understand whether and how state EITCs might be designed to help people move out of poverty. Much information remains to be uncovered regarding whether or not state EITCs are worth the cost and who might benefit from them. More in-depth analysis of the differences in state EITCs, savings options, and spending decisions relative to refunds that also accounts for state tax regressivity—within the context of federal EITCs where state EITCs are intended to magnify the benefit—is important for clarifying the findings in this study. Additionally, future research needs to explore the extent to which EITCs may be funded by the middle class, who likely carry a disproportionate tax burden under the current conditions.

Due to the fact that people living in poverty face difficult financial pressures, it is imperative that individuals living in poverty have access to their own money, as their risk of health and other emergencies is higher than the average. Much more remains to be learned about the pathways to building assets for the least well off. Future research on the barriers to saving and differences in the return on investments from various social positions is essential to establishing the value of IDA programs. This study looked only at IDA programs utilizing TANF funds, but there are a number of other sources of funding and benefit groups. Understanding asset-building requires pulling together knowledge across funding streams and through various mechanisms of provision.

The complexities of race and gender in welfare systems necessitate caution in interpretation. This study highlights the importance of the level of analysis. Poverty governance that increasingly serves private interests through contractual service provision displaces the welfare conflict space. Studies of the enactment of poverty policies are the critical link to understanding the race-gendered politics of the welfare system.

This study also implies that contractual governance networks diminish the impact of institutions. Understanding the regulating functions that institutions might play in welfare systems is less ideologically driven and reflects a more systematic management of contracts. Ideological effects are, however, significantly impactful at the individual level. As citizens buy into increasing social control and accept highly managed labor markets, impoverishment increases. This finding is somewhat troubling, as Soss, Fording, and Schram (2011a) convincingly show that the neoliberal paternalism characterizing welfare reform attempts to reshape the way people living in poverty regulate themselves. And, paternalism lowers levels of voting, political participation, civic participation, and engagement, suggesting that efforts to affect democratic orientations may lead to subsequently increasing regulations. The analysis in this book shows that welfare reforms based on the neoliberal paternalist storyline entrench poverty over time. The implications are that patterns of intense poverty, the internalization of self-regulation, and the trends toward increasing regulations cycle through the welfare policy process without feedback with the potential for learning. People who resist or for whom there are no economic opportunities available are marginalized. Challenges to the neoliberal paternalist storyline are silenced. Evaluation is based almost entirely on technical measures that afford an ever-increasing degree of control. Learning is essential for changing a reality in which more people are increasingly impoverished into one in which poverty alleviation is the norm. More research on the components of the system of poverty governance is critical to understanding the elements of the choice architecture that might be modified to serve antipoverty objectives in a manner that compels the rhetoric to live up to the reality.

Arguably, the most important mechanism for affecting impoverishment might be lowering levels of corruption. The challenge is that current patterns of inequality and corruption undermine the public trust. Trust, in the absence of trustworthy institutions, is misplaced. Consequently, we all have an incentive to address patterns of inequality and corruption that undermine trust. Montinola and Jackman (2002) argue that institutionally defined constraints can challenge corrupt practices. There is also a good deal of evidence that enhancing political competition by lowering barriers to entry and creating direct links between voters and politicians which allow citizens to better hold politicians accountable can discourage corruption (Kunicova and Rose-Ackerman 2005; Persson and Tabellini 2003). However, Brown, Touchton, and Whitford (2011) caution that designing policies to address the institutional components of corruption without ideological checks on powerful interests may be counterproductive.

6

Philanthrocapitalism

•◦————◦•

"New Markets" for Social Services

Poverty governance in the decentralized welfare system increasingly relies on innovative market solutions to generate social value. The instruments for creating opportunities, manipulating transaction costs, and imposing market discipline vary according to the opportunity structures designed in state welfare policies and the state laws of charitable disposition. The evolution of devolution has opened "new markets" for social value creation, and the next phase of the policy cycle is likely to be heavily influenced by private interests. This chapter describes how social entrepreneurship and venture philanthropy are "innovating" poverty governance. By outlining the variation across state contexts and capturing the wealth leveraged by new poverty ventures across the hybrid spectrum, an increasing decentralization of welfare policy is evident, as are efforts by the state to reassert its legitimacy in regulating the instruments of welfare provision as they diversify. This chapter provides a framework for organizing future research on private investments in poverty governance and offers a preliminary outline of poverty ventures aimed at addressing poverty in the United States. This most recent evolution of the welfare system follows from the previous states of welfare. Understanding the extent to which people living in poverty may be affected by privatization of the social sector depends on the perspective of people living in poverty being taken into account by those with the influence to define the public interest.

Social Entrepreneurship: Innovation in Poverty Governance

Social entrepreneurship encompasses "the activities and processes undertaken to discover, define, and exploit opportunities in order to enhance

139

social wealth by creating new ventures or managing existing organizations in an innovative manner" (Zahra et al. 2009, 522), whereas venture philanthropy refers to the financing of innovative social investments. Venture philanthropy is a form of social entrepreneurship in itself. Alternatively, social entrepreneurs may be funded by foundations using the venture philanthropy model. The evolution of these innovative social investments and the social entrepreneurs implementing them characterize the worth and consequence of the social wealth created by these endeavors. The power to differentiate a public and direct the corresponding interest has tremendous potential to affect the opportunities available and shape the access to those opportunities. Moreover, the devolved, contractual nature of governance results in increasingly blurry boundaries between the public, private, and nonprofit sectors in social service delivery systems. As a result, the intentions, functions, and enactment of social objectives are expressed in a complex, competitive, and highly variable display of civic engagement. Some describe the shift in public interest orientation in pluralist terms, suggesting a socialization of the private sector; while others are concerned that the shift is essentially a colonization of the public and nonprofit sectors by the private sector, which may enhance wealth inequalities.

Social entrepreneurship refers to the hybrid spectrum of organizations that attempt to balance civic motives and market logic. Because philanthropic social ventures may also involve cross-sector collaborations, public-private partnerships, and/or contracts for social service delivery implemented by public, private, and/or nonprofit organizations, some venture philanthropists further their objectives by engaging the full spectrum of governance partnerships. These relationships are illustrated in Figure 1C in Appendix C.

The hybrid spectrum includes nonprofits engaged in income generating activities. Those activities include, but are not necessarily limited to, the following:

- cost recovery mechanisms such as special events, conferences, seminars, and fee-for-service; and/or

- earned income revenue streams such as membership dues, sales of publications and products, and consulting programs

Social enterprise, social entrepreneurship, and social entrepreneurs are often used to refer to a field of research or referenced as innovation, despite the fact that the concepts are distinct and suggest different levels of analysis. In terms of the types of entities that might receive venture philanthropy investments, the social enterprise is the level of focus. The social enterprise is characterized by a social purpose, an entrepreneurial approach, and an emphasis on stewardship (Fayolle and Matlay 2010). Social enterprises may be structured as departments or affiliates within an organization or as a separate legal entity—either nonprofit or for-profit. Social enterprise is distinct from the socially responsible business in that the latter operates with the dual purpose of generating shareholder profits while contributing to a social good. In the socially responsible business, every decision is anchored in the company's core values. This is distinct from corporate social responsibility in that for-profit businesses operating under the profit motive and also engaging in philanthropy make business decisions apart from the social values supported by their philanthropy, which is often a program or separate entity under the corporate umbrella.

Broadly speaking, two factors help explain the rise of social entrepreneurship and venture philanthropy: (1) the challenges of the welfare state in the modern global context, and (2) increasing competition within the nonprofit sector (Perrini and Vurro 2006; Robinson 2006). Nonprofits face the pressures of lower financial reserves, increased competition, and amplified pressure to meet performance metrics. Financial support fell as policy was privatized and decentralized in the welfare state (Perrini and Vurro 2006), resulting in reduced government financial support for nonprofits (Wei-Skillern et al. 2007). Lower marginal tax rates in the Bush era also reduced tax savings and the incentive to give to charities, philanthropies, and other nonprofits; the recent recession also contributes to this trend. At the same time, nonprofits face increased public scrutiny and pressure (Boschee 2006). Greater demands for professionalized services and an increasing emphasis on accountability along with escalating competitive pressure among nonprofits for diminishing sources of funding, particularly where there are service redundancies, place tremendous pressure on the nonprofit sector (Alter 2006). Nonprofit organizations are expected to strengthen their evaluation methods, enhance performance, and broaden strategic alliances with increasingly lower levels of financial support. The broad societal trend toward consumerism and moral individualism, in conjunction with the rapidly changing market forces of the new global economy dominated by neoliberal managerial ideals, have produced a social economy in which welfare needs are not met by the state but may be met by social entrepreneurs (see Mayo and Moore 2001). Yet, meeting these social needs relies on exploiting opportunities to create social wealth through mutually beneficial exchange in contexts that have been traditionally undervalued.

One of the defining characteristics of venture philanthropy is its focus on sustainability. Venture philanthropists combine philanthropic grants, subsidies, and earned revenues. By generating earned revenues, venture philanthropists encourage the chosen social enterprises to move toward a market-based self-sufficiency strategy. However, creating self-reliance is difficult, and market sustainability is a constant struggle for organizations with a double bottom line (Raymond 2004). Perhaps more importantly, market-based self-sufficiency may not be a reasonable objective for organizations that serve people who are marginalized by market forces. Many social goods do not lend themselves to market approaches (Bornstein and Davis 2010).

In addition, the mixed motives in the hybrid spectrum present some challenges. First, there is an inherent tradeoff between risk taking and accountability that poses at least the following potential challenges (see Romzek and Dubnick 1987):

1. Complex contracting relationships compound the cross-pressures of accountability and make risk assessments difficult at best; and

2. Even adequately managed risk decreases the likelihood that accountability for performance metrics may be achieved.

Second, while social entrepreneurship and venture philanthropy are characterized as proactive, there are factors in the nonprofit sector that inhibit organizations from being proactive. For example, increasing competition within the nonprofit sector inhibits the collaboration that venture philanthropy intends to foster. Third, there are also factors in the public sector that constrain proactive behavior which are not likely to be remedied by private sector practices. The most striking example of these factors is evident in the provision of services to clients who are perceived as less "deserving." Selecting high performing nonprofits for marketability has the potential to further marginalize services that are undervalued by the market (Ochs 2012). Yet, venture philanthropy is revitalizing the realm of philanthropy, and its evolution has the potential to generate sustainable social value.

While social entrepreneurship and venture philanthropy are revitalizing the social service realm, little is known about the extent to which sustainable organizations may target poverty alleviation for mutual gain. Even less is known about the efficacy of such ventures at addressing poverty.[1] Table 3.1 in Appendix C outlines the venture philanthropy firms that specify poverty as a primary objective. The table also identifies the wealth leveraged by each organization for antipoverty measures. Figure 2C in Appendix C shows the wealth leveraged aggregated at the state level.

The poverty ventures illustrated in Figure 2C reflect the wealth leveraged to address poverty by organizations defining themselves as venture philanthropy firms with antipoverty objectives in their mission statements. The data include all the firms meeting those criteria available from the National Venture Capital Association, the Grantsmanship Center, and the

National Center for Charitable Statistics. They do not necessarily reflect all the wealth leveraged by venture philanthropists to address poverty, as the organizational purposes may be defined in any number of ways. Furthermore, the ways in which the wealth is leveraged to address poverty varies by philanthropic organization. For example, the Appalachian Fund Management Company and the Kentucky Highlands Investment Corporation are interconnected organizations claiming to address poverty by facilitating private sector investment in the region, whereas the Robin Hood Foundation strategically funds nonprofits that provide direct services to disadvantaged members of the New York City community. There are tremendous differences in the amount of wealth leveraged as well as differences in the perspectives on social investment. This preliminary analysis suggests that who gets what, when, and how under these divergent conditions is a function of the ideological perspectives and entrepreneurial strategies employed by the different organizations.

Farther along the hybrid spectrum, Corporate Social Responsibility (CSR) is another private means to expressing public interest in poverty governance. CSRs are generally programs within traditionally private entities that utilize corporate resources for social purposes. The programs may include enhancing volunteerism by allowing employees to spend company time volunteering, encouraging donations through collective company efforts to generate investments in a cause, and/or grant programs for special purposes. The distinguishing characteristics of CSR are the investment in social goals to promote the reputation of the corporation and to promote a particular view of the public interest. Some CSR programs match employee contributions to the organization of their choice rather than having a set of initiatives. Employee-directed programs often result in small gifts that are given most often to religious and educational institutions and animal organizations. Some CSRs include a combination of employee giving with corporate matching programs along with volunteer efforts, and most donate to an array of causes in varying amounts. The number and type of CSR programs vary considerably. Table 3.2 in Appendix C identifies the number of CSR programs in each state, the percentage of top grant making that comes from CSR programs in the state, the number of CSR programs that specifically address poverty in the United States, and the poverty rate. The data suggest that CSR programs addressing poverty in the United States do not appear to be closely connected to need. Considering the extent to which social entrepreneurship is capturing the social service market (see Ochs 2012), the limited investments in antipoverty measures in the United States is notable and deserving of further study. Moreover, there are at least two state-level factors that are of critical import for future research: (1) some states are investing more in antipoverty measures through venture philanthropy, and (2) some states have antipoverty social ventures while many do not have poverty ventures.

State Laws of Charitable Disposition

The decisions in *Dartmouth College v. Woodward* (1819) and *Vidal et al. v. Philadelphia* (1844) establish the bases for incorporation. *The Trustees of Dartmouth College v. Woodward*, 17 U.S. (4 Wheat.) 518 (1819), outlines the application of the Contract Clause to private corporations, distinguishing between public and private charters and setting the stage for the American business corporation. *Vidal et al. v. Philadelphia*, 43 U.S. 127 (1844), provides the first decisive ruling regarding the private authority to establish a charitable trust. It is also interesting to note that the *Vidal* ruling references Acts of the Parliament of England dealing with the regulation of competitive markets and reinforces the doctrine affirming the competency of the corporation and the "incapacity of the poor" in the pursuit of the public interest. The legal legacy establishing the power of private entities to engage in competitive and charitable purposes is central to the discourse on sector boundaries and highlights the primacy of organized efforts legitimized by the state to pursue the interests of the public through assorted means.

Although both Supreme Court decisions favor voluntarism and charity, the ambiguities remaining have led to two divergent legal approaches to regulating charity. The laws of charitable disposition evolved differently in New England, where charitable activities were historically encouraged through tax exemptions. Most other states limited the definition of charitable activities and did little to promote them (see Wright 1992). Consequently, philanthropic activity and voluntarism flourished in states with broadly constructed charity laws, and states with narrowly constructed charity laws restricted the growth of philanthropy and voluntarism.

Rapid growth in the number and size of foundations and greater publicity given to the nonprofit sector in the United States have contributed to increased interest and focus on foundation activities.[2] This increase in interest has also created a corresponding interest from the government and legal sector. However, the legal environment is rarely a coherent regime. There are various levels of government, forms of accountability, types of regulation, and systems of reporting that shape the dimensions of the legal environment. The dimensions of the legal environment include the following (Pross and Web 2003):

- the rules related to legal status;
- the regulation of tax receipts, exemptions, and incentives;

- constraints on contracting; and

- performance metrics accountability systems.

Each of these dimensions varies across levels of government, by contract, and through voluntary regulation.[3] The shape and substance of these legal dimensions serve as the conduits of governance in this context. Table 3.3 in Appendix C outlines the laws of charitable disposition by state. States that require charitable organizations of the types defined in state law seeking to engage in fundraising in the state to register with the state may make the process of registration efficient and allow organizations to network across states by utilizing the Uniform Registration System (URS). Some of those states require supplementary state forms to track organizations raising funds in the state, but the extent to which the supplementary forms are used to ensure that nonprofits continue to act in line with their charters remains unclear. Additionally, the extent to which states that audit charitable organizations may inhibit philanthropy or ensure proper regulation of the sector requires further study.

The legal environment governing nonprofits also varies in terms of the regulation of tax receipts and exemptions at the state and local level, as well as the presence and types of donation incentives that may exist across jurisdictions. Furthermore, the authority over the parameters of exemptions may be the prerogative of state legislatures and/or courts and may vary by subsector across jurisdictions. Yet, when it comes to property tax exemptions, for example, the legal landscape and application of exemptions in practice tend to be fairly similar across jurisdictions (Brody 2010). But when it comes to incentivizing donations, state law determines whether and to what extent charitable donations are encouraged through state tax deductions. Table 3.5 in Appendix C identifies those states with individual income taxes that offer deductions for charitable donations. States that incentivize charitable donations encourage more giving, and may have a more vibrant civic sector as a result. Future research is necessary to understand how tax exemptions for nonprofits and tax incentives for donations affect the reliance on and growth in the nonprofit sectors across states. Understanding the legal regime governing nonprofits requires building knowledge on the extent to which and how states may facilitate voluntarism.

The constraints on contracting that make up part of the legal regime regulating nonprofit social service provision vary according to devolution. Contractual arrangements and professional associations network the poverty governance regime. Yet, the contractual agreements between state, regional, or local agencies and private providers outline the nature of the services provided, expected outcomes, and costs. Efforts by the states to regulate social service contracting have led to various reform efforts. Several states have mandated performance contracting in particular types of social service contracts, requiring payments tied to performance standards and the inclusion of incentives and disincentives for various performance targets; although the nature of contracting often varies by jurisdiction even when performance contracting is mandatory, as the authorizing agency sets the performance standards. The legal environment as it relates to social service contracting requires considerably more study as variation exists along several dimensions.

The attention of government and the legal sector has resulted in changes along several dimensions as it relates to the practice of modern philanthropy. Supervisory legislation has appeared in many different states, and the IRS has started to police the exemption provisions of the tax laws that govern nonprofits. At present, the following states have enacted legislation that stipulates mandatory reporting and/or licensing provisions from foundations: Alabama, Arkansas, California, Colorado, Connecticut, Florida, Hawaii, Illinois, Iowa, Kansas, Kentucky, Louisiana, Maine, Maryland, Massachusetts, Michigan, Minnesota, Mississippi, Missouri, New Hampshire, New Jersey, New Mexico, New York, North Carolina, North Dakota, Ohio, Pennsylvania, Rhode Island, South Carolina, Tennessee, Utah, Virginia, Washington, and West Virginia.[4] It is important to note, however, that foundations may choose to register in those states that do not require licensure or registration as there is a growing movement toward self-regulation in the sector.

The nonprofit sector is now a major component of social service provision, and public and private sources of funding are demanding performance accountability. Due to the fact that nonprofits provide services for which the quality is difficult to observe, quantify, and evaluate and the reality of increasing pressure to *prove* performance, many nonprofits are compelled to engage in self-regulation and evaluation to establish competitiveness. Consequently, nonprofit service providers attempt to solve the trust problem in philanthropy by distinguishing their reputations through licensure, registration, reporting, certifications, accreditation, and various other forms of reputation-enhancing efforts at transparency and performance verification. Oftentimes these efforts are responses to pressures in the sector, but they are also a function of the desire to prevent further intervention on the part of the state to impose accountability measures. This is not to suggest that nonprofits are seeking to circumvent state oversight efforts. While that may be true in some instances, what is more often the case is that nonprofits are intending to define performance standards in a manner that affords a reasonable chance of success under conditions of uncertainty.

Government plays a large role in the realm of philanthropy as a major source of nonprofit revenue as well. Government grants, contracts, and reimbursement from public agencies account for about 36% of the sector's revenue (Raymond 2004). Government policy is pivotal in catalyzing new social ventures by defining the laws, regulations, and support given to social enterprises (Mulgan 2006). For example, organizations that solicit contributions nationwide can utilize the Unified Registration Statement (URS), which allows such organizations in 34 states to file a single form in lieu of separate state registration statements.[5] Although 34 states utilize the URS for multistate filing, the following states that are connected through the URS also require supplementary forms: Arkansas, California, District of Columbia, Georgia, Maine, Minnesota, Mississippi, North Carolina, North Dakota, Tennessee, Utah, Washington, West Virginia, Wisconsin.[6] Governments may utilize technology to minimize transaction costs for nonprofit accountability as well, such as the online charitable registration system available in Colorado, Hawaii, and New Mexico (among a handful of other states) or the e-Postcard required by the IRS. Legal environments that reduce barriers to entry facilitate social entrepreneurship (Mulgan 2006).

Government also defines the flavor of philanthropy. Foundations can either be classified as public or private foundations. Public foundations are supported by a variety of public sources, and private foundations are privately funded or endowed. One million dollars is the minimal opening bid to establish an independent foundation, but each state has its own set of rules for forming and starting a foundation (Raymond 2004). In some states, foundations have to report back to a state official on the status of the organization at certain intervals. Foundations are created in one of two distinct legal forms, either as a corporation or a trust. Corporations are treated as an individual entity by law, but community trusts are treated as a single entity if the trust satisfies several requirements by the IRS affirming that the funds are controlled by a common governing body.[7] Community trusts are often established to attract capital to benefit a specific community, and the funds are generally managed by banks or other corporate trustees. Once the organization is formed under state law, the foundation is required to seek IRS recognition as a tax-exempt charity. With this status, the foundation will not have to pay federal taxes on its income and can receive tax-deductible contributions. However, despite their tax-exempt status, private foundations have to pay a 1 to 2% annual excise tax on net income depending on the amount of grants given each year (Council on Foundations 2008). This tax is incurred to settle the costs the government undertakes to regulate private foundations.

Once established, a private foundation has to follow certain legal requirements. Private foundations are subject to higher scrutiny than public foundations. The foundation's charge is defined in the statement of purposes in its individual charter or deed of trust. These legal limitations vary by state. Excepting Georgia and Pennsylvania, legal standards are generally set in case law and not in statute. Foundations are governed by a set of laws referred to as the laws of charitable disposition. The IRS requires that private foundations give away 5% of their net investment assets (Raymond 2004). Also, private foundations cannot spend more than 15% of their annual charitable budget for administrative expenses and total annual legal and accounting fees should be no more than $5,000 (Council on Foundations 2008).

Many foundations are now encouraged to perform a voluntary legal audit. This is a decision made by the board to systematically review all legal processes and documents to ensure the minimization of legal risks (Andringa and Engstrom 2002). Because of the changing legal and financial landscape surrounding philanthropy, foundations are being held to higher legal standards and accountability demands. Federal law, IRS regulations, state statutes, and court decisions in recent years have started to transform the traditional hands-off approach. At the same time, donors and employees have become more demanding and litigious (Andringa and Engstrom 2002). The regulation of foundations broadly affects the interests that are included and excluded in the pursuit of the mission. Regulatory control and the increasing role of legal authorities in the welfare efforts of foundations have a number of possible implications that are worthy of further study. The increasing oversight of foundation activity most likely represents an assertion of government authority in legitimizing certain foundation activities. Yet, much remains to be learned about how the landscape of private welfare provision affects the type and nature of philanthropy performed and how mounting private influences affect people living in poverty.

In addition to defining the flavor of philanthropy, government utilizes the law to reassert its authority to legitimate organizations and subsequently validate organized interests by structure, purpose, and action arena. Flexible purpose corporations—also known as low-profit limited liability or benefit corporations—have been legally enabled in several states. Efforts are currently underway to get federal legislation passed that would lower hurdles to the creation of such companies, including a quiet push to get preferential tax treatment for them. Table 3.6 in Appendix C outlines the relevant state enabling legislation for the various types of hybrid corporate forms and the effective date for each policy. The hybrid corporation movement began in law when the United Kingdom established the Community Interest Company (CIC) in 2004. Vermont was the first state in the United States to adopt a similar corporate form by establishing the low-profit limited liability company (L3C) in 2008. The L3C legal form allows an organization to insulate investors from individual liability and receive disbursements from investments in charitable purposes. If an L3C discontinues the charitable or educational purposes initially established, it is simply transformed into an ordinary Limited Liability Company (LLC). These new legal forms represent a renewed interest in the state asserting authority in welfare politics.

Benefit corporations sometimes referred to as "B Corps" represent another new organizational form that provides legitimacy to the pursuit of profit for public benefit. B Corps references the certification developed by the nonprofit B Lab to establish credible standards for social entrepreneurship. Certified B Corps are those organizations that pass the socially responsible/sustainable self-audit with at least a "B" rating on the impact assessment and are required to issue an annual benefit report in accordance with B Lab standards. Benefit corporations specify the legal status conferred by the state. Certified B Corps and benefit corporations are somewhat different than L3Cs in that B Corps and benefit corporations define a social purpose in their formative documents. Specifically, fiduciaries are required to consider the impact of the firm's decisions on nonshareholders, the environment, and economic context. Private certification as a B Corps has been a marketing tool for companies since 2006, but Maryland was the first state to establish the benefit corporation as a legal organizational form in 2010, blending state enabling legislation and the third-party certification system. Maryland also established legal recognition for limited liability companies that pursue positive impacts on society and the environment that are measured by a third-party standard.

The Flexible Purpose Corporation (FPC) is a legal corporate form for organizations with at least one "special purpose" that is considered to be a social good defined in the charter. In exchange for promoting environmental sustainability, living wages for employees, or some specific social value that is weighed against the profit motive, boards and management are protected from shareholder liability. The FPC is the legal form intended for use by for-profit companies seeking traditional capital market investments in a socially conscious manner, whereas L3Cs make charitable investments for limited profit, and benefit corporations pursue positive impacts measured by a third-party standard.

These new legal forms assert the distinctions among hybrid corporations that attempt to reflect the relative balance between the civic and market logic. Such enabling legislation lends legitimacy to philanthrocapitalism and affirms the authority of the state in welfare governance. The legal landscape of welfare privatization includes the diverse regulatory strategies governing organizational forms, incentives for voluntarism, and the nature of contracting in poverty governance. Understanding the state of the welfare system requires mapping the institutional boundaries, identifying the regulatory mechanisms across subsectors, and studying the processes that validate some pursuits of the public interest over others.

Opportunities and Challenges of Capitalism in the Public Interest

The investment in innovative approaches to social value creation has the potential to affect the opportunities available and shape access to those opportunities. The types of social wealth leveraged and its perceived value reflect organized pursuits of particular perspectives on the public interest defined in the contractual networks of governance. Increasingly, private businesses, wealthy philanthropists, professional associations, and management influence the objectives and operations of poverty governance. These shifts in influence result in actors across sectors concerning themselves with social welfare, but it remains to be seen whether these concerns produce broad benefits or serve special interests. While actors across sectors enhance their influence in poverty governance, people living in poverty may or may not be included in the process. Future research on welfare privatization must consider the who, how, and why of inclusion and exclusion in antipoverty policy throughout the process.

The hybridization of organizations balancing civic and market motives reflects changes in the civic sector, and changes in the legal landscape represent attempts to legitimate governance. New organizational forms and the regulation of collective action across jurisdictions are a part of the ongoing negotiations regarding the boundaries of welfare institutions and poverty governance. The perceived erosion of the welfare state within the current context of globalization (see Schram 2006b) and the increased competition in the nonprofit sector make conversations about the necessity of need-based care seem controversial or irrelevant. However, the welfare state has privatized, not eroded entirely. Consequently, discussions about welfare dependency appear to focus on false beneficiaries. A focus on false beneficiaries means that welfare analysis that does not account for the system of poverty governance fails to present a story that allows for learning about poverty alleviation. Welfare privatization increases the magnitude of social controls but leaves the subsidies for the private pursuit of the public interest unregulated. So, the private exploitation of welfare is not likely to be any more beneficial than the public exploitation of public works. Ultimately, what might be known about how these dimensions compare can only be understood through systemic analysis.

The challenges to the welfare state under globalization based on real or perceived pressures eroding social investments have shifted influence. Increasing competitive pressures resulting from the blurring of sector boundaries and restricted investments outside of the private sector sort winners and losers efficiently. These sorting mechanisms may select among the most viable to enhance social wealth, but at least two challenges remain. First, selecting for self-sufficiency limits the extent to which we might address existing bias. In fact, the risk of capitalizing on stereotypes may be heightened by cherry picking. Second, the least well off may not be in a position to establish sustainability, and there is evidence that relying on charity is unstable and has a problematic relationship with ideological extremism (see Whitford, Yates, and Ochs 2006). Recent evidence also suggests that the wealthiest Americans give the lowest percentage of their income to charity and prefer to donate to colleges and universities, arts organizations, and museums rather than organizations addressing poverty (Stern 2013). Consequently, care for the least well off continues to be an important aspect of public policy. Yet, these policies are increasingly influenced by people with tremendous wealth who are gradually more isolated from the experiences of people living in poverty. Interestingly, the personal drive to accumulate wealth that contributes to the success of entrepreneurs may also be inconsistent with prosocial attitudes and behaviors.[8]

The mixed logic in the hybrid spectrum of the organizations performing governance functions presents a few issues that deserve further study. Innovations are risky and cannot establish immediate accountability. While reactive and bureaucratic approaches to welfare have well-known problems, proactive approaches to addressing social issues also pose concerns that may be equally problematic. Proactive governance is as likely to result in increasing social control as it is likely to create opportunity. Acting in the interests of others in a narrowly defined manner may produce quantifiable outcomes but runs the risk of serving only narrowly defined interests. The power to define poverty and the marketization of the means to address it favor the individualistic ideal.

The limited investments in poverty in the United States despite increasing impoverishment and the obscure connection between the efforts of social entrepreneurship and need in the United States suggest that marketization may undervalue the least well off or that philanthropic efforts are zero-sum. Undervaluing the least well off is likely to enhance inequality. And, zero-sum philanthropic efforts require good judgment regarding need. Therefore, understanding need is essential to any effort aimed at addressing poverty. Currently, there is no evidence regarding the role of need in poverty governance enacted through philanthrocapitalism.

The legal legacy of incorporation establishes the primacy of private entities and is based on the long held belief that "the poor" are incapable of self-sufficiency or moral behavior. A more accurate view of need is more likely to be revealed as future research explores how people in poverty develop creative ways to adapt to the circumstances of poverty. The legal environment governing charitable organizations reflects the organized actions that serve public objectives legitimated by the state. Whether or not those various organizational forms and charitable missions serve a broad public depends on the extent to which the perspectives of stakeholders, including people living in poverty, are included in definitions of legitimate governance.

Conclusion

Persuasive storytellers interpret politics and affect policy. The interests, values, and motivations of the storytellers are as relevant as the policy object. Lyndon Johnson's 1964 State of the Union Address attempted to redirect war efforts to address economic insecurity. After 50 years, those efforts have been deemed tragic, triumphant, inadequate, and futile by various storytellers trying to redefine the conflict space, change armaments, or shuffle regiments. Civil society is reinforced by stories that foster investments in trust and institutions that are trustworthy. Policy and policy research are forms of storytelling, and stories within a systemic framework yield the greatest understanding of poverty governance. A systemic understanding of poverty governance allows us to trust and verify. The evidence presented in this book shows that a systemic approach to understanding poverty governance is not only possible but essential to antipoverty policy. It also suggests that pulling together knowledge from multiple levels of analysis is crucial to understanding poverty governance and can allow for generalizations about governance broadly.

The social construction of the realm of possibility in welfare policy storytelling today appears to increasingly target a broader contingent of deviants as political and economic incentives align between advantaged groups and politicians. As more "deviants" are constructed in policy storytelling and targeted in policy, wealth is redistributed to subsidize the advantaged in the private sector and exploited for the electoral gain of politicians. The risk is that an increasingly narrow public might likely be represented in policies designed in the degenerative context, and the risks of increasing impoverishment extend beyond those living in poverty. Hacker and Pierson (2010b) point out that the current state of political and economic inequality generates political strategies that attempt to minimize tradeoffs when powerful interests collide with voter preferences rather than responding to the median voter. The most affluent and influential tend to have very pronounced preferences for conservative economic policies and liberal social policies; whereas people in the lowest income brackets tend to be of the opposite opinion on social and economic issues (Gilens 2009; Rigby and Wright 2011; Schlozman et al. 2012). Politicians from both sides capitalize on these cross-cutting opinions, which most often results in the issues concerning people living in poverty being left off the agenda entirely (Rigby and Wright 2013). Vast gaps in income and divergent life circumstances undermine a common sense of concern (Hero 1998), and a divided society characterized by the impoverishment of many and the affluence of a few contributes to increasing income segregation (Jacobs and Soss 2010; Soss and Jacobs 2009), party polarization (McCarty, Poole, and Rosenthal 2006), and ideological polarization (Garand 2010). The well-being of society suffers in numerous ways when inequality defines the social landscape (Wilkinson and Picket 2010), leaving little political or social capital to bridge the increasing cleavages (Alesina and Glaeser 2004).

The opportunities to moderate the degenerative context of welfare politics requires minimizing exploitation by structuring welfare contracts in a manner that coordinates activities and services for mutual benefit. Mobilizing collective action in welfare service provision based on logical reasons to believe that working toward a given objective will be worthwhile for involved parties rather than rationales justifying policies that serve pecuniary interests enhances trust by developing patterns of trustworthiness. Extraordinary storytellers resist opportunism, demonstrate competence, and exhibit trustworthiness. These acts of good will can serve as organizing principles aligning trust and trustworthiness by inspiring belief in a welfare system that does not punitively target the most vulnerable.

Developing a systemic understanding of welfare is an essential part of enhancing the potential for mutually beneficial cooperation. A coherent view of the system of poverty governance is critical to examining the weight of the evidence and relative merits of policy stories. Critical reflection on the welfare conflict space and evidence about the impact of policy choices tell us how well antipoverty objectives are served by given interventions. The persistence and pervasiveness of poverty is an important indicator of the impact of policy on the least well off, and the SST index is the best measure of levels of impoverishment. Assessing the plausible net effects of welfare reforms on poverty over a full policy cycle reveals a great deal about the direction of the state of welfare.

Although Piven and Cloward's (1971, 1993) account of labor regulation through the reach and generosity of welfare programs continues to be an accurate depiction of the relief retraction characterizing modern poverty governance, poverty governance under neoliberal paternalism goes farther, activating the resources of the state to serve markets and manage the demands of labor by reshaping the way people living in poverty regulate themselves in an effort to secure their cooperation (Soss, Fording, and Schram 2011a). Together, neoliberal paternalism imposes a disciplinary agenda that uses state authority enacted through governance practices that facilitate market efficiency, wage work, and behavioral regulation. Soss, Fording, and Schram (2011a) effectively demonstrate that neoliberal paternalist poverty governance increases economic interventions by the state and expands social programs targeting people living in poverty in the state of Florida. Their case illustrates how managerial reforms and privatization orient the state to serve markets, frame feedback, structure practices around market principles, and extend the reach of state authority. The evidence presented in this book shows that the expansion of welfare privatization across states makes it harder for people to move out of poverty in large numbers. This study also suggests that there are myriad points of influence and policy choices that may be promising poverty alleviation strategies. Future research exploring opportunity creation, access, and utilization are essential for understanding how problematic patterns of impoverishment in the aggregate may be affected by various aspects of the system.

Mettler (2011) argues that loans subsidized and guaranteed by the state, tax breaks and incentives, and third-party governance constitute the submerged state. She shows that the submerged state is growing aggressively because politicians get around partisan divisions and institutional gridlock compared to direct spending and visible policy, and the industries that benefit from the vast entitlements use their wealth and influence to defend them. The analysis presented in this book supports Mettler's (2011) contention that the submerged state is growing aggressively, but the story presented here suggests that welfare privatization may be somewhat more nuanced. The diverse motivations and strategies of social entrepreneurs and the efforts to reassert the legitimacy of the state by defining and regulating the social endeavors of private enterprise indicate that the blurred sector boundaries may reemerge. And, the nature of poverty governance under these evolving conditions will remain elusive until the poverty governance research agenda includes a better understanding of social entrepreneurship.

The story told in this book is multifaceted. The states of consciousness about poverty have a long history of being influenced by stories that emphasize moral individualism. The establishment of the welfare state reframes these stories and packages policy to target people according to their perceived social status and political power. Challenges to the welfare state capitalized on stories of moral individualism to devolve and dismantle the welfare system of entitlements. Devolution is a story taking place in a conflict space in which neoliberal arguments for deregulation and privatization met with paternalist calls for government to compel self-regulation. Both the neoliberal and paternalist storylines have several things in common:

- the emphasis on individual responsibility to serve the welfare function;

- the privatization of the welfare conflict space to stabilize the system; and

- the use of administrative reforms to construct a system of poverty governance in which self-regulation is imposed to serve private ends.

The neoliberal paternalistic system of poverty governance is a story about creating a new welfare consciousness. This new consciousness can reflect an illusory state of being if the appropriate level of analysis is not selected. The devolved and contractual welfare state represents states of being that operate in private, nonprofit, and public networks through somewhat fluid contractual configurations of authority functioning as muscular hydrostats. Thus, regulation has both institutional and relational qualities. There is tremendous variation in the story at the periphery of the distribution of discretion, so understanding the system of poverty governance requires evidence about the components, as well as the net effects presented herein.

This book advances a systemic approach to understanding poverty governance by building on the work of Soss, Fording, and Schram (2011a) in two ways:

1. by outlining the range of variation in devolution and privatization across states so that future research may endeavor to test their hypotheses in other contexts in an effort to comprehensively assess the components of the system of poverty governance; and

2. by examining the extent to which the evolution of state policy choices in poverty governance resulting from the political processes evidenced by Soss, Fording, and Schram (2011a) may contribute to aggregate levels of impoverishment over time.

Poverty governance strategies defined by neoliberal paternalism discipline people living in poverty to markets and a morality entrenched in a history of oppression. State welfare reforms emphasizing social order and control consistent with the neoliberal paternalist storylines make it more difficult for people to move out of poverty. In fact, the intensity of poverty expands over time as the working hours of people living in poverty increase, and programs such as IDAs and state EITCs have not significantly aided in the transition out of poverty. This book outlines the extent of variation within the system of poverty governance across U.S. states so that the best evidence from various levels of analysis may be compiled to assess how different policy choices, implementation structures, and enactment practices may affect change in impoverishment, and provides a framework for analyzing the increasingly privatized practice of poverty governance.

The framework for analyzing poverty governance systemically offered in this book organizes antipoverty research. The systemic study of poverty governance centered on poverty alleviation as an organizing principle provides a comprehensive understanding of how antipoverty policy might be designed to promote self-sufficiency with minimal intervention. Each of the following interrelated concepts in the systemic analysis of poverty governance addressed in this book maps the system:

- The structure of governance outlined by the networked, contractual, and interjurisdictional regulatory regime of policies and practices makes up the institutional boundaries that regulate demands and manage the conflict space.

- The aggregate impact of policy choices on opportunities to move out of poverty illustrates how well state policies function as antipoverty policies.

- The experiences of people living in poverty are an integral perspective with the potential to inform policy choices by enhancing mutuality. This study builds on existing research and highlights avenues for enhancing learning by listening to the lived experiences of people surviving in various contexts.

- The organizations enacting social service provision are increasingly private for-profit and nonprofit agencies. This privatization of the scope of conflict presents opportunities to enhance social wealth but also imparts a considerable degree of influence to an ever-narrowing set of interests.

- The history of stories shaping the public consciousness about poverty and welfare shows how the boundaries of "taken for granted assumptions" or "self-evident truths" limit the pursuit of poverty alleviation and the socially constructed boundaries of inclusion.

The outline of the emerging state of affairs that is devolved and privatized highlights mechanisms for organizing a systemic research agenda that offers opportunities to reverse the degenerative course of poverty politics.

The story presented here explores the various states of welfare over time, providing evidence that no other study offers. The states of consciousness regarding welfare have been constructed by storytellers with diverse motivations and interests in an evolving context in which the myth of the self-made man remains ubiquitous. The welfare state in the United States emerged out of the pattern of interactions among those who have influenced perceptions of the public interest and the policy targets, and poverty governance in the devolved welfare state displaces the conflict space. The outline of the structure of devolution across states is an essential contribution to the development of an understanding of the setup for the subsequent rounds of welfare privatization. I show with 18 years of data across all 50 states that welfare privatization has actually made it more difficult for people to move out of poverty in spite of high work effort by people living in poverty. In fact, the more hours TANF participants work the more intense aggregate poverty becomes over time. The pattern of increasing impoverishment among the most marginalized sets the stage for the recasting of social service provision.

Recasting social service provision as new markets with the potential for profitable investments may produce a conflict space in which competition enhances governance and those with resources are invested in the interests of people living in poverty. However, this marketization also runs the risk of constructing a conflict space that serves investors by displacing competition among labor and seeks increasing returns from poverty governance. Markets engender winners and losers. It is crucial to understand the patterns of exchange in these new markets in order to determine the extent to which welfare privatization yields returns that are broadly beneficial. The evidence in this book shows some worrisome patterns resulting from welfare transfers to private business.

The policy process is a means by which values are articulated as problems are defined, goals identified, and solutions outlined in the act of representation as various interpretations and strategies compete in the conflict space. This book reviews the various stories that have been presented about welfare over time and assesses how well the reasons that have served as justifications for welfare reforms produce results that may or may not be in the interest of the broad public. This does not preclude logical argumentation. Rather, it explains the ways in which logic and passion are mechanisms for leveraging influence through storytelling. But, that does not mean that every story is equally valid. The validity of any welfare story has to be measured with the evidence of the impact on poverty. The evidence indicates that the passionate emphasis on individual regulation and the rational, "objective" insistence on private maximization may not be the promising tide that raises all ships.

Over the 18 years in this study, increasing subsidies to facilitate private sector employment priorities have made it more difficult for people living in poverty to move out of poverty. Increasing the working hours of TANF participants has increased aggregate impoverishment, despite efforts to increase asset ownership among people living in poverty. It is likely that devolving the authority over the strategies to pursue the objectives of TANF dilutes efforts to redistribute wealth in a manner that might help people move out of poverty in the aggregate. Structural variations in the level of devolution and the discretionary practices of governance are important factors affecting who might access opportunities and who faces discipline.

As these patterns play out, the exploitation of new markets operates within the context established throughout the evolution of welfare. The people and organizations with the potential for self-sufficiency are not only a matter of perception by those with the resources to define the public interest. Those who might have been afforded access within the devolved system of poverty governance are ripe for investment. At the same time, the people and organizations that have historically been undervalued and have been the subject of disciplinary regimes under welfare devolution are set up for increasing controls.

A Look at the State We're in

The new mentality of governance is characterized by a devolved conflict space in which the pragmatics of guidance is based on two historical practices: (1) reformist traditions emphasizing the need for improvement, and (2) paternalist conventions that insist regulations are in the interests of "the poor," broadly. The political knowledge articulated in neoliberal paternalist poverty governance systematically legitimates the story that separating politics and economics is objective and institutionalizes the practices of "individual responsibility" and "self-improvement" through the networks of service provision. The contracts that make up these networks establish the rules of the game. However, despite the fact that free agency in neoliberal thought relies on mutually beneficial exchange, the contracts are often designed to compel individuals to choose from a limited set of options in which the strategies available to the agent may be restricted in successive iterations. The options and restrictions are based on moral advice and economic rationality "to determine the conduct of others," but may not necessarily be exercised against the interests of the other party (Foucault 1988).

Whether or not the new strategic games instituted by the neoliberal paternalist poverty regime are likely to result in more responsible behavior, opportunities to move out of poverty, or from under domination, depend centrally on two factors: (1) the extent to which poverty alleviation is a contract objective, and (2) the extent to which the contracting parties, particularly the principals, engage in perspective taking and the active cognitive process of correcting the stereotype-based biases that produce patterned errors in judgment. If poverty alleviation is not a policy objective, it is hard to imagine that a rational agent would chose to subject him or herself to an increased work effort without either a substantial amount of force to compel compliance or the internalization of the neoliberal storyline celebrating self-regulation. There are a number of ways in which individual responsibility agreements may undermine choice. The Center for Law and Social Policy outlines a few problematic contractual arrangements.[1] States require TANF participants to complete an employability plan and a personal obligation or family life plan; although some states combine these into a single plan. The following are some conditions of these contracts that have been identified as lacking mutuality:

- circumstances in which the form is designed to limit eligibility or where there is evidence that resistance to the contract terms results in significant losses of assistance;
- forms that list obligations without providing details or the resources to meet those obligations;
- inappropriate obligations that set clients up for failure, including requiring activities without addressing the barriers to fulfilling those obligations; and
- contracts that fail to identify the obligations of the state or the rights of participants.

Clearly establishing mutual obligations is essential to negotiating contractual arrangements that free and equal parties might choose to engage in willingly. However, most states do not clearly identify the obligation of the agency or the rights of participants, or state that poverty alleviation is a contract objective. "Citizens will meet obligations to the collective despite the temptation to free ride as long as they trust other citizens and political leaders to keep up their side of the social contract" (Scholz and Lubell 1998, 411). The language of the contract is an essential component that reveals a great deal about the credible use of authority. The language of the contract is also a very simple thing to change in a manner that aligns trust and trustworthiness. Where trust is the organizing principle in contracting relationships and trust is credibly aligned with trustworthiness, exchange is more likely to be mutually beneficial.

Assimilation into civic relations is conditioned upon the interactions within the contracting experience. The implementation and enactment of contract negotiations, behavioral regulations, and monitoring performance are the functions of the aggregate cognitive processes of numerous individual actors. Perspective taking can often inspire altruistic acts and empathy without having to resort to inducement or coercion. The cognitive process is affected by personal experiences, especially the attribution of "self-like" qualities to another person. People are more likely to identify and empathize with other people if those other people have had or are experiencing similar problems or situations. However, stereotyping may interfere with our ability to empathize with an "other" because the stereotyping process generally occurs outside of our awareness and operates implicitly.

There are reactive and proactive strategies for addressing these habits of thought that can lead us to make errors in judgment. Thought suppression is a reactive strategy to attempt to control stereotype biases that may increase empathy but may also have group-specific limitations (Galinsky and Moskowitz 2000). Proactive control by inhibiting stereotype activation in the first phase of the cognitive process in which the stereotype is accessed from memory by categorical association appears to be a more reliable method of addressing these errors than consciously trying to not stereotype because recognition, strategy, and implementation are all factors that can hinder reactive approaches (Moskowitz and Li 2011; Wegner 1994). The categorization of people into arbitrary groups that promote race, gender, ethnic, religious, or sexuality stereotypes is a goal-directed choice, and altering category selection is an effective proactive method of reducing the activation of the stereotyping process (Moskowitz and Li 2011; Moskowitz and Stone 2011). This is not to suggest that these categories should not be studied— quite the opposite. These findings tell us a great deal about the extent to which our goal-directed choices in targeting people can impact how people might be differentially affected by stereotyping. Therefore, the contracting language, the rhetoric about deserving and deviant policy targets, and the management of discretion are all opportunities to choose broadly beneficial antipoverty goals rather than arbitrary stereotypes.

The devolved and contractual nature of governance implemented through the rhetoric of NPM reforms sets the stage for market solutions to social value creation. The influence of social entrepreneurship on innovating poverty governance varies in accordance with the context set by state laws of charitable disposition. Increasingly, governance is enacted and funded through private organizations along the hybrid spectrum, and the growing influence of private entities on social service delivery requires a framework for assessing the privatization of poverty governance. The outline of the legal landscape within which venture philanthropists concerned with poverty governance operate offers a preliminary framework for understanding welfare privatization.

Organizational hybridization and enabling legislation legitimate philanthrocapitalism and affirm the authority of the state in poverty governance. The regulatory strategies, the incentives for voluntarism, and the nature of contracting are the components of the institutionalization of welfare privatization. However, welfare privatization poses at least two persistent challenges. First, selecting for self-sufficiency is likely to be based on existing biases, absent effective efforts to address stereotypical storylines regarding people living in poverty. Second, voluntarism and philanthropy may be unreliable and have the potential to contribute to polarization. Perhaps more importantly, innovative efforts by volunteers or philanthropists still require good judgment regarding need, and more evidence is necessary to ascertain the extent to which philanthropic efforts may or may not be responsive to need.

Recommendations for Further Inquiry

The current state of poverty governance is based on a lack of consciousness about the circumstances of poverty, despite claims that there have been "changes in our understanding of the causes and consequences of poverty" (Danziger and Haveman 2001, 8). The present state of poverty research may include important contributions to evidence-based practice, but the virtually universal exclusion of the perspectives of people living in poverty from the discourse on welfare reform and study of poverty policy suggests that we have a lot to learn about what it takes to move out of poverty. Studies presenting alternative and critical perspectives on social policy offer important insights regarding the nature of poverty governance. John Gilliom's (2001) stories of how women maintain dignity under circumstances in which the choices are often lose-lose, Julia Jordan-Zachery's (2008) critical analysis of the discursive practices that maintain hierarchies of race, gender, and class, and Soss, Fording, and Schram's (2011b) study of the experiences of caseworkers subject to performance management, which compels a culture of discipline within Florida's welfare-to-work organization, are essential to understanding poverty governance as a system. The components of control and the perspectives of those subject to the disciplinary mechanisms of poverty governance are as important to understanding opportunities to move out of poverty as the aggregate economic conditions of welfare leavers. Understanding the range of conditions experienced within the system of poverty governance is critical for poverty alleviation because ascertaining the circumstances in which opportunities are created and determining the mechanisms of choice that facilitate the actualization of opportunities for the broadest public yield the greatest gains on social investments. Gaps in achievement are opportunities to gain from investments and affect the growing inequality threatening the trust that fuels exchange. This study provides evidence of the net effects of welfare privatization and outlines a systemic framework from which research at various levels, components, and perspectives can contribute to knowledge of poverty governance.

Understanding that policy and policy research are forms of storytelling allows for a more comprehensive view of poverty governance. Critical reflection on the stories told and the interests and potential opportunism of storytellers are essential to assessments of welfare systems. The discourse on poverty defines the realm of possibility and sets the stage in the political theatre. The opportunities, the regulations, and to whom each is directed is a function of the meaning constructed in the framing of people and poverty. Additionally, analyses of the effects of policy choices at various levels reveals a great deal about how the opportunity and regulatory structures may function as antipoverty measures. Avoiding putting together the same puzzles repeatedly requires both the disciplined application of the scientific method and critical reflection on the political discourse.

The opportunism expressed in a degenerative context renders trust misplaced. Increasing the alignment between trust and trustworthiness requires credibility, or the power to inspire belief. Credibly aligning trust and trustworthiness by resisting opportunism, demonstrating competence, and exhibiting trustworthiness enhances opportunities for poverty alleviation when good will is extended by those with policy authority. Trust and trustworthiness can only be developed through credible commitments to a system of governance that functions at all levels to alleviate poverty.

The devolved and restructured system of workfare makes some differences in state choices evident, but all require further study in order to understand their contribution to poverty governance. Some states have repositioned work programs to be managed by departments other than the human/social services offices that implemented AFDC. The management of workfare through departments of labor, economic development, workforce services, or economic opportunity reveals the intention of state governments to direct the labor force and shift influence away from agencies established to provide assistance. States have also established different networks of collaboration or oversight. Future research that explores both the political conditions that produced public-private partnerships in a given context and the contractual arrangements and communication patterns of these distinct collaborative networks on governance is essential to understanding how access and opportunities might be structured to enhance overall welfare.

The vast and varied funding for state-initiated fatherhood programs and research on family well-being is also worthy of further study. The variations in the criteria for understanding the health of marriages and the marriage conflict space appear to have devolved in a manner that necessitates the linking of family therapy and economic well-being research in order to evaluate the extent to which different state programs might have success in supporting healthy relationships. Future research from multiple perspectives is necessary to understand the governance of marriage, particularly as it relates to income, race, gender, and sexuality.

Additionally, programs targeting the "formation and maintenance of two-parent families" as an objective exhibit a degree of variation across states with respect to the emphasis that states place on traditional family units that serve economic ends, rather than on safe, stable homes. Family policies that treat marriage as primarily an economic contract fail to address the volatility that domestic violence introduces. Several states have established standards and procedures to screen for and identify people with a history of domestic violence, refer cases in which there is a history of family violence to counseling and support services (sometimes even compelling participation in TANF self-sufficiency plans), and in some cases waive program requirements to facilitate safety. States that have chosen to certify their Family Violence policies can waive the requirements for those attempting to leave a violent relationship without negatively impacting the state's performance metrics. State policy choices that foster good faith in marriage and place a premium on nonviolence are more likely to promote well-being. Future research is essential to understanding the impact of welfare reform on the feminization of poverty and the relative impact of domestic violence on the lives of women.

The risk to personal safety increases in relationships with a history of violence when a subverted partner attempts to gain self-sufficiency, so the choices states make with regard to domestic violence have a tremendous potential to impact both family violence and TANF objectives in complex ways that require knowledge of empirically based practices in family therapy and an understanding the role institutions play in structuring alternatives and mediating violence. Perhaps more importantly, there are currently no empirically based treatments with demonstrated success at rehabilitating perpetrators of domestic violence, so strategies that attempt to commit partners to their marriage despite the threat to safety may undermine both social and economic goals. Future research may utilize the Domestic Violence and Sexual Assault Data Resource Center, available through the Justice Research and Statistical Association, to examine the extent to which these initiatives serve as effective prevention and intervention measures that reduce the incidence of domestic violence over time.

Understanding the role that diversion plays in the states' strategies for maximizing employment and managing caseloads requires mapping diversion programs in relation to employment strategies over time within each state. Assessing the extent to which diversion programs may assist families in transition, and evaluating how different programs compare in terms of outcomes, will reveal how well a given program may respond to the needs of people in vulnerable circumstances only when the programs are understood as a part of the state's system of welfare provision. Currently, there is no valid method for determining at the state level whether diversion programs operate under regulations that serve people living in poverty or that serve markets, and future research is essential to understanding the role of diversion programs in the welfare system. This book provides a preliminary map of diversion programs so that further research might explore the extent to which diversion strategies address poverty.

The widespread belief that people living in poverty fail to invest their money wisely in assets that grow in value fails to account for the increased risk that comes from experiencing multiple economic hardships. Irrational or arbitrary leaps in logic and pervasive stereotypes affect the implementation of IDA programs, and the fact that the management of many of the accounts is not independent of the discretion of the case manager suggests that much remains to be learned about how these factors may affect who might benefit from these programs and under what conditions opportunities might be maximized. Moreover, the varied funding streams and third-order devolution indicate that analyses at the agency level are necessary to understand the components of asset-building programs. The analysis in this book demonstrates that IDA programs do not appear to offer significant opportunities to move out of poverty in the aggregate. However, further study of the tremendous variations in implementation and enactment is central to establishing the circumstances in which IDA programs might be most effective. It would be interesting to see further research examining the assumptions that affect the independence of IDAs where client groups might vary in the types of investments and prospective outcomes.

The results of the time-series analysis in this study indicate that the presence and structure of IDA programs for TANF participants do not afford people living in poverty opportunities to move out of poverty. The net effects of IDA programs for TANF participants do not suggest a failure of asset-building programs. Eligibility criteria, savings goals, and credit barriers are potential factors affecting the implementation of IDA programs, and more research is necessary to understand whether and how some programs may overcome these impediments to savings. The lack of significant improvements in the circumstances of poverty for TANF participants in various IDA programs does not discount the demonstrable gains that some have made in asset-building programs. Future research is necessary to understand who benefits from IDAs and how those gains might be extended to people who experience higher costs and greater risks in economic and social exchange.

The linkage between work effort, wages, and need is another aspect of the analysis of welfare. The extent to which EITCs assist the least well off has to be weighed against the value of investments made in private business through WOTCs. It is also worth studying the qualitative effects on the least well off. This study provides a framework for future research that may compare tax advantages to the private sector with the tax treatment of people in poverty. Research on taxes and wages across occupational categories may reveal more about how state EITC investments might benefit people as they move out of poverty. In addition, more research is warranted to understand the role of social and political influence on aggregate wages in order to begin to put into perspective the efficacy of the EITC as an antipoverty measure. While the analyses in this study show that minimum wage increases intensify poverty in the aggregate, and that states with a higher minimum wage experience more intense poverty, the mechanisms of action require further clarification. Future research is required in order to understand whether there is a tradeoff between minimum wage standards and employment stability in certain sectors or whether the expanding pool of low-wage labor drowns the most disadvantaged as tides rise.

At present, the best available evidence comes from the administrative data maintained in Wisconsin, which allow for some understanding of WOTC implementation in that state. Due to limited program participation and only temporary employment gains for job seekers, it is imperative that future research examine the employment decisions and eligibility standards that affect the implementation of this incentive. Research that assesses the factors contributing to short job durations is crucial to understanding the extent to which the policy may enhance "workplace diversity" and generate "good jobs" over the long term. There is some evidence that occupational categories may play a role in the separation rates (Gunderson and Hotchkiss 2007). Consequently, workplace diversity policies that do not produce new jobs at competitive wages for diverse groups are unlikely to do more than cycle different people through the few jobs reserved for the target groups, keeping them in competition with one another. Future research is required to evaluate the kinds of opportunities created for targeted groups, compared to the average and compared across different targets.

The use of TANF efforts to mitigate educational gaps in the state workforce varies considerably, as does the focus on different occupational categories. Future research is important in order to assess the extent to which some states may mitigate transaction costs for growth sectors. The relative success of such efforts has to be understood within the context of the system of poverty governance, because the economic outlook, demographic makeup, existing educational gaps, political climate, and institutional mechanisms for facilitating transaction costs are important differences between states that are likely to affect the types of investments and jobs created that TANF clients might access. Perhaps more importantly, additional research to understand the relationship between education and access are crucial to ascertaining who benefits from educational investments and determining how investments that minimize transaction costs and create widespread opportunities might be maximized.

The significance of race in welfare studies is affected by the level of analysis. The salience of race varies across policy domains, time periods, and political jurisdictions. The prevailing cultural stereotypes, the pervasiveness of those stereotypes, and the presence of stereotype-consistent cues determine the likelihood of racially patterned policy outcomes. The Racial Classification Model (RCM) suggests that those who govern poverty are racially diverse, making it more difficult to explain racialized policy outcomes with theories that frame racial minorities as out-groups. The racial threat hypothesis is based on notions of conscious prejudice and does not account for the extent to which racially patterned policy outcomes are positively associated with the degree of policy-relevant contrast in the policy actors' perceptions of racial groups. The lack of a statistically significant relationship between race and impoverishment in the aggregate does not contradict the persistent power of race in poverty governance. Given strong evidence that mobilization based on racial animosity and gender bias (e.g., the "welfare queen") rose and fell in tandem with the racialization of welfare based on stereotypes of black people as lazy (Soss, Fording, and Schram 2011a), it is likely that claims of the declining significance of race fail to account for nuances in implicit racial cues. Future research is necessary to identify the contextual level of analysis appropriate for understanding the impact of racial stereotypes on the choice architecture. Patterns of devolution and privatization conceal racialized patterns of interaction and allow the illusion of choice to explain differences in the actualization of opportunities. Additional research building upon the approach outlined by Soss, Fording, and Schram (2011a) is crucial to understanding the complexities and pervasiveness of stereotypes in social policy processes.

Lone mothers run the highest risk of experiencing deep poverty when income is insufficient for child rearing (Chant 2009). Kelly (2005) finds that female-headed households are a significant factor in increasing inequality over the long term. Women are significantly more likely to be caring for both children and elderly parents, and a considerable portion of the pay gap between men and women is connected to the caregiving roles of women (Heymann 2000). Additionally, women deemed "deviants" by the social welfare system are subordinated and stigmatized by policies that enforce "women's" work and compel conformity to traditional gender roles in the family (Abramovitz 1988, 2006). Service sector industries seek to increase the size of their labor force and decrease wages to increase profits, relying on a vast supply of workers involved in nonmarket institutions. As a result, poverty among women is central to the retention of a large contingent labor force, to facilitate the continued expansion of this sector of the economy (Katz 1989). Furthermore, female-headed households are a heterogeneous category that may include relatively well-off women (Baden and Milward 2000). In fact, women may be significantly better off outside of the traditional household, depending on the division of goods and security within the family (see Abramovitz 1988, 2006; Brush 2006; Peck 2001). However, the lack of evidence of a statistically significant effect on impoverishment by female-headed households in this analysis may reflect differences in labor demands that spread poverty among men, or may suggest that efforts to facilitate greater involvement by men in child rearing might counteract the feminization of poverty in some ways. Future research is necessary to understand how various strategies compare as means to reducing poverty among women and figuring out how these changes may impact families overall.

The establishment of paternity and enforcement of support by states has meant that children are better off under welfare reforms that have facilitated unprecedented family support for women and children. Yet, there are currently no studies that assess the extent to which the devolved and privatized implementation of child support enforcement takes a differential cut out of the support children actually receive across states. Perhaps more importantly, those holding the highest child support debts tend to be among those with no or low reported income and multiple current support orders. Since, the primary reason for the accumulation of child support debt is the interest charges imposed (sometimes by states and private collections agencies), it is important to examine the policies and practices of cost diffusion. Future research may look at the relationships between the costs imposed, the demographics of the target population, population dynamics, and well-being. Recommendations regarding child support enforcement as it impacts impoverishment require more information about how different target groups may be impacted by stricter enforcement regimes and how this might impact the well-being of children.

The welfare reform rhetoric also promised that caseload reductions would reduce welfare dependency. Despite ample evidence disproving the welfare dependency thesis (Katz 1989, 1996, 2001; Schram 2006b; Schram, Soss, Fording 2006), storytellers continue to promote the idea that caseload reductions reduce impoverishment. The analysis in this study reveals no evidence that caseloads impact impoverishment. Future research is necessary to assess whether this finding may be explained by shifting need in an increasingly contingent labor market or may be attributed to variations in implementation. But, the notion of welfare dependency as an individual characteristic is a story that does not appear to be valid in any case, and storytellers intent on promoting the idea of welfare dependency might have more luck finding evidence of dependence in private sector subsidies.

Poverty governance in the decentralized welfare system increasingly relies on innovative market solutions to generate social value. The investment in innovative approaches to social value creation has the potential to affect the opportunities available and shape access to those opportunities. The types of social wealth leveraged and its perceived value reflect organized pursuits of particular perspectives on the public interest defined in the contractual networks of governance. Increasingly, private businesses, wealthy philanthropists, professional associations, and management influence the objectives and operations of poverty governance. These shifts in influence result in actors across sectors concerning themselves with social welfare, but it remains to be seen whether these concerns produce broad benefits or serve special interests. While actors across sectors enhance their influence in poverty governance, people living in poverty may or may not be included in the process. Future research on welfare privatization must consider the who, how, and why of inclusion and exclusion in antipoverty policy throughout the process.

It is often considered intuitively true that accounting for spending and maintaining compliance with funding restrictions may be more efficiently managed with vouchers compared to direct cash assistance, particularly with the utilization of electronic voucher management systems. However, future research on the system design, error rate, and experiences of people from various perspectives in voucher programs may reveal how well this belief holds up in implementation. The ideal of privatization is based on the purported existence of competitive choice, so an evaluation of the extent to which different types of vouchers, and the relative extent of choice in voucher programs, are available may demonstrate how choice may be maximized and how well people utilize their choices.

Furthermore, a research agenda directed at the emerging field of venture philanthropy and its influence on welfare might reasonably be based on the framework outlined in the chapter on philanthrocapitalism in this book. State laws of charitable disposition may be used to explore the following strands of research on philanthropic social ventures:

- *Distinguishing the sector*: There are three distinct but not necessarily mutually exclusive models for engaging venture philanthropy: (1) traditional foundations practicing high-engagement grant making; (2) social value organizations funded by individuals and implemented by a professional staff; and (3) the partnership model in which financial investors become highly engaged with the grantees. These philanthropic models reflect the structure and operations of the foundation as well as symbolize the role the philanthropists envision themselves playing in the generation of social wealth. In addition to philanthropic social ventures defining themselves exclusively as social entrepreneurs, there are also venture capital firms defining themselves in philanthropic terms. These firms include—but are not limited to—City Light Capital, Clean Technology Venture Capital, Good Capital, Renewal2 Investment Fund, Roberts Enterprise Development Fund, Mission Markets, and New Schools Venture Fund. Future research might explore the extent to which these marketing techniques actually reflect a commitment to mutually beneficial exchange in the traditionally underserved markets that they sometimes refer to as "new markets" in an effort to distinguish the sector.

• *Regulation and accountability*: With the rapid growth in the number and size of foundations and the growing publicity given to the nonprofit sector, there is increased interest in and focus on foundation activities. This increase in interest has created a corresponding interest from the government and legal sector. For example, recent state legislation requiring registration and/ or licensing is politically marketed as consumer protection, but it also has the effect of increasing competitive pressure among nonprofits. Future research may look specifically at the various regulations and procedural requirements that inhibit or encourage social entrepreneurship. Understanding the legal environment as a coherent regime requires pulling together evidence from the rules related to legal status as defined by the IRS, as well as differences in state regulations. The regulation of tax receipts, exemptions, and incentives can vary at the federal, state, and local levels. Constraints on contracting vary by funding source and organizational form. And while there are attempts to standardize performance metrics and accountability systems, the variation in outcomes, expectations, measurement, evaluation, and mechanisms of accountability may be best studied through organizational analysis.

• *Governance*: There are at least two streams of governance research: (1) exploring the role that venture philanthropy plays in governance and politics, and (2) establishing knowledge regarding effective organizational governance. Philanthrocapitalism plays an increasing role in poverty governance. Consequently, the governance of philanthropic social ventures also affects the nature of social service provision. Accountable organizational governance is essential to organizational sustainability. However, there is little known about how philanthrocapitalism might affect accountability to a broad public, and understanding how poverty governance increasingly managed through private contracts might affect people living in poverty is an important area of inquiry deserving of critical reflection.

- *Network mapping and operations*: The strategic partnerships and interorganizational investments represent a highly complex pattern of relationships. For example, some of the foundations are also invested in the private equity investments of the other foundations, and many of the strategic partnerships include collaboration with like-minded venture philanthropists in addition to those foundations that operate within a network of affiliated partners. Consequently, network analysis of venture philanthropy could reveal a great deal about the potential for and nature of the transformative power of venture philanthropy. Additionally, this study suggests that organizations are capitalizing on the presumption that private sector management is superior to public and nonprofit sector management. For example, Community Wealth Ventures is a management consulting firm that provides expert guidance to nonprofits pursuing alternative funding strategies or management schemes. Community Wealth Ventures is a subsidiary of Share Our Strength, a nonprofit organization committed to ending childhood hunger in the United States. Interestingly, there are some indications that the pattern of management consultation is, at least in some cases, originating in successful, well-established nonprofits that subsequently established for-profit subsidiaries, affiliates, and/ or venture capital funds. The aggregate origins and the nature of these relationships are aspects of the emerging sector that deserve attention in future research.

- *Developing an understanding of the effect on civil society*: The 990s of education and community development funds indicate that a considerable amount of money is directed toward lobbying activity. This suggests a few streams of research within the civil society strand of a solid research agenda, which include but are not limited to the following: (1) comprehending the effects of the politicization of policy problems or issue areas; (2) understanding social construction at the intersection of issues, opportunities, and entrepreneurs in policy; and (3) empirical evidence regarding shifting influences in political and policy processes. This strand of research has the potential to evaluate whether venture philanthropy reduces or reinforces inequalities of wealth and power.

- *Critical evaluation of core assumptions and normative reflection on social values*: Developing knowledge that is practically applicable and broadly beneficial requires critical and normative discourse regarding the notion as a reasonable idea. Moreover, scholars have noted the importance of gaining an understanding of the political and ethical implications of social entrepreneurship in general (see Fayolle and Matlay 2010), and discourse on the ethics of venture philanthropy and ethical philanthropy is essential in order for the field to have its intended impact.

- *Developing an understanding of how to foster empathy and innovation in the public interest*: A strong research program must also include a multidisciplinary effort to develop effective methods of teaching and sparking innovations that present widespread investments in opportunities rather than fueling a trend in opportunity hoarding. The legal legacy of incorporation establishes the primacy of private entities and is based on the long held belief that "the poor" are incapable. Stories that categorize and stereotype people living in poverty inhibit opportunity creation by perpetuating biases. A more accurate view of need is more likely to be uncovered as future research explores how people in poverty develop creative ways to adapt to the circumstances of poverty. The legal environment governing charitable organizations reflects organized actions serving public objectives legitimated by the state. Whether or not those various organizational forms and charitable missions serve a broad public requires consistently choosing antipoverty objectives over cognitive shortcuts in designing policy.

There are clear opportunities for social entrepreneurship as a vehicle for social value creation. In fact, there is some evidence that the pattern of management consultation, at least in some cases, originated in successful, well-established nonprofits that subsequently established for-profit subsidiaries, affiliates, and/or venture capital funds (see Ochs 2012). The aggregate origins and the nature of these relationships are aspects of the emerging sector that deserve attention in future research. Despite the problems with venture philanthropy, it has created new attention, new networks, and new donors that may generate mutual investments in poverty alleviation. Yet, it is doubtful that the propagation of this model is appropriate for all forms of philanthropy in the public interest.

Appendix A

Table 1.1. Workfare Devolution

TANF CA & WORK PROGRAM DEVOLUTION

State	Organizational Form Administrative Authority	Discretion Eligibility & Benefits	Discretion Available Services	Case Management	Provider Contract Management	Work Verification	Service Provision
AL	state supervised; county administered	state	state	Human Resources	Dept of Labor	Human Resources	TOD
AK	state	state	state	Health & Social Services	Health & Social Services	Health & Social Services	TOD
AZ	state	state	state	Dept of Economic Security	Dept of Economic Security	Dept of Economic Security	TOD
AR	state	state	state	Dept of Workforce Services	Dept of Workforce Services	Dept of Workforce Services	TOD
CA	state supervised; county administered	state	state	Dept of Social Services	Dept of Social Services	Dept of Social Services	TOD
CO	state supervised; county administered	county	county	Dept of Human Services	Dept of Human Services	Dept of Human Services	TOD
CT	state	state	state	Dept of Labor	Dept of Labor	Dept of Labor	TOD
DE	state	state	state	Employment Connection (EC) & Keep A Job (KAJ) contractors collaborate with Division of Social Services	Employment Connection (EC) & Keep A Job (KAJ) contractors collaborate with Division of Social Services	Employment Connection (EC) & Keep A Job (KAJ) contractors collaborate with Division of Social Services	

FL	state	state	Dept of Economic Opportunity	24 Regional Workforce Boards	Workforce Florida, Inc.	TOD
GA	state supervised; county administered	state	county	Dept of Human Services	Dept of Labor	Dept of Human Services & Dept of Labor	TOD
HI	state	state	Dept of Human Services	Dept of Human Services	Dept of Human Services	TOD
ID	state	state	Dept of Health & Welfare	Dept of Health & Welfare	Dept of Health & Welfare	TOD
IL	state	state	Work First contractors	Dept of Human Services	Dept of Human Services	TOD
IN	state	state	Family & Social Service Admin	Family & Social Service Admin	Family & Social Service Admin	TOD
IA	state	county	Dept of Human Services & Iowa Workforce Development	Dept of Human Services & Iowa Workforce Development	Dept of Human Services & Iowa Workforce Development	TOD
KS	state	county	Social & Rehabilitation Services	Social & Rehabilitation Services	Social & Rehabilitation Services	TOD
KY	state	state	Cabinet for Health & Family Services	Cabinet for Health & Family Services	Cabinet for Health & Family Services	TOD
LA	state	state	Office of Family Support	Office of Family Support	Office of Family Support	TOD

Table 1.1. *Continued*

TANF CA & WORK PROGRAM DEVOLUTION

	Organizational Form	Discretion		Case Management	Provider Contract Management	Work Verification	Service Provision
State	Administrative Authority	Eligibility & Benefits	Available Services				
ME	state	state	state	Health & Human Services	Health & Human Services	Health & Human Services	TOD
MD	state supervised; county administered	state	county	Family Investment Admin	Family Investment Admin	Family Investment Admin	TOD
MA	state	state	state	Dept of Transitional Assistance	Dept of Transitional Assistance	Dept of Transitional Assistance	TOD
MI	state	state	state	Dept of Human Services, Michigan Works Assn, & Michigan Rehabilitation Service	Dept of Human Services & the Work Development Agency	Dept of Human Services & the Work Development Agency	TOD
MN	state supervised; county administered	county	state or county	Dept of Human Services & Dept of Employment & Economic Development	Dept of Human Services & Dept of Employment & Economic Development	Dept of Human Services & Dept of Employment & Economic Development	TOD
MS	state	state	state	Dept of Human Services	Dept of Human Services	Dept of Human Services	TOD

MO	state	state	Family Support Division & Missouri Work Assistance contractors	Family Support Division & Dept of Labor	Family Support Division & Missouri Work Assistance contractors	TOD
MT	state supervised; county administered	state	Office of Public Assistance for eligibility management & Work Readiness contractors [WoRC do majority of case mgmt]	Office of Public Assistance	Office of Public Assistance	TOD
NE	state	state	Health & Human Services	Health & Human Services	Health & Human Services	TOD
NV	state	state	Health & Human Services	Health & Human Services	Health & Human Services	TOD
NH	state	state	Health & Human Services	Health & Human Services	Health & Human Services	TOD
NJ	state supervised; county administered	state	Dept of Human Services & Labor & Workforce Development	Dept of Human Services, Labor & Workforce Development, & Economic Development Authority [job creation grants]	Dept of Human Services & Labor & Workforce Development	TOD
NM	state	state	Human Services Dept & NMW contractors	Human Services Dept	Human Services Dept	TOD

Table 1.1. *Continued*

TANF CA & WORK PROGRAM DEVOLUTION

	Organizational Form	Discretion					
State	Administrative Authority	Eligibility & Benefits	Available Services	Case Management	Provider Contract Management	Work Verification	Service Provision
NY	state supervised; county administered	state	county	Office of Temporary & Disability Assistance	Office of Temporary & Disability Assistance	Office of Temporary & Disability Assistance	TOD
NC	state supervised; county administered	county in certain areas	county	Health & Human Services & CBO contractors	Health & Human Services	Health & Human Services	TOD
ND	state supervised; county administered	state	state	Dept of Human Services & CBO contractors	Dept of Human Services	Dept of Human Services	TOD
OH	state supervised; county administered	state	county	Dept of Job & Family Services	Dept of Job & Family Services	Dept of Job & Family Services	TOD
OK	state	state	state	Dept of Human Services	Dept of Human Services	Dept of Human Services	TOD
OR	state	state	county	Dept of Human Services [primary case mgmt] JOBS contractors [service based]	Dept of Human Services	Dept of Human Services	TOD
PA	state	state	state	Dept of Public Welfare	Dept of Public Welfare	Dept of Public Welfare	TOD

RI	state	state	state	Dept of Human Services	Dept of Human Services	Dept of Human Services	TOD
SC	state supervised; county administered	county	state	Dept of Social Services	Dept of Social Services & Dept of Employment & Workforce	Dept of Social Services	TOD
SD	state	state	state	Dept of Social Services	Dept of Social Services	Dept of Social Services	TOD
TN	state supervised; county administered	state	state	Dept of Human Services & regional contractors	5 regional Contractor Zones overseen by Dept of Human Services	Dept of Human Services	TOD
TX	state	state	county	Texas Workforce Commission through TWIST	28 Local WDBs	Texas Workforce Commission	TOD
UT	state	state	state	Dept of Workforce Services	Dept of Workforce Services	Dept of Workforce Services	TOD
VT	state	state	state	Dept for Children & Families Economic Services Division	Dept for Children & Families Economic Services Division	Dept for Children & Families Economic Services Division	TOD; some support services may be provided by DCF
VA	county	state	state	Dept of Social Services	Dept of Social Services	Dept of Social Services	TOD

Table 1.1. *Continued*

TANF CA & WORK PROGRAM DEVOLUTION

	Organizational Form	Discretion		Case Management	Provider Contract Management	Work Verification	Service Provision
State	Administrative Authority	Eligibility & Benefits	Available Services				
WA	state	state	state	Dept of Social & Health Services	Dept of Social & Health Services	Dept of Social & Health Services	TOD
WV	state	state	state	Dept of Health & Human Resources	Dept of Health & Human Resources	Dept of Health & Human Resources	TOD
WI	county	state	county except in Milwaukee where state has direct control	Dept of Children & Families	Dept of Children & Families	Dept of Children & Families	TOD
WY	state	state	state	Dept of Family Services	Dept of Family Services	Dept of Family Services	TOD

Source: State TANF plans (2012), state policy manuals, and most recent, publicly available state work verification plans.

Table 1.2. Program Eligibility According to State TANF Plans (2012)

State	Eligibility Limits (months)	Asset Limits	Vehicle Exemption
AL	60	<60 y/o = $2000 60+ y/o = $3000	all household vehicles exempt from asset limit determination
AK	60	<60 y/o = $2000 60+ y/o = $3001	all household vehicles exempt from asset limit determination
AZ	36 [reduced July 2011 to 24 months]	$2,000	all household vehicles exempt from asset limit determination
AR	24	$3,000	1 vehicle/household
CA	60 [reduced July 2011 to 48 months]	$2,000	1 vehicle/licensed driver; total value <$4651
CO	60	$2,000	1 vehicle/household
CT	60 month total time limit to receiving assistance, including extensions	$3,000	$9,500
DE	36	$1,000	$4,650
FL	48	$2,000	$8,500
GA	48	$1,000	$1500/$4650
HI	60	$5,000	all household vehicles exempt from asset limit determination
ID	24	$2,000	$4,650
IL	60	$2000 [1 person]; $3000 [2 people]; +$50 each additional person in household	1 vehicle/household
IN	60	$1,000	$5,000
IA	60	$2,000	1 vehicle/household
KS	60	$2,000	all household vehicles exempt from asset limit determination

Table 1.2. *Continued*

State	Eligibility Limits (months)	Asset Limits	Vehicle Exemption
KY	60	$2,000	all household vehicles exempt from asset limit determination
LA	60	$2,000	all household vehicles exempt from asset limit determination
ME	Families in which an adult member has received assistance for 60 months will continue to receive assistance provided that they are complying in all respects with TANF program rules. [adopted 60 month limit beginning July 2011]	$2,000	1 vehicle/household
MD	60	$2,000	all household vehicles exempt from asset limit determination
MA	No Limits	$2,500	$10000 [FMV]/$5000[EV]
MI	48	$3,000	all household vehicles exempt from asset limit determination
MN	60	$2,000	$7,500
MS	60	$2,000	1 vehicle/household
MO	60	$1,000	1 vehicle/household
MT	60	$3,000	1 vehicle/household
NE	60	$4000/$6000	1 vehicle/household
NV	60	$2,000	1 vehicle/household
NH	60	$1,000	1 vehicle/household
NJ	60	$2,000	$9,500
NM	60	$3,500	all household vehicles exempt from asset limit determination
NY	60	$2000/$3000	$4,650

Table 1.2. *Continued*

State	Eligibility Limits (months)	Asset Limits	Vehicle Exemption
NC	60	$3,000	1 vehicle/adult
ND	60	$3000/$6000/$25 each additional over 2 in household	1 vehicle/household
OH	60	no limit	all household vehicles exempt from asset limit determination
OK	60	$1,000	$5,000
OR	60	$2,500	$10,000
PA	60	$1,000	1 vehicle/household
RI	48	$2,500	1 vehicle/adult
SC	60	$2,500	1 vehicle/licensed driver
SD	60	$2,000	1 vehicle/household
TN	60	$2,000	$4,600
TX	60	$1,000	$4,600
UT	36	$2,000	$8,000
VT	No Limits	$1,000	1 vehicle/adult
VA	60	no limit	all household vehicles exempt from asset limit determination
WA	60	$1,000	$5,000
WV	60	$2,000	1 vehicle/household
WI	60	$2,500	$10,000
WY	60	$2,500	$15,000

Source: State TANF plans and state policy manuals.

Table 1.3. Cash Assistance and Work Program Names by State

State	Program
AL	Family Assistance Program (FA)
AK	Alaska Temporary Assistance Program (ATAP)
AZ	Employing & Moving People Off Welfare & Encouraging Responsibility (EMPOWER)
AR	Transitional Employment Assistance (TEA)
CA	California Work Opportunity & Responsibility to Kids (CALWORKS)
CO	Colorado Works
CT	JOBS FIRST
DE	TANF [A Better Chance (ABC) initially]
FL	Welfare Transition Program
GA	TANF
HI	TANF
ID	Temporary Assistance for Families in Idaho (TAFI)
IL	TANF
IN	TANF—cash assistance; Indiana Manpower Placement & Comprehensive Training (IMPACT)—work program
IA	Family Investment Program (FIP)
KS	Kansas Works
KY	Kentucky Transitional Assistance Program (K-TAP)
LA	Family Independence Temporary Assistance Program (FITAP)—cash assistance; Strategies to Empower People (STEP)
ME	TANF work program—cash assistance; Additional Support for People in Retraining and Employment (ASPIRE)—work program
MD	Family Investment Program (FIP)
MA	Transitional Aid to Families with Dependent Children (TAFDC)—cash assistance; Employment Services Program—work program
MI	Family Independence Program (FIP)
MN	Minnesota Family Investment Program (MFIP)
MS	TANF
MO	Beyond Welfare or Temporary Assistance
MT	Families Achieving Independence in Montana (FAIM)

Table 1.3. *Continued*

State	Program
NE	Employment First
NV	TANF
NH	Family Assistance Program (FAP) or Financial Assistance for Needy Families (FANF)—financial aid for work-exempt families; New Hampshire Employment Program (NHEP)—financial aid for work-mandated families
NJ	Work First New Jersey (WFNJ)
NM	NM Works
NY	Family Assistance (FA)
NC	Work First
ND	Training, Employment, Education Management (TEEM)
OH	Ohio Works First (OWF)
OK	TANF
OR	Families First
PA	Pennsylvania TANF
RI	Family Independence Program (FIP)
SC	Family Independence
SD	TANF Worker Supplement Program includes Transition Employment Allowance (TEA)
TN	Families First
TX	Texas Works—cash assistance; Choices—work program administered by Texas Workforce Commission
UT	Family Employment Program (FEP)
VT	Aid to Needy Families with Children (ANFC)—cash assistance; Reach Up—work program
VA	Virginia Initiative for Employment, Not Welfare (VIEW)
WA	WorkFirst
WV	West Virginia Works
WI	Wisconsin Works (W-2)
WY	Personal Opportunities with Employment Responsibility (POWER)

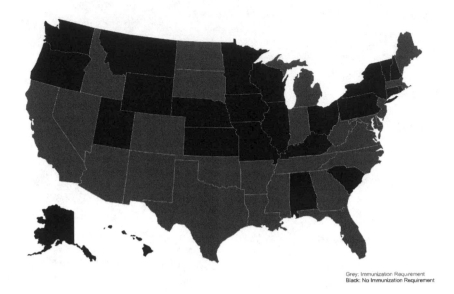

Grey: Immunization Requirement
Black: No Immunization Requirement

Figure 1A. Immunization Requirements as a Condition of TANF Eligibility

Table 1.4. Eligibility of Lawful Permanent Residents (LPRs) for State-Funded TANF CA While Ineligible for Federally-Funded TANF

State	LPR eligibility for state-funded TANF CA (2011)
AL	No
AK	No
AZ	No
AR	No
CA	Yes*
CO	No
CT	Yes for those pursuing citizenship (some exemptions)*
DE	No
FL	No
GA	No
HI	No
ID	No
IL	Only those leaving a violent relationship
IN	No
IA	Only those leaving a violent relationship
KS	No
KY	No

Table 1.4. *Continued*

State	LPR eligibility for state-funded TANF CA (2011)
LA	No
ME	Only those who meet hardship criteria*
MD	Yes
MA	No
MI	No
MN	Yes for those pursuing English literacy and citizenship*
MS	No
MO	No
MT	No
NE	No
NV	Only those leaving a violent relationship
NH	No
NJ	Only those leaving a violent relationship
NM	Yes*
NY	Yes—*Safety Net Assistance Program*
NC	No
ND	No
OH	No—denied even after 5 year period of federal ineligibility
OK	No
OR	Yes*
PA	Yes*
RI	No
SC	No
SD	No
TN	Yes
TX	No
UT	Yes*
VT	Yes*
VA	No
WA	Yes*
WV	No
WI	Yes*
WY	Yes*

Eligibility may be affected by deeming the income and/or resources of the sponsor part of the benefit criteria

Source: National Immigration Law Center. 2011. "State Funded TANF Replacement Programs." *Guide to Immigrant Eligibility for Federal Programs.* Available online at www.nilc.org. Cite last visited July 24, 2014.

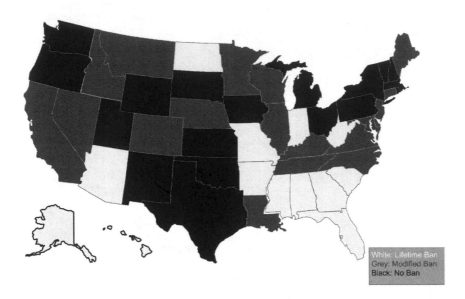

Figure 2A. State Drug Disqualification Policies

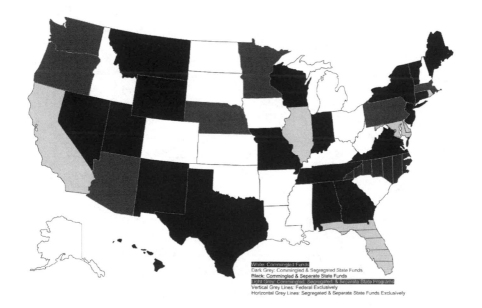

Figure 3A. State Choices in Funding Streams for TANF CA

Table 1.5. State Choices in Family Policies

State	Family Cap	State Nuclear Family Policies & Initiatives	Federally Certified Family Violence Option (Wellstone Murray Amendment)	Domestic Violence Considered Good Cause for Exemption from Work Requirements	Exemption from Time Limits for Families Escaping Domestic Violence	Time Limit Extension for Families Escaping Domestic Violence	No Domestic Violence Exemptions or Extensions
AL	No	Fatherhood Program under the Dept. of Child Abuse & Neglect Prevention (AL) Children's Trust Fund	Yes	No	Yes	No	
AK	No	N/A	Yes	Yes	No	Yes	
AZ	Yes	Two-Parent Employment Program (TPEP)	Yes	Yes	No	No	
AR	Yes	N/A	Yes	No	Yes	Yes	
CA	Yes	N/A	Yes	Yes	Yes	Yes	
CO	No	CO DHS Responsible Fatherhood Grant ($2m)	Yes	No	No	Yes	
CT	Yes	CT DSS Responsible Fatherhood Grant ($1m)	No	Yes	No	Yes	
DE	Yes	N/A	Yes	Yes	Yes	No	

Table 1.5. *Continued*

State	Family Cap	State Nuclear Family Policies & Iniatives	Federally Certified Family Violence Option (Wellstone Murray Amendment)	Domestic Violence Considered Good Cause for Exemption from Work Requirements	Exemption from Time Limits for Families Escaping Domestic Violence	Time Limit Extension for Families Escaping Domestic Violence	No Domestic Violence Exemptions or Extensions
FL	Yes	Commission on Marriage & Family Support Initiatives	Yes	Yes	No	Yes	
GA	Yes	Healthy Marriage Initiative & Fatherhood Initiative	Yes	Yes	No	Yes	
HI	No	Commission on Fatherhood (no state or fed funding = exclusively donations)	Yes	Yes	Yes	No	
ID	No	N/A	No	No	No	No	*
IL	No	Illinois Fatherhood Initiative	Yes	No	No	No	
IN	Yes	Indiana Fathers & Families	No	No	Yes	Yes	
IA	No	N/A	Yes	Yes	No	No	
KS	No	N/A	Yes	No	No	No	*
KY	No	N/A	Yes	No	Yes	Yes	
LA	No	N/A	Yes	Yes	Yes	Yes	
ME	No	N/A	No	Yes	No	Yes	

MD	No	Maryland Responsible Fatherhood Programs (urban)	Yes	Yes	Yes	No
MA	Yes	N/A	Yes	No	No	Yes
MI	No	N/A	No	Yes	No	No
MN	Yes	N/A	Yes	No	Yes	No
MS	Yes	N/A	No	Yes	Yes	Yes
MO	No	N/A	Yes	Yes	No	No
MT	No	N/A	Yes	No	No	No *
NE	No	N/A	Yes	No	Yes	Yes
NV	No	N/A	Yes	No	No	Yes
NH	No	N/A	Yes	Yes	No	Yes
NJ	Yes	N/A	Yes	No	Yes	No
NM	No	N/A	Yes	Yes	No	Yes
NY	No	Strengthening Families Through Stronger Fathers (urban pilot programs)	Yes	No	No	Yes
NC	Yes	N/A	Yes	No	No	No *
ND	Yes	N/A	Yes	Yes	No	Yes *
OH	No	Ohio Fatherhood Initiative (managed by Ohio Commission on Fatherhood)	No	No	No	No

Table 1.5. *Continued*

State	Family Cap	State Nuclear Family Policies & Iniatives	Federally Certified Family Violence Option (Wellstone Murray Amendment)	Domestic Violence Considered Good Cause for Exemption from Work Requirements	Exemption from Time Limits for Families Escaping Domestic Violence	Time Limit Extension for Families Escaping Domestic Violence	No Domestic Violence Exemptions or Extensions
OK	No	OK DHS Healthy Marriages Grant ($549,791)	No	No	No	No	*
OR	No	N/A	Yes	Yes	No	Yes	
PA	No	Fatherhood Initiatives (community-based centers funded by the state)	Yes	Yes	No	No	
RI	No	N/A	Yes	No	Yes	Yes	
SC	Yes	Center for Fathers & Families (Healthy Marriage & Responsible Fatherhood DRA grant); Fatherhood Initiatives (funded by Sisters for Charity)	Yes	No	No	No	*
SD	No	N/A	No	No	No	No	*
TN	Yes	N/A	Yes	Yes	Yes	No	

		TX HHS Healthy Marriages Grant ($900,000)				
TX	No	TX HHS Healthy Marriages Grant ($900,000)	Yes	Yes	Yes	No
UT	No	N/A	Yes	No	No	Yes
VT	No	N/A	Yes	Yes	No	No
VA	Yes	N/A	No	Yes	Yes	No
WA	No	N/A	Yes	Yes	No	No
WV	No	N/A	Yes	Yes	No	No
WI	No	N/A	No	No	No	No *
WY	No	N/A	Yes	No	Yes	Yes

Source: This data on family policies was compiled from and cross-checked with the most recent state TANF plans and policy manuals, the ACF, the Urban Institute Welfare Rules Database, and the GAO.

Table 1.6. State Policy Specific to the Eligibility of Strikers

State	State TANF Policies Regarding the Eligibility of Strikers
AL	strikers excluded
AK	no policy statement specific to strikers
AZ	voluntary strikers not excluded; eligibility based on pre-strike gross income
AR	no policy statement specific to strikers
CA	households with striking members excluded from eligibility
CO	no policy statement specific to strikers
CT	no policy statement specific to strikers
DE	strikers ineligible for food stamp program
FL	no policy statement specific to strikers
GA	no policy statement specific to strikers
HI	no policy statement specific to strikers
ID	no policy statement specific to strikers; participants are explicitly restricted from using support services for professional or trade union dues
IL	Families that include a striker only qualify for assistance if they would have been eligible prior to the strike, and benefits do not increase as a result of a strike. Lockouts are not considered strikes.
IN	no policy statement specific to strikers
IA	People participating in a strike are ineligible, and the entire family is ineligible if parents are participating in a strike.
KS	households with striking members excluded from eligibility
KY	Participants in a strike are ineligible for Medicaid.
LA	FITAP benefits exclude families in which a caretaker or stepparent is participating in a strike, and any other member of the household participating in a strike will be excluded in the benefits calculation
ME	Households with a person on strike are ineligible unless they were eligible the day before the labor dispute, and eligible households cannot receive additional SNAP assistance due to the income loss of the striker.
MD	no policy statement specific to strikers
MA	A natural parent or adoptive parent on a strike on the last day of the calendar month disqualifies the entire assistance unit regardless of their whether that individual striker is included in the application. Individuals who are not natural or adoptive parents who are

Table 1.6. *Continued*

State	State TANF Policies Regarding the Eligibility of Strikers
	participating in a strike are ineligible during the period of the strike. A dependent child on a strike disqualifies the entire unit for assistance. If assistance was paid prior to a strike that lasted until the last day of the month, the grant is recovered, and assistance is denied until the strike is over.
MI	Strikers, their spouses, and children are ineligible.
MN	no policy statement specific to strikers
MS	A "principle wage earner" on strike disqualifies assistance units applying to the separate state program for two-parent families.
MO	no policy statement specific to strikers
MT	The administrative rule 37.78.222 denies TANF cash assistance to strikers.
NE	no policy specific to strikers
NV	A natural parent or adoptive parent on a strike on the last day of the calendar month disqualifies the entire assistance unit. Individuals other than natural or adoptive parents participating in a strike on the last day of a month are ineligible for benefits in that month.
NH	no policy specific to strikers
NJ	no policy specific to strikers
NM	no policy specific to strikers
NY	Strikers who qualify for food stamps are subject to the work requirements. A household member who is a federal, state, or local government employee participating in a strike is deemed a voluntary separation from employment and is evaluated in accordance with the rules related to such a voluntary quit. Individuals who are dismissed from federal, state, or local government employment due to participating in a strike are deemed to have voluntarily quit without good cause.
NC	no policy specific to strikers
ND	Households do not qualify for increased allotments from SNAP due to the loss of wages resulting from a strike, and striking members are ineligible unless they would have been eligible the day prior to the strike. Employees unable to work as a result of striking employees are not considered strikers. Employees who are not part of the bargaining unit on strike but fear personal injury or death if picket lines are crossed are not considered strikers.

Table 1.6. *Continued*

State	State TANF Policies Regarding the Eligibility of Strikers
OH	no policy specific to strikers in TANF plan or state policy; striker ineligibility present in some county program policies
OK	The entire assistance unit is considered ineligible for TANF and SNAP in any month that a natural or adoptive parent participates in a strike, whether or not that person is included in the benefit. An individual other than a natural or adoptive parent participating in a strike on the last day of any month is excluded from the benefit in that month.
OR	A filing group is ineligible for TANF, SNAP, or EA in any month that a parent participates in a strike. If the striker is not a parent in the assistance unit, only the striking individual is ineligible; in which case, the household income including the striker's income before the strike is used in calculating food need.
PA	The entire assistance unit is considered ineligible for TANF and SNAP in any month that a natural or adoptive parent participates in a strike, whether or not that person is included in the benefit. A striking member of the budget group other than a natural or adoptive parent disqualifies that individual and not the entire budget group.
RI	no policy specific to strikers
SC	Individuals who are caretaker relatives in the assistance unit are subject to sanction for participating in a strike. Refusing to seek, accept, or leaving employment due to a strike is considered noncompliance. The entire family is ineligible for the entire month in which a natural or adoptive parent participates in a strike, and benefits will be recouped from those participating in a strike on the last day of the month in which benefits were paid.
SD	Participation cannot be denied because of a strike unless the strike has been enjoined under the Taft Hartley Labor-Management Relations Act or an injunction has been issued under the Railway Labor Act. However, strikers participating in the Food Stamp program are required to work.
TN	Households with striking members are ineligible for Food Stamps unless the household was eligible the day prior to the strike, and the striking members income prior to the strike is used in calculating benefits. A household cannot receive an increase in benefits due to a strike, but a household eligible prior to a strike remains eligible.

Table 1.6. *Continued*

State	State TANF Policies Regarding the Eligibility of Strikers
TX	The "refusal in combination with others" to "provide services to one's employer" is considered a strike in Texas, and strikers are ineligible for TANF and SNAP benefits.
UT	no policy specific to strikers
VT	no policy specific to strikers
VA	strikers ineligible for D-SNAP
WA	Strikers remain eligible for CA and medical programs.
WV	no policy specific to strikers
WI	no policy specific to strikers
WY	Assistance units with a striking member are ineligible for SNAP unless eligible the day prior to the strike. Eligibility for POWER is not allowed for any assistance unit that has a member participating in a strike.

Source: This data on state policies specific to organized labor was compiled from and cross-checked with the most recent state TANF plans and policy manuals as well as state legislation.

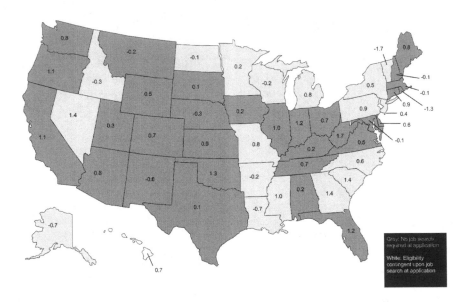

Figure 4A. State Transaction Costs & Eligibility Management with Corresponding Pre-Recession Changes in Poverty Rates

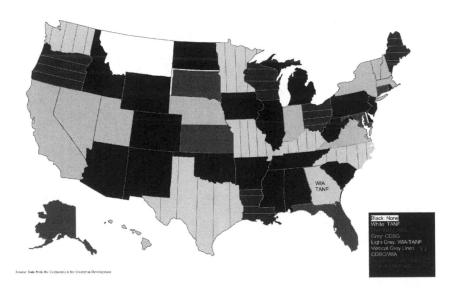

Figure 5A. Employment Strategies Using Federal Block Grants to Support Micro-enterprise

Table 1.7. Total TANF Dollars Spent on Subsidies for Employers from 2004–2009

State	TANF Dollars Spent on Work Subsidies					
	2009	2008	2007	2006	2005	2004
AL	0	0	0	0	0	0
AK	99,039	146,833	250,478	275,909	361,537	251,809
AZ	59,405	8,930	1,960	3,553	7,347	7,290
AR	100,341	119,208	133,956	151,276	128,337	-4,837
CA	12,240,232	2,667,209	2,742,005	2,566,856	2,915,195	2,112,749
CO	138,298	0	0	0	0	-273
CT	0	0	0	0	0	0
DE	0	0	0	0	0	0
FL	197,403	-265,336	766,494	249,513	140,511	256,767
GA	0	0	0	0	0	0
HI	5,292,937	0	0	0	0	0
ID	0	0	0	0	0	0
IL	251,463	0	0	0	0	0
IN	0	0	0	0	0	0
IA	0	0	0	0	0	0
KS	0	0	0	0	0	0
KY	1,740,725	3,077,776	2,149,306	314,984	3,677,179	787,474
LA	C	0	0	0	0	0
ME	C	0	0	0	-64,493	1,282,138
MD	572,596	467,535	499,875	567,951	216,527	714,909

Table 1.7. Continued

State	TANF Dollars Spent on Work Subsidies					
	2009	2008	2007	2006	2005	2004
MA	−35,202	57,198	2,224,763	102,447	1,884,150	2,163,499
MI	185,146	542,220	0	0	0	0
MN	0	0	0	0	0	0
MS	114,693	170,725	147,272	36,130	23,585	257,750
MO	0	−29,799,202	0	29,799,202	0	4,398
MT	37,084	0	0	0	0	0
NE	−30,475,693	−1,334,507	4,075,140	15,885,353	11,849,707	12,663,433
NV	0	0	0	0	0	0
NH	102,910	81,099	6,927	25,555	14,290	0
NJ	1,732,265	555,157	477,781	0	0	4,347
NM	775,211	615,847	593,660	376,550	349,908	866,191
NY	10,761,850	1,480,456	3,591,929	4,799,600	22,526,649	15,574,184
NC	41,147	13,223	225	−435	126	574
ND	0	0	0	0	0	0
OH	1,775,180	39,776	6,516,224	12,701,844	21,026,872	6,719,418
OK	158,723	0	0	0	0	0
OR	275,504	233,141	847,248	800,704	1,278,784	1,060,418
PA	6,550,060	6,121,304	4,130,258	4,006,266	4,422,565	5,476,765
RI	15,369	22,368	25,200	44,488	30,793	40,064

SC	0	0	0	0	0	0
SD	0	0	0	0	0	0
TN	0	0	0	0	0	0
TX	3,126,550	1,650,191	–602,607	3,125,570	4,755,699	3,999,082
UT	122,452	5,622	56,098	99,035	103,067	112,636
VT	0	0	0	0	0	0
VA	29,600	20,600	12,000	6,300	219,744	2,249,136
WA	21,578,601	16,778,042	9,016,830	10,913,927	10,416,437	11,696,122
WV	0	0	0	0	0	0
WI	44,717	5,505	32,831	20,940	29,326	4,411
WY	0	0	0	0	0	0

Source: The TANF dollars spent on work subsidies are from the Center for Law and Social Policy. It should also be noted that work subsidies come from a variety of sources, including federal WIA funds, state departments of labor or economic opportunity, and public-private partnerships with state and/or local governments. The figures listed in this table are exclusively TANF dollars and do not reflect the total subsidies to employers.

Table 1.8. Share of TANF Dollars Spent on Work First Strategies (2009)

| State | Share of Total TANF Dollars Spent on Work First Strategies (2009) | | | |
	Transportation or Support Services	Education & Training	Work Subsidies	Other Work Expenses
AL	4.00%	0.40%	0.00%	13.00%
AK	1.50%	0.00%	0.10%	11.10%
AZ	0.20%	0.00%	0.00%	3.00%
AR	3.10%	5.70%	0.10%	12.50%
CA	3.00%	0.60%	0.20%	6.20%
CO	1.60%	0.20%	0.00%	0.10%
CT	1.10%	0.00%	0.00%	3.70%
DE	0.40%	0.10%	0.00%	0.90%
FL	0.60%	0.60%	0.00%	5.70%
GA	3.00%	0.50%	0.00%	2.90%
HI	0.80%	17.00%	1.50%	20.50%
ID	0.30%	0.20%	0.00%	15.30%
IL	0.30%	3.90%	0.00%	2.10%
IN	0.00%	5.70%	0.00%	0.00%
IA	2.90%	0.10%	0.00%	8.40%
KS	4.80%	1.00%	0.00%	0.10%
KY	2.30%	2.10%	0.60%	6.70%
LA	2.10%	3.30%	0.00%	0.40%
ME	15.00%	0.60%	0.00%	9.70%
MD	0.90%	0.30%	0.10%	6.40%
MA	0.10%	1.30%	0.40%	0.20%
MI	0.20%	0.50%	0.00%	6.50%
MN	1.10%	0.20%	0.00%	14.20%
MS	19.70%	3.60%	0.10%	18.20%
MO	0.00%	0.00%	0.00%	6.50%
MT	0.00%	18.60%	0.10%	3.70%
NE	0.00%	0.00%	−28.80%	49.10%
NV	3.90%	0.10%	0.00%	3.80%
NH	1.90%	1.20%	0.10%	9.60%
NJ	1.70%	2.00%	0.20%	6.30%

Table 1.8. *Continued*

State	Transportation or Support Services	Education & Training	Work Subsidies	Other Work Expenses
NM	0.50%	0.00%	0.40%	7.10%
NY	0.20%	0.00%	0.20%	3.00%
NC	0.80%	0.40%	0.00%	7.70%
ND	5.30%	0.10%	0.00%	8.70%
OH	1.70%	0.40%	0.10%	2.90%
OK	8.50%	0.00%	0.10%	0.00%
OR	2.30%	0.80%	1.40%	6.50%
PA	3.20%	0.60%	0.60%	12.50%
RI	4.00%	0.00%	0.00%	5.60%
SC	5.20%	13.40%	0.00%	0.40%
SD	0.10%	0.00%	0.00%	13.80%
TN	0.00%	0.00%	0.00%	15.80%
TX	0.20%	1.40%	0.40%	7.70%
UT	3.10%	1.60%	0.10%	22.40%
VT	8.90%	0.00%	0.00%	0.30%
VA	3.30%	0.30%	0.00%	19.10%
WA	0.30%	2.10%	1.50%	4.70%
WV	10.70%	0.00%	0.00%	0.90%
WI	0.30%	0.50%	0.00%	4.70%
WY	1.10%	1.60%	0.00%	0.00%

Source: The TANF dollars spent on work first strategies are from the Center for Law and Social Policy. It should also be noted that each of these categories of spending may come from a variety of sources which also vary across states, including federal WIA funds, CDBG, governor's initiatives, state legislative allocations and trust funds for workforce development and/or education enhancement, state departments of labor or economic opportunity, and public-private partnerships with state and/or local governments. The figures listed in this table are exclusively TANF dollars and do not reflect the priority of any one category overall.

Table 1.9. State Sanction Policies Regulating Personal Responsibility & Work Compliance

State	Personal Responsibility Sanction Severity	Max Sanction for Work Noncompliance
AL	Entire assistance unit loses eligibility for twelve months.	Loss of CA for 6 months
AK	The entire assistance unit loses its benefit. The case is closed and the family must reapply to receive further benefits.	CA reduced for 12 months
AZ	Entire assistance unit loses eligibility for one month or until compliance, whichever is longer.	Loss of CA for 1 month
AR	After the 9th month of non-compliance, the case will be closed.	Loss of CA for 3 months
CA	The needs of the sanctioned individual are not included for benefit calculation; however, their income (after standard disregards) and assets are still included for eligibility and benefit calculation purposes. The individual is sanctioned until compliance. If the head is sanctioned, the benefit is issued to a protective payee. For an individual subject to sanction for at least three months, vouchers or vendor payments for at least rent and utility payments are issued.	CA reduced for up to 6 months
CO	Unit is ineligible for assistance for 3 months or until compliance, whichever is longer. A new assessment and Individual Responsibility Contract must be completed before assistance can be reissued.	Loss of CA for 3–6 months (varies by county)
CT	For recipients who have not reached time limit: Entire assistance unit loses benefit eligibility for three months and must reapply for assistance after the sanction period. For recipients who have had their time limit extended: Entire assistance unit loses benefit eligibility for the remainder of the extension and does not qualify for additional extensions.	Loss of CA for 3 months
DE	Case is closed.	Loss of CA for life

FL	Loss of benefits for the entire assistance unit for 3 months or until the individual who failed to comply does so, whichever is later. Upon meeting this requirement temporary cash assistance will be reinstated to the date of compliance or the first day of the month following the penalty period. Assistance may still be provided to children under 16 in the unit; these benefits are issued to a protective payee.	Loss of CA for 3 months
GA	Unit is ineligible for benefits. There is no opportunity to comply to cure the sanction.	Loss of CA until compliance
HI	Unit is ineligible for benefits for three months or until compliance, whichever is longer.	CA reduced for 6 months
ID	The family is ineligible for benefits for lifetime.	Loss of CA for life
IL	Unit is ineligible for benefits for 3 months or until compliance with activities requirements, whichever is longer.	Loss of CA for 3 months
IN	Case is closed until compliance.	CA reduced until compliance
IA	Unit is ineligible for benefits for 6 months. Sanction continues after 6 months until sanctioned parent signs a family investment agreement and completes 20 hours of eligible education/work activities.	Loss of CA for 6 months
KS	The entire unit is ineligible for benefits until compliance.	Loss of CA for 2 months
KY	Unit is ineligible for benefits until compliance	CA reduced until compliance
LA	The case is closed for 3 months or until compliance, whichever is longer.	Loss of CA for 3 months or until compliance, whichever is longer

Table 1.9. *Continued*

State	Personal Responsibility Sanction Severity	Max Sanction for Work Noncompliance
ME	The needs of the sanctioned individual are not included for benefit calculation; however, the sanctioned parent's income (after disregards listed below) and assets are still included for eligibility and benefit calculation purposes. The individual is sanctioned for 6 months or until compliance, whichever is longer. If the head is sanctioned, the benefit is issued to a protective payee. Disregards include amount equal to the standard of need for support of non-categorically eligible dependents living in the household with the sanctioned parent, alimony and child support payments to persons outside the household, and payments to dependents of the sanctioned parent who live outside the household. If the unit head is sanctioned, the benefit is issued to a third party payee.	CA reduced for 6 months or until compliance, whichever is longer
MD	Unit is ineligible for benefits until the sanctioned individual complies with activities requirements for 30 days.	Loss of CA until 30 days of consecutive compliance
MA	n.a.	Loss of CA unless allowed to participate in community service
MI	Case is closed for 12 calendar months.	Loss of CA for 1 month or until compliance
MN	Case is closed for one month or until compliance, whichever is longer.	CA reduced
MS	Unit is permanently disqualified from receipt of benefits.	Loss of CA for life
MO	Benefit is reduced by 25 percent. The individual is sanctioned for 3 months or until compliance, whichever is longer.	CA reduced for 3 months or until compliance, whichever is longer

MT	The case is closed and the family is ineligible for six months.	CA reduced for 12 months
NE	Termination of benefits for the entire family for twelve months or until compliance, whichever is longer	Loss of CA until end of time limit
NV	Termination of assistance until compliance	CA reduced for 1 month
NH	The grant amount is reduced by 2/3 of the Adjusted Payment Standard (the amount of the grant after the adult portion has been removed). After 8 weeks of continuous non-compliance, or 3 non-consecutive months of non-compliance within a 12-month period, assistance is terminated.	CA reduced until compliance
NJ	Assistance unit's cash assistance case is closed for a minimum one-month period. Assistance unit must reapply in order to receive further cash assistance benefits.	Loss of CA for 3 months
NM	The unit's benefits are terminated and the case is closed for 6 months. The unit must reapply and are treated as new applicants with respect to meeting cooperation requirements.	Loss of CA until compliance
NY	The assistance unit's benefit is reduced pro rata by the sanctioned individual's share; however, their income (after standard disregards) and assets are still included for eligibility and benefit calculation purposes. The individual is sanctioned for 6 months or until compliance, whichever is longer. If unit head is sanctioned, benefits issued to protective payee.	CA reduced
NC	If the non-exempt recipient fails to comply with requirements for three consecutive months, the unit's benefits will be terminated.	Loss of CA
ND	The needs of the individual are not included for benefit calculation, however, their income (after standard disregards) and assets are still included for eligibility and benefit calculation purposes. The unit is sanctioned for one month. If no compliance after one month, entire case goes into closure following penalty month. Sanction cannot be imposed for more than 12 months.	Loss of CA until compliance

Table 1.9. *Continued*

State	Personal Responsibility Sanction Severity	Max Sanction for Work Noncompliance
NV	Termination of assistance until compliance	CA reduced for 1 month
NH	The grant amount is reduced by 2/3 of the Adjusted Payment Standard (the amount of the grant after the adult portion has been removed). After 8 weeks of continuous non-compliance, or 3 non-consecutive months of non-compliance within a 12-month period, assistance is terminated.	CA reduced until compliance
NJ	Assistance unit's cash assistance case is closed for a minimum one-month period. Assistance unit must reapply in order to receive further cash assistance benefits.	Loss of CA for 3 months
NM	The unit's benefits are terminated and the case is closed for 6 months. The unit must reapply and are treated as new applicants with respect to meeting cooperation requirements.	Loss of CA until compliance
NY	The assistance unit's benefit is reduced pro rata by the sanctioned individual's share; however, their income (after standard disregards) and assets are still included for eligibility and benefit calculation purposes. The individual is sanctioned for 6 months or until compliance, whichever is longer. If unit head is sanctioned, benefits issued to protective payee.	CA reduced
NC	If the non-exempt recipient fails to comply with requirements for three consecutive months, the unit's benefits will be terminated.	Loss of CA
ND	The needs of the individual are not included for benefit calculation, however, their income (after standard disregards) and assets are still included for eligibility and benefit calculation purposes. The unit is sanctioned for one month. If no compliance after one month, entire case goes into closure following penalty month. Sanction cannot be imposed for more than 12 months.	Loss of CA until compliance

State	Description	Outcome
OH	The unit is ineligible for benefits for six months or until the failure/refusal ceases, whichever is longer. Assistance groups that do not submit signed compliance forms to end the failure/refusal by a specified date will not have benefits reinstated and will be required to reapply.	Loss of CA for 6 months
OK	The unit is ineligible for cash assistance until compliance.	Loss of CA until compliance
OR	Unit is ineligible for benefits until compliance and must go through the application process (including initial job search) upon reapplication.	Loss of CA until compliance
PA	If sanction occurs within the first 24 months of assistance, the needs of the sanctioned individual are permanently excluded for benefit calculation; however, their income (after standard disregards) and assets are still included for eligibility and benefit calculation purposes. If sanction occurs after 24 months of assistance, the entire assistance unit is permanently ineligible.	Loss of CA for life
RI	Cash assistance to the entire unit is terminated, effective on the next payroll date after the adverse action period.	CA reduced
SC	The case is closed until the unit is in compliance for 30 days.	Loss of CA until 30 days of consecutive compliance
SD	The case is closed for at least one month, and the unit must reapply for assistance; until compliance.	Loss of CA
TN	Unit is ineligible for benefits until compliance has been demonstrated for 5 days.	Loss of CA for 3 months
TX	The TANF case is closed. To receive assistance again, the family must reapply and demonstrate cooperation for 30 days. If they reapply, and they voluntary quit their job or they didn't meet the school attendance requirement, they face a full family sanction when they reapply.	CA reduced for 6 months

Table 1.9. *Continued*

State	Personal Responsibility Sanction Severity	Max Sanction for Work Noncompliance
UT	Financial assistance is sanctioned for two full months. The client must reapply for financial assistance, and complete a trial participation period before financial benefits are authorized.	Loss of CA until compliance
VT	Benefits are reduced by $225 per month if sanctioned adult has 12 or more cumulative months of sanctions or if a recipient is sanctioned after 60 or more cumulative months of benefits. After two weeks of resumed activity participation, recipient benefits are restored to the pre-sanction level.	Loss of CA until compliance
VA	Monthly benefit will be suspended for a minimum of six months and will continue until compliance.	Loss of CA for 6 months
WA	The family's grant amount is reduced by the non-compliant participant's share or 40%, whichever is larger; any remaining benefit is paid to a protective payee. The sanction remains in effect until the individual is compliant for 4 weeks; after 4 weeks of compliance, benefits are restored to their pre-sanction level. If the participant refuses to participate 6 months in a row, the case may be closed.	Loss of CA until compliance
WV	Unit is ineligible for benefits for 6 months or until compliance, whichever is later.	Loss of CA for 6 months
WI	Unit is ineligible for benefits in that component for life. Unit may receive benefits again if s/he becomes eligible for a different component.	Loss of CA for life
WY	The family's benefits are terminated until compliance.	Loss of CA for 1 month

Source: The data on sanction policies were compiled from the most recent state TANF plans and 2012 state policy manuals. Additional information regarding the initial state policy choices is available through the Urban Institute's Welfare Rules Database, which compiled data on state TANF policies from 1998–2000 tracked by the State Policy Documentation Project. Available online at www.spdp.org. Cite lasted visited July 24, 2014.

Table 1.10. State Diversion Strategies (2012)

State	Diversion Programs
AL	No Formal Diversion Program
AK	cash payment for up to 3 months only once in 12 month period and maximum 4 times in a lifetime
AZ	Eligibility for diversion assistance requires meeting all eligibility requirements for cash assistance except the Jobs Program as well as: 1) Being eligible for $1 of cash assistance benefits in the application month or next 2 months; 2) not having received diversion in the last 4 months; 3) not having received cash assistance in the month of application; 4) not having an open cash assistance sanction; 5) not being employed and on absence from work All Two-Parent Employment Program (TPEP) families are eligible for diversion cash payments for up to 3 months and must be processed as such.
AR	cash loan up to 3 months provided only once in a lifetime
CA	Diversion assistance is only offered to CalWORKS applicants and may be in the form of cash payments or services; maximum diversion payments vary by county; diversions available as often as needed for up to $4000 annually and $10000 lifetime
CO	applicant/recipient must demonstrate need for a specific item or type of assistance, such as cash, supportive services, housing, or transportation; vendor or cash payments up to $1000 available twice in a lifetime
CT	cash payment for up to 3 months only once in 12 month period and maximum 2 times in a lifetime
DE	Diversion Assistance is paid to vendors up to $1500 for parents either (a) currently employed but having a problem that jeopardizes the job or (b) promised a job but need help in order to accept the job. Non-parent caretaker relatives are not eligible for Diversion Assistance.
FL	Florida has three separate diversion programs. Up-front diversion is for individuals in need of assistance due to unexpected circumstances or emergency situations. Relocation assistance is available for individuals who reside in an area with limited employment opportunities and experience one of the following: geographic isolation, formidable transportation barriers, isolation from extended family, or domestic violence that threatens the ability of a parent to maintain self-sufficiency. Exemptions to work participation and hardship extensions available to vulnerable but "diligent" participants.*
GA	If applicant either: (1) has full-time job, but is on unpaid leave due to his or her temporary illness or the illness of a family member (under 4 months) and meets gross income test, or (2) employed and eligible for less than maximum amount of cash assistance and declines it, cash payment for up to 4 months once in a lifetime

Table 1.10. *Continued*

State	Diversion Programs
HI	cash payment for up to 8 months once in 60 months
ID	cash payment for up to 3 months available once in a lifetime; each payment counts toward time limit
IL	An applicant who has found a job that will make him/her ineligible for cash assistance or who wants to accept the job and withdraw his/her application for assistance is eligible for a one-time payment in order to begin or maintain employment.
IN	No Formal Diversion Program
IA	vendor payment up to $2000 available once every 12 months
KS	lump sum non-recurrent diversion payment of $1000 available to first time applicants to meet immediate short-term needs; diversion inapplicable if need exceeds $1000; ineligible for TANF for 1 calendar year upon receipt of diversion [implemented 2012]
KY	vendor payment up to $1300 twice in a lifetime but no more than once every 24 months
LA	Although it still exists in the law, Louisiana's diversion program has not received funding since September 2002.
ME	caretaker relative or parent must be employed or looking for work to qualify for vendor payment for up to 3 months available once in a lifetime
MD	cash payment for up to 3 months as often as needed
MA	No Formal Diversion Program
MI	lump sum CA once in 12 months does not count toward time limit for 4 months of diversion eligibility; max payment can be received for up to 3 months
MN	Minnesota's Diversionary Work Program (DWP) is mandatory for all units applying for TANF. DWP consists of four months of intensive employment services, focused on helping the participant obtain an unsubsidized job before entering welfare. After the four months are complete, the participant may reapply for TANF as an applicant (the unit will not be eligible for the higher earned income disregard used for recipients). The following types of units are exempt from mandatory participation in DWP and may apply for TANF benefits directly: (1) child only cases, (2) one-parent families that include a child under 12 weeks of age, (3) minor caregivers without a school diploma or GED, (4) caregivers age 18 or 19 without a high school diploma or GED who choose to have an employment plan with an educational component

Table 1.10. *Continued*

State	Diversion Programs
MS	No Formal Diversion Program
MO	No Formal Diversion Program
MT	No Formal Diversion Program
NE	diversion mandatory for nonexempt eligible clients; cash payment for emergency then automatic transition to TANF
NV	lump sum CA as often as needed; does not count toward time limit; variable eligibility; max payment = $1000
NH	cash payment or voucher to provide crisis stabilization for the hard-to-employ
NJ	Applicants for WFNJ/TANF must participate in the diversion program (Early Employment Initiative) if they: (1) have a work history that equals or exceeds four months of full-time employment in the last 12 months; (2) have at least one child; (3) appear to meet TANF eligibility requirements; (4) are not in immediate need; (5) and do not meet criteria for a deferral from work requirements. Participants receive an activity payment and are required to pursue an intensive job search for 15 to 30 days, while their TANF application is being processed. If participants secure employment and withdraw their application, they are eligible to receive a one time lump-sum payment to assist in the transition to employment. If no employment is secured, then the applicant is referred back for traditional assistance
NM	Diversion only available to assist applicant to keep a job, accept a bona fide offer of employment, or remedy an emergency situation or unexpected short-term need in the form of cash payment for up to 3 months twice in a lifetime
NY	There are three types of diversion payments: 1) Diversion Transportation Payment (non-recurring payment for employment-related transportation expenses) 2) Diversion payment (non-recurrent, short-term payment to be used for crisis items such as moving expenses, storage fees, or household structural or equipment repairs). 3) Diversion Rental Payment (short-term diversion payment for rent)
NC	Designed to deal with a specific crisis situation or episode of need; not intended to meet recurrent need; cash payment for up to 3 months available once every 12 months
ND	No Formal Diversion Program
OH	county discretion; lump sum CA or vendor payment; variable eligibility and max payment; does not count toward time limit

Table 1.10. *Continued*

State	Diversion Programs
OK	To qualify a person must be employed or have a bona fide offer of employment and the family must meet assistance income and resources eligibility. Diversion assistance cannot be used for reimbursement of expenses already paid, to pay fines, or fees associated with criminal offenses. A stepparent may be included in the diversion assistance benefit. Payments made to vendors for up to 3 months available once in a lifetime.
OR	No Formal Diversion Program
PA	To qualify, applicants must have an expectation of receiving income and must have a recent work history (within 90 days of application) or job skills training. Cash payments are possible for up to 3 months once every 12 months.
RI	Diversion is only available to applicants. The unit must not receive assistance payments during the 12 months prior to the date of application and the adult member of the unit must not have terminated employment within 60 days of application for benefits. Cash payments are available for up to 3 months once in a lifetime.
SC	2008 pilot in 1 county for crisis stabilization; cash payment based on applicant needs
SD	vendor or cash payment for up to 2 months as often as needed
TN	lump sum CA once in a lifetime; $1200 max
TX	cash payment up to $1000 available once every 12 months
UT	To receive a diversion payment, the unit must pass all eligibility and income tests and be eligible for a financial payment of at least one dollar. Cash payments are available for up to 3 months as often as needed, but payments count toward time limits.
VT	Reach First—new applicants experiencing a financial crisis but likely to be stable in 4 months provided emergency assistance without counting toward time limit
VA	vendor or cash payment for up to 4 months available once every 60 months
WA	cash payment up to $1500 available once every 12 months
WV	cash payment for up to 3 months available once in a lifetime
WI	Referred to as Job Access Loans; $1600 cash loan available once every 12 months
WY	No Formal Diversion Program

*FL also implements an abstinence-focused teen parent and pregnancy prevention diversion program through the Dept. of Health authorized by the FL legislature that does not use TANF or MOE funds.

Source: The data on sanction policies were compiled from the most recent state TANF plans and 2012 state policy manuals.

Table 1.11. Independent/Individual Development Account Programs in State TANF Systems

State	IDA Program Model	Permitted Uses of Allowable Assets	Match Rate	Account Limit	% Unbanked Households (2009)
AL	None	n.a.	n.a.	n.a.	11.6%
AK	None	n.a.	n.a.	n.a.	4.3%
AZ	Contribution Limits	Allowable educational or training costs, first home purchases, business capitalization costs leading toward self-sufficiency	no matching	$9,000	7.5%
AR	Account Limits	n.a.	3:1	$2000/person; $4000 max	10.1%
CA	Account Limits	Purchase of home, post-secondary education, start a new business, retirement	county option	county option	7.7%
CO	No Contribution Limits	home purchase, business capitalization, or higher education	county option	unlimited	6.9%
CT	No Contribution Limits	Assets set aside for post secondary education of a dependent child; IRAs, Keoghs, 401k plans are all excluded.	no matching	unlimited	5.3%
DE	Contribution Limits	Self-sufficiency needs including education expenses, employment start-up needs, entrepreneurship, or purchase of a vehicle or home	no matching	$5,000	5.6%

Table 1.11. *Continued*

State	IDA Program Model	Permitted Uses of Allowable Assets	Match Rate	Account Limit	% Unbanked Households (2009)
FL	Contribution and Account Limits	Funds in an IDA can be used by eligible participants for purchasing a first home, paying for post-secondary education, transportation, assistive technology or capitalizing a business. IDAs are comprised of participant's savings from earned income and may be matched by funds controlled by the regional workforce board.	1:1	$1000/year; $3000/lifetime	7.0%
GA	Contribution Limits	Post-secondary educational expenses, first home purchase, business capitalization	no matching	$5,000	12.2%
HI	None	n.a.	n.a.	n.a.	2.9%
ID	None	n.a.	n.a.	n.a.	6.7%
IL	Limited State Matching	Must be used to start a business, purchase a home for a first-time buyer, pay for postsecondary educational expenses, or purchase an automobile.	1:1 with max match of $1000	no contribution limit but maximum match of $1000	6.2%
IN	Unlimited Contributions with State Matching	For postsecondary education or purchasing a home or business	3:1 up to $300/year	unlimited	7.4%

IA	Virtually Unlimited with State Matching	Post secondary education or job training, buying a home or home improvement, starting a small business, or medical emergencies.	15–25%	$50,000	4.7%
KS	Unlimited Contributions without Matching	Post-secondary education; first home purchase; business capitalization; Assistance Technology Savings	no matching	unlimited	6.4%
KY	Unlimited Contributions without Matching	Must be used for a down payment on a house, college fund, or establishing a self-employment business; may also be used for emergency home repairs	no matching	$5,000	11.9%
LA	Contribution Limits	Educational expenses for higher education, training programs, or payments for work related clothing, tools or equipment. IDAs can be established for educational expenses, the first-time purchase of a home, and/or business capitalization expenses.	no matching	$6,000	8.7%
ME	Somewhat Limited Contributions with Variable State Matching	Up to $10,000 of nonrecurring lump sum income may be disregarded if used within 30 days for Family Development Accounts, educational expenses, purchase of a home, repairs to vehicle or home, or for a business start up; allows for some spending in certain emergencies as determined by caseworker	variable	$10,000 plus interest	2.6%

Table 1.11. *Continued*

State	IDA Program Model	Permitted Uses of Allowable Assets	Match Rate	Account Limit	% Unbanked Households (2009)
MD	County Administered without State Matching	For education, buying a home or starting a business	county option [4]	variable	5.6%
MA	None	n.a.	n.a.	n.a.	4.1%
MI	Limited Contributions with State Matching	Post-secondary educational expenses, a first home purchase, or business capitalization.	up to 3:1 depending on purpose	$1,000	6.7%
MN	Limited Contributions with State Matching	Home Ownership, Post-Secondary Education, and Small Business Development	3:1	$3,000	2.6%
MS	None	n.a.	n.a.	n.a.	16.4%
MO	None	n.a.	n.a.	n.a.	8.2%
MT	No Contribution Limits	Discretion of community organizations; TANF funds have not been utilized, but some TANF clients access	2:1 up to $4000	unlimited	3.8%
NE	None	n.a.	n.a.	n.a.	5.4%
NV	Unlimited with State Matching	First home purchase, post secondary educational expenses, or business capitalization	not reported	unlimited	6.9%

State	Type	Purpose	Matching	Contribution Limit	Percent
NH	Unlimited with State Matching	Purchasing a first home; financing post-secondary education; financing a new business	3:1	unlimited	2.2%
NJ	Limited Contributions with State Matching	Moneys, matching contributions, and interest from separate approved IDAs are totally exempt. The funds must be designated for one of the following purposes: (1) purchase of a home, (2) educational/training expenses, (3) purchase of a vehicle, or (4) purchase of a business.	1:1	up to $1500/year for 3 years	7.4%
NM	Contribution Limits	Post-secondary education for dependent child, first time home buyer, business capitalization, home improvements, vehicle acquisition	no matching	$1,500	11.4%
NY	Unlimited Contributions with State Matching	Individual Development Accounts for post-secondary education, buying first home and business capitalization	variable	unlimited	9.8%
NC	Limited with State Matching	First home purchase; business capitalization; post-secondary education; trust funds for children are excluded	up to 1:1	$2,000	8.2%
ND	None	n.a.	n.a.	n.a.	4.8%
OH	Limited Contributions with State Matching	Post-secondary education, first time home purchase, establishment of a business	county discretion up to 2:1	county discretion	7.1%
OK	Contribution Limits with Matching	Education, purchase of home, start of new business	matching based on income up to $500/year or up to 4 years	$2,000	9.8%

Table 1.11. *Continued*

State	IDA Program Model	Permitted Uses of Allowable Assets	Match Rate	Account Limit	% Unbanked Households (2009)
OR	Unlimited with State Matching	Education account in which the participant's employer contributes $1 for every hour the participant works.	$1/hour worked	unlimited	5.7%
PA	Federal Assets for Independence (AFI) funds may be used to match	Family Savings Account (FSA) administered by Department of Community & Economic Development for homeownership, postsecondary education, business capitalization, home repair, car purchase, or computer purchase related to employment or education	discretionary	$10,000	5.1%
RI	None	n.a.	n.a.	n.a.	6.2%
SC	Contribution Limits	Funds deposited into an IDA, including lump sum income deposited within thirty days of receipt. May be used for education, job training, business start-up, the purchase of a vehicle, or the purchase of a home.	no matching	$10,000	10.2%
SD	None	n.a.	n.a.	n.a.	4.8%
TN	Contribution Limits	May be used for post-secondary education, small business development, home ownership, and transportation needs	no matching	$5,000	9.9%

State					
TX	Limited Contributions with State Matching	TANF-certified IDA accounts are for paying for a college education, purchasing a home or starting a business. Only count as a resource any deposits into an IDA not made with earnings or EITC, or any withdrawals from an IDA made for non-allowable purposes. Assets for Independence Act (AFIA) IDAs follow the same rules as TANF IDAs. All other IDAs not meeting one of the qualifying purposes (paying for college education, purchasing a home, or starting a business) are counted as a resource, and interest is counted as unearned income. The exception to this rule is any IDA certified as meeting the Social Security criteria for a Plan to Achieve Self-Sufficiency (PASS).	IDA entity can use TANF funds to match up to $2000/year of earned income (excluding EITC refund)	discretionary by IDA entity	11.7%
UT	None	n.a.	n.a.	n.a.	1.7%
VT	Limited Contributions with State Matching	Purchasing a home; education; starting a business.	1:1 state limit; 2:1 limit with funds from partnership with Central Vt Community Action Council	$500/year min with max of $2000 for individual; $1000/year min with max $4000 for family; must commit to at least 1 year of saving	4.2%

Table 1.11. *Continued*

State	IDA Program Model	Permitted Uses of Allowable Assets	Match Rate	Account Limit	% Unbanked Households (2009)
VA	Contribution Limits	IDA funds are limited to purchase a home, start a business or attend post-secondary education.	no matching	$5,000	5.1%
WA	Limited Contributions with State Matching	$3000 of a savings account or Certificate of Deposit may be excluded. Entire amount in IDA may be excluded. An IDA is a trust fund established with a Community Based Organization which will match the contributions of the recipient for one of the following purposes: post secondary education, small business development, or first time home purchase	2:1 up to $4000	$4000/contractor; $2000/client; maximum allowable $6000	3.9%
WV	None	n.a.	n.a.	n.a.	6.3%
WI	County Administered without State Matching	Purchase of a home, starting a small business, post-secondary education	no matching	county discretion	4.3%
WY	None	n.a.	n.a.	n.a.	4.0%

Source: Data on state IDA program details from the 8th annual report to Congress and the Center for Social Development at Washington University St. Louis; also available on the Urban Institute's WRD. Data on unbanked households from FDIC's National Survey of Unbanked and Underbanked Households. Washington, DC: Federal Deposit Insurance Corporation, 2009.

Table 1.12. Spending from Federal TANF Dollars on Independent/Individual Development Accounts Across States Relative to the Percent Change in Asset Poverty

State	Match Rate	Percent Change in Asset Poverty Rate (2006–2009)	TANF Dollars Spent on IDAs					
			2009	2008	2007	2006	2005	2004
AL	n.a.	19.5%	0	0	0	0	0	0
AK	n.a.	unknown	0	0	0	0	0	0
AZ	no matching	34.1%	0	0	0	0	0	0
AR	3:1	14.3%	840,280	575,677	1,432,347	482,319	410,246	397,283
CA	county option	30.2%	0	0	0	0	0	0
CO	county option	36.3%	0	0	0	0	0	0
CT	no matching	8.0%	0	0	0	0	0	0
DE	no matching	10.3%	0	0	0	0	0	0
FL	1:1	43.5%	0	0	0	0	0	0
GA	no matching	31.9%	0	0	0	0	0	0
HI	n.a.	9.6%	0	0	0	0	0	0
ID	n.a.	31.1%	0	0	0	0	0	0
IL	1:1 with max match of $1000	26.9%	0	0	0	0	0	0
IN	3:1 up to $300/year	19.4%	0	0	0	0	0	0

Table 1.12. *Continued*

State	Match Rate	Percent Change in Asset Poverty Rate (2006–2009)	TANF Dollars Spent on IDAs					
			2009	2008	2007	2006	2005	2004
IA	15–25%	25.4%	0	0	0	0	0	0
KS	no matching	0.4%	0	0	0	0	0	0
KY	no matching	18.7%	0	0	0	0	0	0
LA	no matching	−12.2%	1,337,745	646,630	308,818	0	31,079	3,012,347
ME	variable	5.2%	0	0	0	0	0	0
MD	county option [4]	11.5%	0	0	0	0	0	0
MA	n.a.	10.1%	0	0	0	0	0	0
MI	up to 3:1 depending on purpose	30.1%	200,000	158,125	325,383	519,207	929,873	711,321
MN	3:1	40.1%	0	0	0	0	0	0
MS	n.a.	34.1%	0	0	0	0	0	0
MO	n.a.	9.6%	0	0	0	0	0	0
MT	2:1 up to $4000	−19.7%	0	0	0	0	0	60,127
NE	n.a.	30.4%	0	0	0	0	0	0
NV	not reported	71.8%	0	0	0	0	0	0
NH	3:1	7.9%	0	0	0	0	28,701	76,679

NJ	1:1	34.3%	-50,804	430,463	179,241	0	151,228	378,893
NM	no matching	16.7%	0	0	0	0	0	0
NY	variable	9.3%	0	0	0	0	0	0
NC	up to 1:1	6.3%	0	1,000	0	0	0	0
ND	n.a.	-17.9%	0	0	0	0	0	0
OH	county discretion up to 2:1	24.5%	42,630	22,833	3,034	0	0	0
OK	matching based on income up to $500/year for up to 4 years	16.4%	0	0	0	0	764	5,349
OR	$1/hour worked	7.7%	0	0	0	0	0	0
PA	AFI [discretionary]	9.7%	0	0	0	0	0	0
RI	n.a.	24.9%	0	0	0	0	0	0
SC	no matching	-2.0%	0	0	0	0	0	0
SD	n.a.	34.9%	0	0	0	0	0	0
TN	no matching	19.2%	0	0	0	0	0	0
TX	IDA entity can use TANF funds to match up to $2000/year of earned income (excluding EITC refund)	16.0%	0	0	40,604	-456,846	820,199	1,977,968

Table 1.12. Continued

State	Match Rate	Percent Change in Asset Poverty Rate (2006–2009)	TANF Dollars Spent on IDAs					
			2009	2008	2007	2006	2005	2004
UT	n.a.	–17.7%	0	0	0	0	0	0
VT	1:1 state limit; 2:1 limit with funds from partnership with Central Vt Community Action Council	unknown	0	0	0	0	0	0
VA	no matching	50.9%	0	1,239	0	8,088	12,836	11,111
WA	2:1 up to $4000	14.2%	0	0	0	0	206,764	432,237
WV	n.a.	4.2%	0	0	0	0	0	0
WI	no matching	14.6%	0	0	0	0	0	–9,015
WY	n.a.	15.4%	0	0	0	0	0	0

Source: Data on the spending of federal TANF dollars from the Center for Law and Social Policy Data Finder. Data on the percent Change in Asset Poverty from the Survey of Income and Program Participation. Washington, DC: U.S. Department of Commerce, Census Bureau, calculated by the Bay Area Council Economic Institute.

Table 1.13. State Child Support Enforcement Strategies

State	Interest	State OCSE Fees	Legal Limitations on Collections Fees by Private Collection Agencies (PCAs)	Modifications for Incarceration	Arrears Adjustments for Incarcerated Parents with Modified Orders	Debt Compromise Program
AL	12%	fees for sliding scale application fee = $5–$25 charged only to those who do not receive FA, Medicaid, or foster care services; $25 annual collection fee if at least $500 collected; $10 tax intercept fee; $125.50 to apply for IRS action to collect back support of at least $750; $10 fee each time a Federal payment is offset for child support purposes deducted from automatic payments	None	Incarcerated parents may apply for a reduced support order	Forgive interest only	case-by-case
AK	6%	annual collection fee of $25 charged to custodial parent who has never received TANF/AFDC for each fiscal year after $500 has been collected; reimburse for genetic tests, attorney fees, and process server fees charged to parent ordered to pay	None	Incarcerated parents	Forgive state-owed	pilot

Table 1.13. *Continued*

State	Interest	State OCSE Fees	Legal Limitations on Collections Fees by Private Collection Agencies (PCAs)	Modifications for Incarceration	Arrears Adjustments for Incarcerated Parents with Modified Orders	Debt Compromise Program
AZ	1%	annual collection fee of $25 charged to custodial parent who has never received TANF/AFDC for each fiscal year after $500 has been collected	None	Incarceration cases automatically reviewed for a reduced support order	state settlement program for "life changing events"	case-by-case
AR	1%	The following legal fees are charged to custodial parties who do not receive TEA, Medicaid, or whose child does not receive ARKids 1st: $25 application fee; base costs of 13% (up to $18) per month child support is received; $80 to initiate any court action; $100 when initiated court action settled out-of-court; $150 in-court settlement fee; $250 trial fee; all actual court costs deferred to custodial parent; $35 fee charged for each levy resulting in monetary recovery from a participating financial institution or levy against	AR Code §17-24-101 – §17-24-403, effective 4/13/2009: no collection fee in excess of 50% of the total actually collected on all accounts; no minimue charge in excess of $1 on any partially or totally collected account	No ban, but courts do not favor modification	No policy	no program

		an insurance claim; $25 federal offset fee each year there is an assessment; annual collection fee of $25 charged to custodial parent who has never received TANF/AFDC for each fiscal year after $500 has been collected.			
CA	1%	annual collection fee of $25 charged to custodial parent who has never received TANF/AFDC for each fiscal year after $500 has been collected	CA Family Code, Div 9 §5610-5616, effective 9/29/2006: all orders and agreements must include a collection fee not to exceed 33 1/3 percent of the total arrears and not to exceed 50% of the private collection fee	Incarceration cases automatically reviewed for reduced or suspended support order	Forgive state-owed principal and interest	fully implemented program
CO	8%	annual collection fee of $25 charged to custodial parent who has never received TANF/AFDC for each fiscal year after $500 has been collected	§12-14.1-105, effective 7/1/2006: maximum fee cannot exceed 35% of any amount collected, and no other fees	Incarcerated parents may apply for a reduced support order	No policy	case-by-case

Table 1.13. *Continued*

State	Interest	State OCSE Fees	Legal Limitations on Collections Fees by Private Collection Agencies (PCAs)	Modifications for Incarceration	Arrears Adjustments for Incarcerated Parents with Modified Orders	Debt Compromise Program
CO *continued*			except a contingency fee for collection can be charged by private collection agencies			
CT	0	annual collection fee of $25 charged to custodial parent who has never received TANF/AFDC for each fiscal year after $500 has been collected	§36a-805, effective 6/20/2001: prohibits the imposition of any charge or fee that exceeds 25% of the overdue support actually collected	Incarcerated parents may apply for a reduced support order but not likely granted if the offense was against custodial parent or child	No policy	pilot
DE	0	annual collection fee of $25 charged to custodial parent who has never received TANF/AFDC for each fiscal year after $500 has been collected	none	Incarceration is considered voluntary unemployment, and the law does not permit reduced support orders		

FL	0	annual collection fee of $25 charged to custodial parent who has never received TANF/AFDC for each fiscal year after $500 has been collected	none	Incarcerated parents may apply for a reduced support order post incarceration	No policy	case-by-case
GA	"legal rate" = 7%	annual collection fee of $25 charged to custodial parent who has never received TANF/AFDC for each fiscal year after $500 has been collected and $25 non-refundable application fee for those not currently receiving TANF	§10-1-393.10, effective 7/1/2009: fees in excess of 1/3 of the total child support collected are prohibited	Incarceration is considered voluntary unemployment, and the law does not permit reduced support orders	Forgive state-owed principal and interest	case-by-case
HI	10%	annual collection fee of $25 charged to custodial parent who has never received TANF/AFDC for each fiscal year after $500 has been collected	HRS §443B-9(a), effective 4/22/1994: fees cannot be collected from a debtor, but attorney's fees or commission may be collected up to 25% of the unpaid principal by filing suit	Incarcerated parents may apply for a reduced support order	No policy	case-by-case

Table 1.13. Continued

State	Interest	State OCSE Fees	Legal Limitations on Collections Fees by Private Collection Agencies (PCAs)	Modifications for Incarceration	Arrears Adjustments for Incarcerated Parents with Modified Orders	Debt Compromise Program
ID	5% + base rate (base rate varies annually from 5.375%–11.375%)	annual collection fee of $25 charged to custodial parent who has never received TANF/AFDC for each fiscal year after $500 has been collected and a $25 fee per transaction for the attachment of a state tax refund	§26-2229, §26-2229A: fees in excess of 50% of the amount collected on any account prohibited	Incarcerated parents may apply for a reduced support order	No policy	no program
IL	9%	annual collection fee of $25 charged to custodial parent who has never received TANF/AFDC for each fiscal year after $500 has been collected	§225 ILCS 425/2.04 (a-10), effective 12/31/2005: fee of no more than 29% imposed, but collection fees cannot extend beyond the collection contract	Incarcerated parents may apply for a reduced support order	Forgive state-owed principal and interest	case-by-case

IN	1.5% per month	annual collection fee of $25 charged to custodial parent who has never received TANF/AFDC for each fiscal year after $500 has been collected in addition to a $55 fee per case annually assessed by IN Code 33-37-5-6	None	Incarcerated parents may apply for a reduced support order		no program
IA	10%	annual collection fee of $25 charged to custodial parent who has never received TANF/AFDC for each fiscal year after $500 has been collected in addition to a $25 application fee	None	Incarcerated parents may apply for a reduced support order	Forgive state-owed principal and interest	pilot
KS	12%	annual collection fee of $25 charged to custodial parent who has never received TANF/AFDC for each fiscal year after $500 has been collected in addition to a 4% collection fee for services provided to those who are not receiving TANF	requires compliance with KS rules of professional conduct (K.S.A. 50-623 et seq.) and SC Rule 226	Incarceration is considered voluntary unemployment, and the law does not permit reduced support orders	No policy	limited pilot

Table 1.13. *Continued*

State	Interest	State OCSE Fees	Legal Limitations on Collections Fees by Private Collection Agencies (PCAs)	Modifications for Incarceration	Arrears Adjustments for Incarcerated Parents with Modified Orders	Debt Compromise Program
KY	12%	annual collection fee of $25 charged to custodial parent who has never received TANF/AFDC for each fiscal year after $500 has been collected	None	Incarcerated parents may apply for a reduced support order	No policy	case-by-case
LA	varies annually; legal rate 9.75%	annual collection fee of $25 charged to custodial parent who has never received TANF/AFDC for each fiscal year after $500 has been collected in addition to a $25 application fee for those not currently receiving TANF	None	No ban, but courts do not favor modification	No policy	case-by-case
ME	15%	annual collection fee of $25 charged to custodial parent who has never received TANF/AFDC for each fiscal year after $500 has been collected, and employers or the department administering payment may charge $2 per transaction	§2109, effective 11/22/2003: fees can only be assessed on the amount actually received	Incarcerated parents may apply for a reduced support order	No policy	case-by-case

MD	10%	annual collection fee of $25 charged to custodial parent who has never received TANF/AFDC for each fiscal year after $500 has been collected in addition to a $25 annual fee to the state for cases collecting $3500 in support within a 12 month period	None	Incarcerated parents may apply for a reduced support order	Forgive state-owed principal and interest	pilot
MA	varies; legal rate = 6–12%; revised to 0.5–1% in 2010	annual collection fee of $25 charged to custodial parent who has never received TANF/AFDC for each fiscal year after $500 has been collected	None	Incarcerated parents may apply for a reduced support order	Forgive interest only	pilot
MI	8% annual surcharge; reduced in 2012 to variable rate tied to 5 year US Treasury Note	annual collection fee of $25 charged to custodial parent who has never received TANF/AFDC for each fiscal year after $500 has been collected	None	Incarcerated parents may apply for a reduced support order within 14 days of sentencing for periods of more than 1 year	Forgive state-owed principal and interest	fully implemented program

Table 1.13. *Continued*

State	Interest	State OCSE Fees	Legal Limitations on Collections Fees by Private Collection Agencies (PCAs)	Modifications for Incarceration	Arrears Adjustments for Incarcerated Parents with Modified Orders	Debt Compromise Program
MN	varies; legal rate = 6%	annual collection fee of $25 charged to custodial parent who has never received TANF/AFDC for each fiscal year after $500 has been collected in addition to a $25 application fee	None	Incarcerated parents may apply for a reduced support order	Forgive state-owed principal and interest	case-by-case
MS	set by judge after hearing; legal rate = 8%	annual collection fee of $25 charged to custodial parent who has never received TANF/AFDC for each fiscal year after $500 has been collected in addition to a $25 application fee	None	Incarcerated parents may apply for a reduced support order	No policy	no program
MO	1% per month	annual collection fee of $25 charged to custodial parent who has never received TANF/AFDC for each fiscal year after $500 has been collected in addition to a $10 annual service fee to the state	None	Incarcerated parents may apply for a reduced support order	No policy	no program

MT	0	annual collection fee of $25 charged to custodial parent who has never received TANF/AFDC for each fiscal year after $500 has been collected	None	Incarceration is considered voluntary unemployment, and the law does not permit reduced support orders	Forgive state-owed principal and interest	fully implemented program
NE	10%	annual collection fee of $25 charged to custodial parent who has never received TANF/AFDC for each fiscal year after $500 has been collected	None	Incarceration is considered voluntary unemployment, and the law does not permit reduced support orders		fully implemented program
NV	2% over prime	annual collection fee of $25 charged to custodial parent who has never received TANF/AFDC for each fiscal year after $500 has been collected in addition to an application fee determined by the collection jurisdiction in the state only imposed on those not currently receiving public assistance	None	Incarcerated parents may apply for a reduced support order	Forgive interest only	case-by-case
NH	10%	annual collection fee of $25 charged to custodial parent who has never received TANF/AFDC for each fiscal year after $500 has been collected	None	Incarcerated parents may apply for a reduced support order	No policy	case-by-case

Table 1.13. Continued

State	Interest	State OCSE Fees	Legal Limitations on Collections Fees by Private Collection Agencies (PCAs)	Modifications for Incarceration	Arrears Adjustments for Incarcerated Parents with Modified Orders	Debt Compromise Program
NJ	Federal HHS rates; vary quarterly from 10.75%–13.875%	annual collection fee of $25 charged to custodial parent who has never received TANF/AFDC for each fiscal year after $500 has been collected	None	Incarcerated parents may apply for a reduced support order	No policy	case-by-case
NM	8.75%	fees for families not on TANF may include a $60 fee for locating a parent, $250 fee for establishing support obligation, $150 for modification, $250 fee for support enforcement, $25 fee per tax intercept, and applicable court fees in addition to the annual collection fee of $25 charged to the custodial parent who has never received TANF/AFDC for each fiscal year after $500 has been collected	fee agreement but no expressed fee limitation	Incarcerated parents may apply for a reduced support order	No policy	pilot

NY	9%	annual collection fee of $25 charged to custodial parent who has never received TANF/AFDC for each fiscal year after $500 has been collected	§20–494.1 c, effective 11/26/2003: application fees prohibited and interest or fees in excess of 15% of child support collected is prohibited	Incarceration is considered voluntary unemployment, and the law does not permit reduced support orders	No policy
NC	legal rate = 8%	annual collection fee of $25 charged to custodial parent who has never received TANF/AFDC for each fiscal year after $500 has been collected in addition to a $25 non-refundable application fee charged only to those not currently receiving public assistance	None	Incarcerated parents may apply for a reduced support order	No policy
ND	12%; administratively reset at 6.5% in 2012	annual collection fee of $25 charged to custodial parent who has never received TANF/AFDC for each fiscal year after $500 has been collected; cases exempt from the federally imposed annual fee are charged a $2.10 monthly fee	None	Incarceration is considered voluntary unemployment, and the courts impute minimum wage	No policy

no program

fully implemented program

fully implemented program

Table 1.13. *Continued*

State	Interest	State OCSE Fees	Legal Limitations on Collections Fees by Private Collection Agencies (PCAs)	Modifications for Incarceration	Arrears Adjustments for Incarcerated Parents with Modified Orders	Debt Compromise Program
OH	10%	annual collection fee of $25 charged to custodial parent who has never received TANF/AFDC for each fiscal year after $500 has been collected in addition to a $0.75 transaction fee and $0.40 balance inquiry fee for use of the e-QuickPay card at ATMs	None	Incarcerated parents may apply for a reduced support order	No policy	case-by-case
OK	10%	annual collection fee of $25 charged to custodial parent who has never received TANF/AFDC for each fiscal year after $500 has been collected	§118.4 B.: fees, including attorney fees, cannot exceed 50% of the child support collected	Incarceration is considered voluntary unemployment, and the courts impute minimum wage; although there is no ban on modifications	Forgive state-owed principal and interest	case-by-case
OR	9%	annual collection fee of $25 charged to custodial parent who has never received	§ORS 25.020 (3)(d)(B): interest and fees cannot	Incarcerated parents may apply for a reduced support order	No policy	fully implemented program

PA	legal rate = 6%	TANF/AFDC for each fiscal year after $500 has been collected in addition to a $1 service fee upon application	exceed 29% of child support received unless legal fees accrue	Incarcerated parents may apply for a reduced support order	No policy	case-by-case
RI	12%	annual collection fee of $25 charged to custodial parent who has never received TANF/AFDC for each fiscal year after $500 has been collected in addition to a $20 fee charged to applicants who are not currently on public assistance	None	Incarcerated parents may apply for a reduced support order	Forgive state-owed principal and interest	case-by-case
SC	14%	annual collection fee of $25 charged to custodial parent who has never received TANF/AFDC for each fiscal year after $500 has been collected in addition to a $25 non-refundable application fee	None	No ban, but courts do not favor modification	No policy	case-by-case

Table 1.13. *Continued*

State	Interest	State OCSE Fees	Legal Limitations on Collections Fees by Private Collection Agencies (PCAs)	Modifications for Incarceration	Arrears Adjustments for Incarcerated Parents with Modified Orders	Debt Compromise Program
SD	1% per month	annual collection fee of $25 charged to custodial parent who has never received TANF/AFDC for each fiscal year after $500 has been collected	None	Incarceration is considered voluntary unemployment, and the law does not permit reduced support orders	No policy	case-by-case
TN	12%	annual collection fee of $25 charged to custodial parent who has never received TANF/AFDC for each fiscal year after $500 has been collected	None	Incarcerated parents may apply for a reduced support order	No policy	no program
TX	12%	annual collection fee of $25 charged to custodial parent who has never received TANF/AFDC for each fiscal year after $500 has been collected; cases that receive registry-only services through the State Disbursement Unit are charged $3 for each month support is received (both fees do not accrue simultaneously)	None	Incarcerated parents may apply for a reduced support order	No policy	fully implemented program

	Interest rate	Fees		Incarcerated parents	Forgive state-owed principal and interest	fully implemented program
UT	Federal rates; vary quarterly from 10.75%–13.875%	annual collection fee of $25 charged to custodial parent who has never received TANF/AFDC for each fiscal year after $500 has been collected in addition to $0.01 fee charged to applications from those not on public assistance but paid from state funds; The following fees may also be charged to parents not on public assistance: a fee up to $25 for federal tax intercept and $15 finance charge for state tax intercept, a $5 fee not to exceed $10/month to process payments to debts (except public assistance debt), and a $3.50 fee not to exceed $7/month for each income withholding payment	None	Incarcerated parents may apply for a reduced support order	Forgive state-owed principal and interest	fully implemented program
VT	determined by judge; legal rate = 12%	annual collection fee of $25 charged to custodial parent who has never received TANF/AFDC for each fiscal year after $500 has been collected; a $5 monthly fee is charged to clients receiving OCS services without submitting an application for each support order	None	Incarcerated parents may apply for a reduced support order	Forgive state-owed principal and interest	fully implemented program

Table 1.13. Continued

State	Interest	State OCSE Fees	Legal Limitations on Collections Fees by Private Collection Agencies (PCAs)	Modifications for Incarceration	Arrears Adjustments for Incarcerated Parents with Modified Orders	Debt Compromise Program
VA	legal rate = 8%	annual collection fee of $25 charged to custodial parent who has never received TANF/AFDC for each fiscal year after $500 has been collected; a $25 fee for services charged to applicants who reapply within six months of requesting case closure	None	Incarceration is considered voluntary unemployment, and the courts impute minimum wage; Legislation to allow review has been introduced but has not passed		no program
WA	12%	annual collection fee of $25 charged to custodial parent who has never received TANF/AFDC for each fiscal year after $500 has been collected	None	Incarcerated parents may apply for a reduced support order	Forgive state-owed principal and interest	fully implemented program
WV	10%	annual collection fee of $25 charged to custodial parent who has never received TANF/AFDC for each fiscal year after $500 has been collected	§48-1-307 (j), effective 4/14/2001: interest and fees cannot exceed 10% of the principal	Incarcerated parents may apply for a reduced support order	Forgive interest only	fully implemented program

WI	1% per month	annual collection fee of $25 charged to custodial parent who has never received TANF/AFDC for each fiscal year after $500 has been collected; genetic testing charged on a sliding scale divided between parents (no fee charged to man when tests show he is not the father); court fees for modifying orders paid by parent requesting change if the family is not receiving public assistance; tax intercept fee of 10% not to exceed $25; employers allowed to assess up to $3 for each withholding; $65 fee for processing payments each year on each court case	None	Incarcerated parents may apply for a reduced support order	Forgive state-owed principal and interest	pilot
WY	10%	annual collection fee of $25 charged to custodial parent who has never received TANF/AFDC for each fiscal year after $500 has been collected	None	Incarcerated parents may apply for a reduced support order	No policy	case-by-case

Source: Data on the interest, fees, and legal limitations on private collections fees compiled from the Federal Office of Child Support Enforcement and resources provided by each state's Office of Child Support Enforcement. Data on modifications and adjustments for incarceration are from the Center for Law and Social Policy, and data on debt compromise programs are from the Administration for Children and Families.

Table 1.14. State Drug Screening Policies

State	Drug Screening
AL	no drug testing
AK	no drug testing
AZ	HB 2678 [passed in 2008]: Arizona Department of Economic Security requires urine drug test paid for by the state for welfare recipients when there is "reasonable cause", and those who test positive for illegal drugs are denied cash assistance for 12 months.
AR	no drug testing
CA	AB 2389 [failed in 2008-2009 session]: attempted to require random drug urine testing of CalWorks participants
CO	no state requirement for drug testing; authority devolved to 64 county Human Services agencies
CT	no drug testing
DE	no drug testing
FL	HB 353 [passed July 1, 2011]: requires all applicants for federally-funded TANF assistance pass a drug test before receiving assistance; does not apply to those currently receiving aid; applicants required to pay for tests themselves but reimbursed for the cost of the test if the results are negative for illegal drugs; does not apply to federal food stamp program
GA	HB 464 [currently in House Second Readers]: proposal to require randomly selected drug testing at the expense of the recipient/applicant for no more than 1 test per year; failing a drug test would result in ineligibility for cash assistance; failure to comply would be treated as a failed test resulting in ineligibility
HI	HB 2923 [considered in 2004] proposal to allow for the random testing of welfare recipients; also applied to SNAP
ID	A non-testing drug screen is a condition of TANF eligibility, and treatment is included in the work plan when addiction is present.
IL	The implementation of TANF in this state includes identifying substance abuse problems that inhibit employment and requiring that the recipient cooperate in addressing it or face case closure.
IN	HB 1452 [under consideration]: proposal requires testing for applicant/recipients based on "reasonable suspicion"; positive test for illegal drugs would result in 6 months of ineligibility and/or individual may reapply after completing treatment; proposal limits eligibility for state Medicaid as a result of positive drug test but may allow for treatment costs to be paid by the Division of Mental Health and Addiction

Table 1.14. *Continued*

State	Drug Screening
IA	Individuals who report substance abuse as a work barrier are required to identify and comply with various steps and goals outlined with the case worker in the Family Investment Agreement.
KS	The implementation of TANF in this state includes identifying substance abuse problems that inhibit employment and requiring that the recipient cooperate in addressing it or face case closure. HB 2275 [passed House and hearing before Senate Public Health and Welfare Committee February 24, 2010]: would require all recipients to agree to random drug screening, positive drug tests would result drug treatment, and failure to comply and/ or failing 3 drug tests would result in denial of further state aid
KY	HB 208 [introduced January 7, 2011]: requires screening test as an initial condition of public assistance and once each subsequent year of assistance; results no admissible in criminal proceeding "without the consent of the person being tested"; assistance denied if individual refuses state-paid drug treatment
LA	HB 137 [considered on May 12, 2009 and involuntarily deferred in House Health & Welfare Committee]: proposal sought to expand drug testing to 50% of adult TANF recipients; HB 7 [passed House and under consideration in Senate]: proposal requires random drug testing of 20% of recipients of cash assistance, and those who fail drug testing require rehabilitation
ME	This state's policy is described as being in line with workplace standards which permits the use of tests when there is a "compelling reason" to administer, and the discretion over such matters is left to the case workers. Maine DHHS does not drug test TANF recipients who do not have drug-related felony convictions.
MD	HB 7/SB 671 [passed in 2000]: integrates child welfare and substance abuse treatment to provide comprehensive assessments of substance use disorders and coordinate treatment based on a collaborative intervention model for serving child welfare families, which includes those on cash assistance; no drug testing required of TANF recipients; screening for intervention broadly
MA	H.974 [2011 session]: proposal would require random testing of those with prior drug convictions; testing positive would result in state placement in treatment under the state's mandatory health insurance coverage program
MI	HB 4090 [passed 1999]: statewide random drug testing of all welfare recipients challenged in courts (Marchwinski v. Family Independence Agency, No 99cv10393 & Marchwinski v. Howard 319 F.3d258 2003); struck down as a violation of the Fourth Amendment protection against unreasonable searches in 2003; revised versions under consideration

Table 1.14. *Continued*

State	Drug Screening
MN	HF 331 [introduced 2011-2012 no Senate companion]: proposal seeks to require drug and alcohol screening for determining eligibility, including random drug screening for TANF recipients at the discretion of the case worker; denial of benefits for negative test result until "pattern of negative results satisfies the agency"; applicants/recipients pay full costs of testing
MS	HB 1291 [under consideration in 2011 regular session]: proposal seeks to require random drug testing linked to eligibility; criminal penalties for "willful violations" of drug testing requirements
MO	HCS HB 73 & 47 [passed leg - take effect by default if not vetoed by July 14]: requires drug test for each work-eligible applicant for TANF benefits where "reasonable suspicion" based on screening by the Department of Social Services; testing positive for illegal drugs results in ineligibility for TANF benefits for 3 years from the date of the administrative hearing decision regarding the drug test if they refuse treatment or if they test positive a second time; eligible household members will continue to receive benefits through third-party
MT	HB 1152 [failed House vote in 2011]: would have required drug testing of applicants/recipients for "reasonable suspicion"
NE	no drug testing
NV	no drug testing
NH	no drug testing
NJ	A3858/S2851 [introduced February 22, 2011]: proposes the use of random drug testing for Work First New Jersey program benefits
NM	HB 210 [died in 2011 session]: attempted to require applicants/recipients submit to drug testing as a condition of eligibility; positive drug tests would result in drug treatment, during which time the individual would remain eligible unless he/she fails to complete treatment; also intended to deny low-income energy assistance to those who test positive if payment is in the form of direct assistance to the recipient
NY	A non-testing drug screen is a condition of TANF eligibility, and treatment is included in the work plan when addiction is present.
NC	DRH90083-LR-97C [2011 session]: proposal to require negative drug test to be eligible for unemployment or welfare benefits
ND	left to the discretion of the case worker in the employability plan
OH	no drug testing

Table 1.14. *Continued*

State	Drug Screening
OK	SB 390 [approved by Senate and under consideration in House]: seeks to require drug testing linked to eligibility; positive drug test would require treatment
OR	The implementation of TANF in this state includes identifying substance abuse problems that inhibit employment and requiring that the recipient cooperate in addressing it or face case closure.
PA	HB 1297 /SB 719 [passed House on April 27, 2011/consideration in Senate 2011-2012 Regular Session]: would establish drug testing for 20% of the public assistance recipients convicted of drug-related felony in the previous 5 years or who are on probation for a felony drug conviction every 6 months randomly assigned; refusal or positive drug test would result in ineligibility or loss of benefits for TANF, food stamps, General Assistance, and state supplemental assistance but does not impact Medicaid eligibility; county administered pilot program began January 2012
RI	H 6249 [introduced June 14, 2011]: proposal would require all applicants for cash assistance pass a drug test paid for by applicant; positive drug test would result in 12 months ineligibility unless individual can document the successful completion of treatment, which would allow individual reapply after 6 months
SC	The state pays for drug testing required by prospective employers. If the test is positive for illegal drugs, the case worker utilizes the options available to address the problem, including treatment referral.
SD	HB 1152 [failed House vote in 2011]: would have required drug testing of applicants/recipients for "reasonable suspicion"
TN	HB 0230 [assigned to s/c General Sub of HHR February 9, 2011]: proposal requires drug test for TANF recipients; positive drug test would result in ineligibility for 12 months after test
TX	no drug testing
UT	Utah Human Services Code provides for referral to court-ordered drug screening test when it is determined to be an issue of child welfare
VT	debated but no drug testing required
VA	Applicants required by law to disclose any felony drug conviction(s).
WA	support services for drug screen test when required by employer; individuals eligible for WorkFirst do not have to be referred to receive treatment

Table 1.14. *Continued*

State	Drug Screening
WV	HB 3007 2009 [died, redrafted, and failed to pass House Health and Human Resources Committee]
WI	Any applicant or participant convicted of a drug felony in the past 5 years is required to take a drug test as a condition of eligibility.
WY	HB0072 [failed February 12, 2008]: failing or refusing a drug test required for employment would constitute disqualification from unemployment and public assistance benefits

Source: Public records of state legislatures and state TANF policy manuals.

Appendix B

In 1982, Amartya Sen argued that antipoverty policies should satisfy certain ethically defensible criteria based on the assumption that policies are valuable when they account for the least well off without making others less well off. They are as follows:

1. the *homogeneity axiom* requires the index is invariant to changes in the scale of income distribution and the poverty line;

2. the *focus axiom* requires that the index does not depend only on the income levels of the poor;

3. the *impartiality axiom* prohibits the index itself from depending on the identity of individuals;

4. the *replication invariant axiom* holds that the index should not change if it is calculated based on an income distribution that is the k-fold replication of the original income distribution;

5. the *monotonicity axiom* maintains that a reduction in a poor person's income, holding other incomes constant, increases the poverty index;

6. the *continuity axiom* requires that the index is a function of individual incomes; and

7. the *transfer axiom* holds that the index increases whenever a pure transfer is made from a poor person to someone with more income.

This study utilizes the poverty intensity measure proposed by Sen (1976, 1982) with modifications introduced by Thon (1979) and Shorrocks (1995) to examine the impact of the various states of welfare policy on opportunities to escape impoverishment. It is calculated in Stata 10 using Census data, Health and Human Services (HHS) data, and data from the Bureau of Labor Statistics. Sen's impoverishment index responds to changes in the income of the poor but is not solely dependent on the incomes of the poor. And, the index is sensitive to transfers from the poor to the wealthy. Not all markets are positive sum, so in those cases in which the wealthy increase their profits by minimizing the cost of labor and/or diffusing costs to consumers, the poverty index increases. Additionally, the Sen index is invariant to changes in the scale of the income distribution and changes in the poverty level. So, if everyone is made better-off, the poverty index will not increase. I use the Sen index instead of the poverty level because the federal poverty level fails to account for the quality of life as it is based on gross income, assumes need is only three times the basic food need, does not include the long-term unemployed, and does not account for the extent to which increasingly regressive taxes disparately impact the impoverished. Moreover, the minimum needs gap (which is the ratio of household income to poverty line or other measure of min needs) does not take into account the actual numbers of the poor or income transfers among them. The Sen index is also better than a simple gini coefficient because the Sen index accounts for the marginal impact on the poor rather than merely income inequality. The gini coefficient tells us how much inequality there is in the distribution of incomes. It is expressed as a ratio from 0 (indicating absolute equality) to 1 (indicating perfect inequality). The Sen index used in this study is based on the modified Sen index (the Sen-Shorrocks-Thon [SST] index) proposed by Shorrocks (1995),[1] which can essentially be viewed as a product of the poverty rate, average poverty gap ratio,[2] and one plus the gini coefficient across the population. The measure takes into account the numbers of the poor, their shortfall in income relative to the minimum needs line, and the degree of inequality in the income distribution. It tells us how the least well off are doing compared to those who are better off. Sen's measure of impoverishment indicates the amount of work it would take for the poor to move out of poverty in significant numbers. Basically, it reflects the average of the number of people living in poverty and the extent of their poverty weighted by the degree of income inequality. The higher the index—the wider the poverty gap—the more persistent poverty is for more people, and the more difficult it is for the poor to improve their circumstances relative to those better off.

Sen's axiomatic approach to the measurement of poverty captures the intensity of poverty through measures of impoverishment. The SST Index is most commonly used in comparative approaches to understanding welfare states in the international system. However, there are no studies of the factors affecting impoverishment in the United States to date, and perspective on the factors that affect impoverishment in the United States is essential to understanding the system of poverty governance. Table 2.1 describes the measurement, source, and summary statistics for this dependent variable and for the independent variables.

Table 2.1. Variable List for the Analysis of Impoverishment across U.S. States over Time (1990–2008)

Variable	Source	Mean	SD	Range
Impoverishment	SST Index = (poverty rate)*(average poverty gap)*(1 + gini coefficient for the population); Measure of poverty intensity where impoverishment is the average of the headcount and poverty gap measures weighted by the gini coefficient (Sen 1976; Shorrocks 1995; Thon 1979); calculated in Stata 10 using Census data, HHS data, and BLS data; 150 observations (18.75%) imputed in the calculation of this variable for a strongly balanced panel.	31.62	11.18	1.61–79.11
Workfare	Variable reflecting the enactment of workfare policies across states; 0 = pre-PRWORA; 1 = state implementation of PWORA; 2 = state implementation of WIA; 3 = state implementation of DRA. State Policy Documentation Project http://spdp.org.	1.26	1.12	0–3
Workrate	Rates of working hours for TANF recipients. State Policy Documentation Project http://spdp.org. Administration for Children and Families http://www.acf.hhs.gov/programs/ofa/data-reports/annualreport6/ar6index.htm.	22.93	22.16	0–98.2
State EITC	Variable distinguishing states with refundable EITCs; −1 = no state income tax; 0 = state income tax but no refundable EITC; 1 = state EITC. Neumark, D. and W. Wascher. 2001, "Using the EITC to Help Poor Families: New Evidence and a Comparison with the Minimum Wage," National Tax Journal 54(2): 281–317. Stacy Dickert-Conlin and Scott Houser. "EITC and Marriage," National Tax Journal 55(1): 25–40, March 2002. State Online Resource Center. "50 State Resource Chart," 27 July 2005 http://www.stateeitc.org/map/2005_stateeitc_chart.xls.	−0.67	0.61	−1–1

Variable	Description			
Independent Development Accounts	Measure of the form of independent development accounts; 0 = none, 1 = pilot, 2 = amount limits, 3 = not limited, 4 = limited w/matching option, 5 = unlimited w/matching option	1.10	1.67	0–5
Cost of Living	Cost of living across states; William D. Berry, Richard C. Fording, "An Annual Cost of Living Index for the American States, 1960–1995," *Journal of Politics* 62(2): 550–67. Bureau of Labor Statistics www.bls.gov. U.S. Department of Commerce Bureau of Economic Analysis www.bea.gov.	156.93	60.85	76.61–251.77
Unemployment	Unemployment rate, measured as percentage of states labor force that it is out of work. *Geographical Profile of Employment and Unemployment.* Bureau of Labor Statistics.	5.11	1.38	2.2–11.2
Population Density	Population in 1000s per square mile (excluding water). *The Statistical Abstract of the United States.*	177.09	192.35	0.97–1128.04
Black Population^2	Percent black population squared to reflect the curvilinear relationship. *The Statistical Abstract of the United States.*	629.47	3689.68	0.003–58545
Female-Headed Households	Percentage of households in the state headed by women; 1990–2002 data from the Center for Law and Social Policy www.clasp.org; 2003–08 data from the Annie E. Casey Foundation.	19.59	11.60	10.49–53
High School Education	High school graduation rate. *The Statistical Abstract of the United States.*	80.84	6.98	37–92.7
Welfare Caseloads	Number of families receiving benefits in 1000s. U.S. Department of Health and Human Services Administration for Children and Families. http://www.acf.hhs.gov/news/stats/case-fam.htm.	61703	106975	269–919471

Russell L. Hanson, 2000,

Table 2.1. *Continued*

Variable	Source	Mean	SD	Range
Government Ideology	Ideology index of primary state political institutions. Lower index scores reflect more conservative ideology, and higher index scores reflect more liberal ideology. William D. Berry, Evan J. Ringquist, Richard C. Fording, Russell L. Hanson, "Measuring Citizen and Government Ideology in the American States, 1960–93." *American Journal of Political Science* 42(1) (Jan. 1998): 327–48. Updates available online at http://www.bama.ua.edu/~rcfording/stateideology.html.	50.26	12.86	23.64–74.05
Citizen Ideology	Ideology index of the state's citizens. Lower index scores reflect more conservative ideology, and higher index scores reflect more liberal ideology. William D. Berry, Evan J. Ringquist, Richard C. Fording, Russell L. Hanson, "Measuring Citizen and Government Ideology in the American States, 1960–93." *American Journal of Political Science* 42(1) (Jan. 1998): 327–48. Updates available online at http://www.bama.ua.edu/~rcfording/stateideology.html.	50.09	15.21	8.45–95.97
Corruption	Federal public corruption convictions by state. U.S. Department of Justice. 2004. "Report to Congress on the Activities and Operations of the Public Integrity Section."	17.70	23.10	0–144
Minimum Wage	Inflation adjusted value of the state minimum wage.	4.58	0.26	4.04–5.03

Estimating the net effects of welfare reforms on impoverishment using panel data requires a strongly balanced panel (no missing observations). The data utilized in this study represent the best available measures of each of the variables over a full cycle of the policy process, and the time period covered reflects the most up-to-date information on each variable with imputation that is within reasonable standards (see Abayomi, Gelman, and Levy 2008).

Table 2.2. Generalized Least Squares Regression of Factors Affecting Impoverishment Across States (1990–2008)

Variable	Coefficient	Significance
Workfare	4.2005550 (0.4769481)	***
Workrate	0.0604561 (0.0152755)	***
State Refundable EITC	0.3739283 (0.4311905)	
Independent Development Accounts (IDAs)	0.1395054 (0.1983022)	
Black Population^2	0.0000736 (0.0000725)	
Cost of Living^2	0.0000340 (0.0000130)	**
Unemployment Rate $_{[n-1]}$	0.9215597 (0.2246960)	***
Population Density	0.0049081 (0.0013307)	***
Female-Headed Households	−0.0011947 (0.0346941)	
High School Education	−0.2746915 (0.0579847)	***
Welfare Caseload	−0.0000004 (0.0000023)	
Government Ideology $_{[n-1]}$	0.0377709 (0.0248509)	
Citizen Ideology $_{[n-1]}$	−0.0852467 (0.0197740)	***
Corruption	0.0477337 (0.0120274)	***
Minimum Wage	2.9917080 (1.2681410)	**

Table 2.2. *Continued*

Variable	Coefficient	Significance
Constant	27.9158400	***
	(8.7837690)	
Observations = 950		
Groups = 50		
Wald Chi^2 (15) = 403.02***		

Note: Models estimated using STATA 10. Standard errors in parentheses are heteroskedastic.

***Indicates significance at 0.001 level

**Indicates significance at 0.01 level

The data utilized in this study consists of a panel of U.S. states from 1990 to 2008. A feasible generalized least squares regression tests the net effects of each of the variables on impoverishment. Calculation of the Variance Inflation Factors (VIF) reveals no problematically high levels of multicollinearity. However, a Cook-Weisberg test for heteroskedasticity reveals a Chi^2 of 87.10 with a significance reaching the 0.01 level, indicating that a generalized least squares regression requires correction for heteroskedasticity.

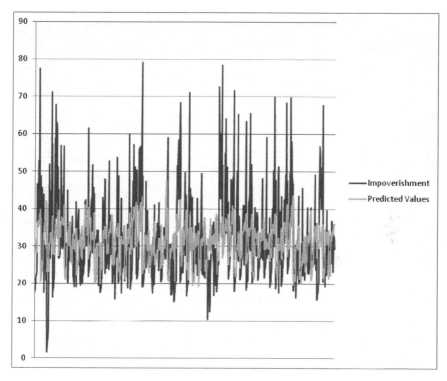

Figure 1B. Net Rates of Impoverishment and Model Predictions from the GLS Regression of the Net Effects of Workfare (1990–2008)

Welfare Reform Legislation	Impoverishment
SSA (AFDC)	25.74
PRWORA (TANF)	29.94
WIA	34.14
DRA	38.34

Figure 2B. Marginal Impact of Welfare Reform Legislation on Impoverishment

TANF Work Rates	Impoverishment
90	35.07
80	34.47
70	33.87
60	33.27
50	32.67
40	32.07
30	31.47
20	30.87

Rates of working hours for TANF recipients

Poverty intensity or difficulty moving out of poverty

Figure 3B. Impact of the Rates of Working Hours of TANF Participants on Impoverishment

Table 2.3. Budgeting Basic Needs by Family Structure in a Sample of States (2002 & 2007)

Family Structure	One Parent One Child (2002)	One Parent One Child (2007)	Two Parents One Child (2002)	Two Parents One Child (2007)	One Parent One Child (2002)	One Parent One Child (2007)	Two Parents One Child (2002)	Two Parents One Child (2007)	One Parent One Child (2002)	One Parent One Child (2007)	Two Parents One Child (2002)	Two Parents One Child (2007)
State	AL	AL	AL	AL	KS	KS	KS	KS	CA	CA	CA	CA
Housing	$577	$690	$577	$690	$691	$754	$691	$754	$1,124	$1,595	$1,124	$1,595
Food	$265	$317	$448	$514	$265	$317	$448	$514	$265	$317	$448	$514
Child Care	$600	$421	$600	$421	$488	$560	$488	$560	$485	$557	$485	$557
Trans-Portation	$272	$339	$387	$482	$255	$318	$358	$447	$222	$277	$321	$401
Health	$307	$232	$395	$319	$263	$216	$336	$303	$221	$185	$299	$243
Taxes	$341	$231	$287	$358	$220	$251	$261	$305	$305	$523	$348	$530
Monthly Total	$2,589	$2,471	$3,071	$3,073	$2,440	$2,674	$2,390	$3,188	$2,997	$3,913	$3,449	$4,346
Annual Total	$31,068	$29,656	$36,852	$36,879	$29,280	$32,090	$34,680	$38,250	$35,964	$46,956	$41,388	$52,146
Minimum Wage Deficit	($21,180)	($15,736)	($17,076)	($17,103)	($19,392)	($18,170)	($14,904)	($10,410)	($20,604)	($31,596)	($10,668)	($21,426)
Poverty Rate	15%	15%	15%	15%	10%	12%	10%	12%	13%	13%	13%	13%

Source: Economic Policy Institute, Basic Family Budgets

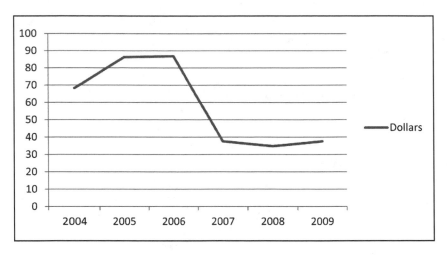

Figure 4B. Work Subsidies to the Private Sector

Appendix C

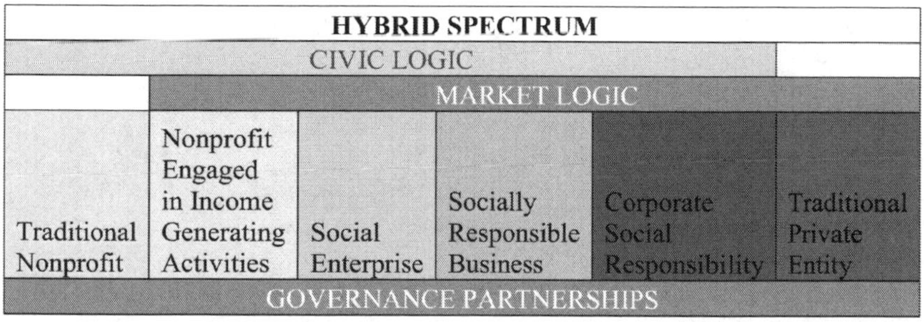

HYBRID SPECTRUM					
CIVIC LOGIC					
MARKET LOGIC					
Traditional Nonprofit	Nonprofit Engaged in Income Generating Activities	Social Enterprise	Socially Responsible Business	Corporate Social Responsibility	Traditional Private Entity
GOVERNANCE PARTNERSHIPS					

Figure 1C. Hybrid Spectrum in Governance Partnerships

Table 3.1. Poverty Ventures Based in the U.S.

Poverty Venture	Year	State	Assets	Grants & Investments	Wealth Leveraged	Focus
Clarence Foundation	2002	CA	$14,436	$29,510	2.044	Global Investment in Social Entrepreneurship
Clarence Foundation	2003	CA	$44,906	$6,300	0.140	Global Investment in Social Entrepreneurship
Clarence Foundation	2004	CA	$65,303	$41,500	0.635	Global Investment in Social Entrepreneurship
Clarence Foundation	2005	CA	$58,002	$109,300	1.884	Global Investment in Social Entrepreneurship
Clarence Foundation	2006	CA	$80,782	$37,465	0.464	Global Investment in Social Entrepreneurship
Clarence Foundation	2007	CA	$127,561	$122,790	0.963	Global Investment in Social Entrepreneurship
Clarence Foundation	2008	CA	$133,992	$80,575	0.601	Global Investment in Social Entrepreneurship
Clarence Foundation	2009	CA	$3,274	$66,929	20.443	Global Investment in Social Entrepreneurship
REDF	2004	CA	$5,700,000	$783,450	0.137	SF Bay Area Investment in Social Entrepreneurship
REDF	2005	CA	$4,500,000	$759,030	0.169	SF Bay Area Investment in Social Entrepreneurship
REDF	2006	CA	$6,700,000	$569,800	0.085	SF Bay Area Investment in Social Entrepreneurship
REDF	2007	CA	$7,500,000	$705,800	0.094	SF Bay Area Investment in Social Entrepreneurship
REDF	2008	CA	$6,200,000	$683,250	0.110	SF Bay Area Investment in Social Entrepreneurship
REDF	2009	CA	$4,400,000	$479,890	0.109	SF Bay Area Investment in Social Entrepreneurship
REDF	2010	CA	$8,200,000	$508,060	0.062	SF Bay Area Investment in Social Entrepreneurship

Organization	Year	State				Project
Women Are Dreamers Too	2003	GA	$7,726	$0	0.000	Human Service Provision Micro Enterprise Training Atlanta Area
Women Are Dreamers Too	2004	GA	$8,509	$0	0.000	Human Service Provision Micro Enterprise Training Atlanta Area
Women Are Dreamers Too	2005	GA	$10,825	$0	0.000	Human Service Provision Micro Enterprise Training Atlanta Area
Women Are Dreamers Too	2006	GA	$10,293	$0	0.000	Human Service Provision Micro Enterprise Training Atlanta Area
Women Are Dreamers Too	2007	GA	$7,577	$0	0.000	Human Service Provision Micro Enterprise Training Atlanta Area
Women Are Dreamers Too	2008	GA	$349	$0	0.000	Human Service Provision Micro Enterprise Training Atlanta Area
Women Are Dreamers Too	2009	GA	$349	$0	0.000	Human Service Provision Micro Enterprise Training Atlanta Area
Appalachian Fund Management Company	2007	KY	$79,539	$5,000	0.063	Fund Management Promoting Economic Development in Appalachian Corridor
Appalachian Fund Management Company	2008	KY	$98,400	$0	0.000	Fund Management Promoting Economic Development in Appalachian Corridor
Appalachian Fund Management Company	2009	KY	$192,114	$160,000	0.833	Fund Management Promoting Economic Development in Appalachian Corridor
Appalachian Fund Management Company	2010	KY	$48,670	$20,000	0.411	Fund Management Promoting Economic Development in Appalachian Corridor

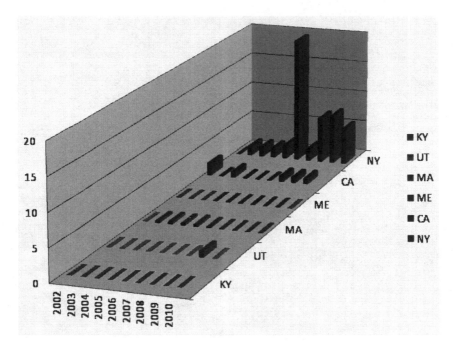

Figure 2C. Wealth Leveraged by Poverty Ventures across States (2002–10)

Table 3.2. Corporate Social Responsibility (CSR) Programs & Poverty

		Corporate Social Responsibility			
State	CSRs	Percentage of Top Grantmaking from CSR	CSR Programs Addressing Poverty in the US	Percentage of CSRs Addressing Poverty	Poverty Rate (2009)
AL	31	0.197%	2	6%	16.6
AK	12	0.134%	0	0%	11.7
AZ	*52	0.180%	3	6%	21.2
AR	13	0.003%	2	15%	18.9
CA	248	0.024%	2	1%	15.3
CO	34	0.026%	0	0%	12.3
CT	49	0.424%	2	4%	8.4
DE	5	0.000%	0	0%	12.3
FL	70	0.088%	2	3%	14.6
GA	53	0.285%	4	8%	18.4
HI	15	0.076%	3	20%	12.5
ID	5	0.005%	0	0%	13.7
IL	124	0.140%	3	2%	13.2
IN	40	0.110%	1	3%	16.1
IA	39	0.120%	4	10%	10.7
KS	21	0.130%	2	10%	13.7
KY	18	0.170%	2	11%	17.0
LA	14	0.000%	0	0%	14.3
ME	16	0.160%	6	38%	11.4
MD	32	0.040%	3	9%	9.6
MA	95	0.253%	4	4%	10.8
MI	60	0.100%	7	12%	14.0
MN	80	0.370%	6	8%	11.1
MS	4	0.010%	0	0%	23.1
MO	49	0.110%	10	20%	15.5
MT	4	0.027%	1	25%	13.5
NE	14	0.040%	6	43%	9.9
NV	12	0.100%	2	17%	13.0
NH	11	0.120%	1	9%	7.8
NJ	53	0.290%	4	8%	9.3
NM	5	0.017%	1	20%	19.3
NY	142	0.130%	3	2%	15.8
NC	27	0.327%	3	11%	16.9
ND	2	0.202%	0	0%	10.9
OH	89	0.274%	7	8%	13.3
OK	17	0.080%	5	29%	12.9
OR	19	0.300%	3	16%	13.4
PA	96	0.559%	4	4%	11.1

Table 3.2. *Continued*

		Corporate Social Responsibility			
State	CSRs	Percentage of Top Grantmaking from CSR	CSR Programs Addressing Poverty in the US	Percentage of CSRs Addressing Poverty	Poverty Rate (2009)
RI	13	0.440%	3	23%	13.0
SC	14	0.130%	2	14%	13.7
SD	5	0.030%	3	60%	14.1
TN	30	0.180%	4	13%	16.5
TX	140	0.151%	1	1%	17.3
UT	13	0.030%	0	0%	9.7
VT	7	0.050%	3	43%	9.4
VA	56	0.140%	6	11%	10.7
WA	32	0.010%	1	3%	11.7
WV	2	0.000%	0	0%	15.8
WI	74	0.110%	3	4%	10.8
WY	1	0.000%	0	0%	9.2
TOTALS	1962	6.892%	134	7%	

*Turf Paradise Foundation dissolved 03/30/2012 due to failure to file annual report

Source: The Grantsmanship Center and the Census Bureau.

Note: Poverty programs refer to those that define assistance to low-income individuals or impoverished communities as a specific initiative but does not necessarily include education, health, or other related programs. The mission statements and list of grantees were used to determine whether the program addressed poverty in the U.S. CSR programs addressing poverty in the US may or may not focus on local, regional, state, and/or beyond but contribute to at least one organization addressing the needs of people living in poverty in that state. CSRs include those programs based in the state; although CSR programs based in other states may be among the top grantmakers contributing to a given state.

Table 3.3. State Laws of Charitable Disposition

State	State Policies of Charitable Disposition	Fundraising Registration Required	URS	Audit	Supp State Forms
AL	Al. Code Sec. 13A-9-70 et seq. & Chapter 3, Title 10A	YES	YES	NO	0
AK	AS 45.68.010 et seq., Chapter 10.20, and 9 AAC 12.010 et seq.	YES	YES	NO	0
AZ	ARS 44-6551-44-6561, ARS Title 42, Chapter 5, and AAC Title 15, Chapter 5	YES	YES	NO	0
AR	Ark. Code Ann. § 4-28-401 & 4-33-101 et seq.	YES	YES	YES	1
CA	Cal. Govt Code §§ 12580-12596; Cal. Code of Regulations, Title 11 §§ 300-310, 999.1-999.4; Bus. & Prof. Code Sec. 17510-17510.85; 22930; Cal. Corp Code Sec. 5250; Cal Code-Division 2 [5000-10841]	YES	YES	YES	1
CO	Colorado Charitable Solicitations Act (Title 6, Article 16, C.RS.) and CRNCA 7.121.101-7.137.301	YES	NO, but 6-16-104.3 gives Sec authority to link existing state efile to URS when "practicable"	NO	N/A
CT	C.G.S. §21A-175, et seq. and CRNCA "Chapter 602"	YES	YES	YES	0
DE	DE Code Title 6, Chapter 19	NO	N/A	N/A	N/A
FL	Fla. Stat. § 617, 212, and 496	YES	NO	NO	N/A

Table 3.3. *Continued*

State	State Policies of Charitable Disposition	Fundraising Registration Required	URS	Audit	Supp State Forms
GA	O.C.G.A. §43-17-1 et seq;; Ga Code Ann. §14-3	YES	YES	YES	1
HI	Hawaii Revised Statutes §467B, 414D, & 429	YES	YES	NO	0
ID	Idaho Title 48 and Title 30, Chapter 3	NO	NO	NO	N/A
IL	760 ILCS 55/1; 225 ILCS 460/1; 805 ILCS 105-150	YES	YES	YES	0
IN	Indiana Code 23-17-3-2	NO	N/A	N/A	N/A
IA	IA Code § 504	NO	N/A	N/A	N/A
KS	KSA Chapter 17-101 through 17-7709 (KGCC)	YES	YES	YES	financial statement
KY	K.R.S. §367.650 and K.R.S. Chapter 273	YES	YES	NO	0
LA	La. R.S. 51:1901-1904; La. Admin. Code, Title 16, Part III, Chapter 5, Sec. 515; La. Title 12	YES	YES	NO	0
ME	9 M.R.S.A. Chapter 385, Sec. 5001-5018; Title 13-B	YES	YES	YES	1
MD	Ann. Code, Bus. Reg. Art., Sec. 6-101 to 7-701; § 14-301 through 302; § 15-407; § 3-513; § 11-204; Title 5	YES	YES	YES	0
MA	Mass. Gen. Law, Chapters 12 & 68; M.G.L. 156B, s.9 and s.11-13; M.G.L. 180	YES	YES	YES	0
MI	MCLA §400.271 and the Nonprofit Corporation Act 162 of 1982	YES	YES	YES	0

	Statute				
MN	Minnesota Statutes ch. 309 and ch. 317A	YES	YES	YES	1
MS	Miss. Code Ann. Sec. 79-11	YES	YES	YES	1
MO	Sec. 407.450, et seq, RSMo supp. 1988 and MO Rev Stat § 355	YES	YES	NO	attach solicitations
MT	Title 35, Chapter 2	NO	N/A	N/A	N/A
NE	21-1901 to 21-19,177 Nebraska Nonprofit Corporations Act	NO	N/A	N/A	N/A
NV	NRS Chapter 82	NO	N/A	N/A	N/A
NH	RSA 7:19 through 7:32-I; RSA Chapter 292; RSA 564-B	YES	YES	YES	attach conflict of interest policy
NJ	NJSA 45:17A-18 though 45; NJSA 15A	YES	YES	YES	0
NM	NMSA Article 22, Sec 57-22; NMAC Article 12.3.3; NMSA 53-8-3 TO53-8-33	YES	YES	YES	0
NY	NYCRR Title 13, Chapter 5; Article 7-A, Executive Law; N.Y.NPC.LAW § 101	YES	YES	NO	0
NC	NCGS Ch. 55A and Ch. 131F	YES	YES	NO	1
ND	No. Dak. Century Code, Chapter 50-22; Tile 10-24 through 10-28	YES	YES	NO	2
OH	Ohio Revised Code Ch. 1716; 109:1-1, 109.23 and ORC 1702 [effective until 5/22/2012]	YES	YES	NO	0
OK	Title 18, Section 1001 (OGCA)	YES	NO	NO	N/A

Table 3.3. *Continued*

State	State Policies of Charitable Disposition	Fundraising Registration Required	URS	Audit	Supp State Forms
OR	Ore. Rev. Stat. 128.610-129 & 65; Ore. Admin Rules § 137, Division 10	YES	YES	NO	0
PA	PA Code Title 19; 10 P.S. Sec. 162.1; Chapter 41	YES	YES	YES	0
RI	R.I.G.I. Title 7, Ch. 7.6; Title 5, Ch. 53.1	YES	YES	YES	0
SC	South Carolina Uniform Code Title 33, Ch. 31 and 56	YES	YES	NO	0
SD	Codified Laws Title 47, Ch. 22-28	NO	N/A	N/A	N/A
TN	TN Code Annotated Sec. 48-51-101 through 48-68-105 and 48-101-501	YES	YES	YES	2
TX	Texas Bus. Orgs. Code Chapter 22	NO	N/A	N/A	N/A
UT	Utah Code Ann. Title 16-6A	YES	YES	NO	1
VT	Title 11B Vermont Nonprofit Corporations Act and Title 9.2	NO	N/A	N/A	N/A
VA	Code of Virginia 57-48 to 57-69; Va. Code Title 13.1, Chapter 10	YES	YES	YES	0
WA	RCW Title 19.09 and Title 24; WAC 458-20-169	YES	YES	YES	1
WV	WV Code Ch. 31E and Ch 29-19	YES	YES	YES	1
WI	Wis. Statutes Ch. 181, Wis. Admin Code Ch. RL5	YES	YES	YES	3
WY	Wyoming Nonprofit Corp. Act W.S. Title 17 Ch. 19	NO	N/A	N/A	N/A

Table 3.4. State Regulation of Foundations

ACCOUNTABILITY TO STATES: FOUNDATIONS

Mandatory reporting and/or licensing provisions	No state licensing or reporting requirements
AL	AK
AR	AZ
CA	DE
CO	GA
CT	ID
FL	IN
HI	MT
IL	NE
IA	NV
KS	OK
KY	OR
LA	SD
ME	TX
MD	VT
MS	WI
MI	WY
MN	
MS	
MO	
NH	
NJ	
NM	
NY	
NC	
ND	
OH	
PA	
RI	
SC	
TN	
UT	
VA	
WA	
WV	

Table 3.5. State Incentives for Charitable Donations

State Individual Income Tax Incentives for Charitable Donations	No State Individual Income Tax Incentives for Charitable Donations	No State Individual Income Tax
AL	CT	FL
AK	IL	NV
AZ	IN	NH
AR	LA	SD
CA	MA	TN
CO	MI	TX
DE	NJ	VT
GA	OH	WA
HI	PA	WY
ID	WV	
IA		
KS		
KY		
ME		
MD		
MN		
MS		
MO		
MT		
NE		
NM		
NY		
NC		
ND		
OK		
OR		
RI		
SC		
UT		
VA		
WI		

Table 3.6. State Laws Governing Hybrid Corporate Forms

L3C	BLLC	Benefit Corporations	Flexible Purpose (FPC)
IL (805 ILCS 180) 2010	MD. Code Ann. Corps & Ass'ns § 4A (2011)	Cal. Corp. Code § 14600-14622 (2012)	Cal Corp. Code § 2500-3503 (2012)
LA (HB 1421/Act 417) 2010		Haw. Rev. Stat. Ann. § 420D (2011)	
ME (H 819) 2011		MD. Code Ann. Corps & Ass'ns § 5-6C (2010)	
MI (Sec. 450.4101 et seq) 2009		NJ Stat. Ann § 14A (2011)	
NC (H769/SB308) 2010		VT Stat Ann. Tit. 11A § 21 (2010)	
RI (H5279) 2012		VA Code Ann § 13.1-782 through 788 (2011	
UT (Tit. 48, Ch. 02c) 2009			
VT (Tit. 11, Ch. 21) 2008			
WY (Tit. 17, Ch. 15) 2009			

Conceptual Appendix

Credible commitment: refers to the development of social norms that foster long-term investments and undermine opportunistic behavior; Shepsle (1991) defines a commitment as credible in the motivational sense when people want to continue to honor commitments at the time of performance and a commitment as credible in the imperative sense when the performance is coerced or discretion is disabled.

Degenerative politics: activities associated with governance "characterized by its exploitation of derogatory social constructions, manipulations of symbols or logic, and deceptive communication that masks the true purpose of policy" (Schneider and Ingram 2005, 11).

Devolution: refers to the process by which the power to design social policy within federal guidelines and the authority to manage social service provision has transferred to subnational units of government.

Feminization of poverty: refers to three distinct poverty trends (see Heymann 2000; McLanahan, Sorenson, and Watson 1989; Pearce 1978): (1) the higher incidence of poverty among women; (2) that women are more likely to experience more severe poverty; and (3) that poverty among women is more persistent as women are at greater risk of being long-term poor.

Market logic: refers to an understanding of social exchange based on the notion that society is comprised of aggregations of self-interested, utility-maximizing individuals in which the central feature of social organization is the maintenance of property rights.

Moral individualism: use of religious principles and the emphasis on the interpretations of religious teachings that focus on individual choices and serve to untangle social obligations or duties.

Mutuality in exchange: refers to the give and take that is freely and independently agreed upon but not necessarily equal; the reciprocal balance over the long term and the maintenance of the free will of all parties is a priority over strict equality at a given moment in time.

Neoliberalism: employs the instruments of governance to create market opportunities, manipulate transaction costs, and impose market discipline (see Brown 2006); Neoliberalism is both an economic theory and an approach to international economic development. Neoliberal economic logic is a supply-side theory, focusing on deregulation of business and individual initiative to understand welfare.

Paternalism: capitalizes on managerial reforms to monitor behavioral expectations, discipline people to market logic, and reinforce social status (Soss, Fording, and Schram 2011a).

Philanthrocapitalism: represents the shifting influence over public priorities to private interests through the financing of social investments using the strategies of venture philanthropy and the implementation of those endeavors through social enterprise.

Poverty governance: a concept that can be defined structurally, normatively, critically, and in terms of politics and ideology. Structurally, poverty governance refers to the contracting networks, intergovernmental grants, public and private sector loans and loan guarantees, and intricate interjurisdictional regulatory regimes (Lynn, Heinrich, and Hill 2000). Normatively, poverty governance refers to processes of governing carried out by laws, norms, power, or language. These processes define the boundaries of inclusion and exclusion, normalcy and deviance, and compliance and disruption (see Bevir 2012). Neoliberal paternalist poverty governance is implemented through devolved authority, increasingly privatized, enacted through diffuse networks of contracted providers, and operates in a competitive environment in which performance metrics dominate evaluations.

Privatization: refers to three distinct mechanisms that diffuse the government monopoly on services: (1) vouchers, (2) welfare transfers to the private sector (e.g., Work Opportunity Tax Credits), and (3) contracting out; welfare privatization also refers to the increasing privatization of the conflict space.

Race-gendered moral order: use of moral reasoning to justify the stratification of wealth and access to opportunities by manipulating social constructions of identity and knowledge in a manner that devalues women and people of color in particular (see, e.g., Jordan-Zachery 2009).

Social constructions: postmodern notion that knowledge and identity are understood through the lenses of experience and manipulated through symbolism, language, logic, and communication.

Social entrepreneurship: encompasses "the activities and processes undertaken to discover, define, and exploit opportunities in order to enhance social wealth by creating new ventures or managing existing organizations in an innovative manner" (Zahra et al. 2009, 522).

Subjects of governance: refers to the people within the province of the authorities defining the boundaries of inclusion and exclusion, normalcy and deviance, and compliance and disruption through the laws, policies, actions, and affairs of order maintenance.

Venture philanthropy: refers to the financing of social investments; differs from traditional philanthropy in that venture philanthropy is conceived of as "highly engaged" partnerships using business metrics to evaluate impact and strategic management focused on sustainability.

Notes

Introduction

1. See Lynn, Heinrich, and Hill (2000) for the most widely accepted structural definition of governance under the neoliberal logic.

2. See Bevir (2012) for a philosophical examination of the meaning of governance in various contexts and usages.

3. Schram, Soss, Houser, and Fording (2009) outline the disciplinary practices that serve to enforce the normative boundaries and social order under welfare reform.

4. Foucault (1991) defines the concept of governmentality as the practices, mentalities, rationalities, and techniques by which subjects learn to self-govern. The exercise of control through acts of governing under neoliberal paternalism are persuasively explained by Schram, Soss, Houser, and Fording (2009).

Chapter 1. Framing the Welfare Policy Process

1. Refer to Herrick and Stuart (2005) for a history of precolonial welfare in North America.

2. For a comprehensive understanding of the construction of identity and status, see Ore (2003), and for a thorough depiction of the legal construction of the trans-Atlantic slave trade, see Finkelman (2002).

3. See Katz (1996) for a complete social analysis of the history of welfare in the United States.

4. Kluegel and Smith (1986), Ladd (1993), and Sidel (1996) use survey evidence to show that Americans tend to believe that poverty is a result of individual failure or poor moral character, and Golding and Middleton (1982) and Martindale (1996) find that media perpetuate these stereotypes.

5. Wilson (2011) describes how Katrina drew public awareness to the plight of urban poverty. He goes on to outline the role public policies such as redlining and highway construction have played in amplifying racial and economic segregation, how the economic forces of employment discrimination and technological and global economic shifts have geographically concentrated poverty, and how cultural stereotypes and isolated intragroup interactions fuel these trends.

6. See Iyengar (1991).

7. See Schneider and Ingram (1997) for the most widely accepted understanding of how the social construction of policy targets may lead to democratic discovery or limit participation and debate.

8. Barrett (1995) effectively establishes the "strong consensus" among black women in state legislatures that poverty is a priority.

9. See Gilens (1996, 1999).

10. See Avery and Peffley (2001).

11. Mendelberg (2001) outlines the political strategies that manipulate racial and gender biases for individual political gain.

12. Quadagno (1996) establishes the role of race in redirecting the war on poverty to a war on welfare crime and then crime generally.

13. Abramovitz (1996) provides a historical analysis of welfare policy, illustrating how the feminization of poverty over time has made it easier for politicians to scapegoat women, and Jordan-Zachery (2009) shows how stereotypes of black women are manipulated to justify policy formulations that punish women of color.

14. See Schneider and Ingram (2005).

15. See Soss, Fording, and Schram (2011a).

16. Hugh Heclo (2001, 183) describes how the complicated history of federalism culminated in an "inadvertent bipartisanship" as party control shifted at different levels of government.

17. Refer to Gring-Pemble (2001) for a narrative analysis of how the rhetoric of welfare reform facilitated elite discourse, discouraged alternative perspectives, and delegitimized the public voices of clients and feminists, particularly women of color. Refer to Naples (1997) for an analysis of how the Congressional hearings on welfare reform constructed a consensus by excluding critical stakeholders and delegitimizing dissent, redefining the social contract in increasingly gendered and individualistic terms.

18. See Sabatier (1999).

19. The realities of the qualitative, lived experiences of people surviving poverty are an equally valid and important subject of study. They also contribute significantly to the systemic understanding of poverty governance that might be designed to alleviate poverty. This study focuses on aggregate opportunities to move out of poverty, but builds on the qualitative work essential to the systemic framework proposed in this book (see e.g.; Abramovitz 2006; Collins and Mayer 2010; Gilliom 2001; Hays 2004; Jordan-Zachery 2009).

20. McEvily, Perrone, and Zaheer (2003) outline the causal pathways that align trust and trustworthiness, which may be applied to the context of poverty governance.

21. Refer to Gring-Pemble (2001) for a narrative analysis of how the rhetoric of welfare reform facilitated elite discourse, discouraged alternative perspectives, and delegitimized the public voices of clients and feminists, particularly women of color. Refer to Naples (1997) for an analysis of how the Congressional hearings on welfare reform constructed a consensus by excluding critical stakeholders and delegitimizing dissent, redefining the social contract in increasingly gendered and individualistic terms.

Chapter 2. The Evolution of Devolution

1. U.S. Department of Health and Human Services. 2008. "Indicators of Welfare Dependence: Annual Report to Congress, 2008." Washington, D.C. Available online at http://www.hhs.gov. Last updated December 30, 2008. Lasted visited July 21, 2014.

2. U.S. Department of Health and Human Services. "FY 2011 TANF Contingency Fund and Supplemental Grant Awards Summary." Available online at http://www.acf.hhs.gov/programs/ofa/policy/im-ofa/2011/im201104/im201104_contingency_fund.html. Site last visited July 21, 2014. Supplemental grants were provided to the following 17 states at a reduced rate in 2011: Alabama, Alaska, Arizona, Arkansas, Colorado, Florida, Georgia, Idaho, Louisiana, Mississippi, Montana, Nevada, New Mexico, North Carolina, Tennessee, Texas, and Utah.

3. Some examples that illustrate the variation in personal responsibility contracts are available online through the following links: https://www.azdes.gov/main.aspx?menu=358&id=5279; http://www.dads.state.tx.us/forms/H1073/; Family & Social Services Admin form 47073 in searchable state database: http://www.in.gov/icpr/3030.htm. Site last visited July 21, 2014.

4. The procedures for calculating eligibility and benefit levels are available through the Urban Institute's Welfare Rules Database.

5. Despite the fact that existing evidence shows no support for the notion that welfare recipients are dependent (Primus 1999), deviant (Gilliom 2001), unmotivated to work, or incapable of saving (Danziger, Haveman, and Plotnick 1981). The welfare dependency thesis was a long-ago disproven notion revived by scholars with oppressive inclinations.

6. It should be noted that reasonable and very important arguments about the necessity of adequate supervision and the importance of family involvement in children's development and later life chances were also integral to the discourse but failed to reconcile the complex dilemmas of work responsibilities and care giving obligations (see e.g., Akerloff and Yellen 1996; Bowles, Gintis, and Grove 2005).

7. See Beryl Radin (2006) for the most influential critical analysis of performance metrics.

8. For a compelling analysis of the state-sanctioned family norm policies as a part of the oppressive structures that perpetuate poverty among the most marginalized communities, see Julia Jordan-Zachery (2007).

9. A relatively recent description of the full spectrum of state-by-state variations in efforts to promote marriage is available online at http://www.clasp.org/admin/site/publications_archive/files/0158.pdf. Site last visited July 21, 2014.

10. Non-displacement provisions are enumerated in TANF (42 U.S.C. § 607(f)) and the WIA (29 U.S.C. § 2931(b)(3)) to prevent the subsidized work from replacing existing unsubsidized work.

11. Sondra Youdelman and Paul Gestos, *Wages Work! An Examination of the NYC's Park Opportunities Program (POP) and its Participants* (New York: Community Voices Hear, 2004).

12. It is worth noting that a good deal of variation in workforce development is evident at the city level. Bennett and Giloth (2007) provide a thorough examination of economic development strategies across five U.S. cities, highlighting the importance of equitable development in sustainable growth through workforce investments in long-term labor market retention in careers offering family self-sufficiency.

13. Soss, Fording, and Schram (2011a) provide a comprehensive understanding of how the politics of social control capitalizes on the fragmented and privatized nature of poverty governance, exacerbating social cleavages.

14. RTW states are those states with laws securing employee rights to choose whether or not to participate or contribute to unions, with some exceptions for rail workers, airline employees, and workers on a federal enclave.

15. Brodkin, Fuqua and Thoren (2002) show how discretionary power affects the access to opportunities and is an excellent example of how important research of this kind informs welfare policy.

16. The NHEP makes their job readiness portfolio available online at http://www.dhhs.state.nh.us/dfa/tanf/documents/portfolio.pdf. Site last visited July 21, 2014.

17. A detailed table of the specific employment strategies and opportunity structures utilized by each state is available at https://docs.google.com/viewer?a=v-&pid=sites&srcid=ZGVmYXVsdGRvbWFpbnxwcm9mZXNzb3JvY2hzfGd4OjRmYT U3YjE4YThlYTZmYTI. Site maintained by the author.

18. The details of the EITC and the WOTC are outlined in the section on PRWORA-related programs of this chapter.

19. A detailed table describing the types of educational opportunities afforded by each state along with the other employment strategies is available at https://docs.google.com/viewer?a=v&pid=sites&srcid=ZGVmYXVsdGRvbWFpbnxwcm9m ZXNzb3JvY2hzfGd4OjRmYTU3YjE4YThlYTZmYTI. *Site maintained by the author.*

20. See Brodkin and Majmundar (2010) for a review of the organizational research on welfare practices.

21. Refer to Soss, Fording, and Schram (2011a) for a thorough analysis of how neoliberal paternalism operates as a poverty governance regime that calls upon moral individualism, utilizes behavioral discipline, and imposes the preeminence of market rationales to manage the way people in poverty govern themselves.

22. The language employed by HHS is interesting. The notion that noncompliance is a disease requiring a "cure" executed by the state suggests that individual participants may not reasonably resist without being considered "sick" and in need of correction or treatment. It might remind one of the mythical condition identified by Samuel Cartwright in 1851, drapetomania.

23. The Center for Law and Social Policy stores policy variations and maintains data on relevant state outcomes. Available online at www.clasp.org. Site last visited July 21, 2014.

24. The exemptions for good cause vary considerably across states, and the application of good cause exemptions represent another area in which discretion affects patterns of practice. Evidence suggests that the boundaries of discretion related to good cause exemptions at the state level are partisan (Keiser and Soss 1998) and that the use of discretion at the street-level enactment varies in complex ways according to caseworker values (Maynard-Moody and Musheno 2003; Watkins-Hayes 2009), although not independent from the organizational forces that shape the use of discretion in predictable ways (Soss, Fording, Schram 2011b).

25. The Center for Social Development at Washington University—St. Louis provides detailed information on state asset-building initiatives, and myriad resources on asset-building approaches are cataloged by the Community-Wealth project of The Democracy Collaborative at the University of Maryland. Available online at http://www.community-wealth.org/strategies/index.html. In addition, the Corporation for Enterprise Development has an IDA directory online at http://cfed.org/programs/idas/directory_search/. Sites last visited July 21, 2014.

26. The Center for Social Development in the George Warren Brown School of Social Work at Washington University in St. Louis tracks state asset building policies, funding sources for asset-building projects, and coalitions facilitating asset-building strategies. Available online at http://csd.wustl.edu/Pages/default.aspx. Site last visited July 21, 2014.

27. It has long been understood that conspicuous consumption is a mechanism for distinguishing oneself from the "other" (see Veblen 1994 [1899]).

28. Chao and Schor (1998) test the independence assumption as it relates to consumer demand and demonstrate that status purchasing is the norm and that it is more likely among those with status. In other words, most people invest in status, and those who can afford to are more likely to do so, contrary to the stereotype.

29. Refer to Carpenter (2008) for a comprehensive review of the research on IDA programs at various levels of analysis.

30. Fragile Families data is available online at http://www.fragilefamilies.princeton.edu/documentation.asp. Site last visited July 21, 2014.

31. See Jordan-Zachery (2007) for a critical analysis of how racialized patriarchy imposes the heaviest costs on black women.

32. Refer to the annual reports and statistics maintained by the ACF. Available online at http://www.acf.hhs.gov/programs/cse/pubs/index.html#annual. Site last visited July 21, 2014.

Chapter 3. The States of PRWORA-Related Welfare Programs

1. The University of Kentucky Center for Poverty Research maintains an extensive dataset on state-level variables related to poverty and state poverty policies. Available online at http://www.ukcpr.org/. Site last visited July 21, 2014.

2. For example, Denver, Colorado, implemented a local EITC pilot program in 2002 that was financed with TANF funds but was suspended in 2004 due to lack of funds.

3. See Eissa and Hoynes (2006), Hoffman and Seidman (2002), Hotz and Scholz (2003), and Meyer and Holtz-Eakin (2002) for literature reviews on EITCs.

4. The most compelling research on the complex relationship between work effort and wages comes from tests of principal-agent models (see Fehr and Gächter 2000; Fehr, Gächter, and Kirchsteiger 1997; Whitford and Lee 2008; Whitford and Miller 2007).

5. The details of the WOTC and the programs that make it up are available online from the IRS at www.irs.gov and the Department of Labor at www.doleta.gov. Sites last visited July 21, 2014.

6. The Government Accounting Office finds no evidence that worker separation is due to employer strategies to increase tax credits. The report to the Chairman, Subcommittee on Oversight, Committee on Ways and Means, House of Representatives on the Work Opportunity Tax Credit is available online at http://www.gao.gov/new.items/d01329.pdf. Site last visited July 21, 2014.

7. The National Labor Exchange maintains links to each state's workforce agency and is available online at http://us.jobs/state-workforce-agencies.asp. The directory of state WOTC coordinators is available through the Department of Labor online at http://www.doleta.gov/business/incentives/opptax/State_Contacts.cfm. Sites last visited July 21, 2014.

8. Data on household food security, hunger and poverty statistics, SNAP participation rates, and community food projects is available from the USDA online at http://snap.nal.usda.gov/professional-development-tools/hot-topics-z/food-insecurity-and-hunger. Site last visited July 21, 2014.

9. James Ohls and Fazana Saleem-Ismail, "The Emergency Food Assistance System—Findings from the Provider Survey." Report FANRR-16-1 by the USDA Economic Research Service, 2002.

10. FRAC is a national nonprofit organization that lobbies for policies addressing hunger. FRAC also maintains data on hunger, food hardship, food access and affordability, national and state food program data, SNAP participation, and poverty data. Available online at http://frac.org/reports-and-resources/. Site last visited July 21, 2014.

11. For the purposes of this discussion, I use SCHIP in reference to the original formulation, and refer to the program as CHIP since the program reauthorization in 2009.

12. U.S. Congress. 1997. Balanced Budget Act of 1997: Report of the Committee on the Budget, House of Representatives. 105th Congress, First Session, to accompany H.R. 2015. Washington, DC, 2101a.

13. The final report on the ELE experiments is available online at http://aspe.hhs.gov/health/reports/2013/ELE/ELE%20Final%20Report%20to%20ASPE%2012%2011%2013.pdf. Site last visited July 21, 2014.

14. The Kaiser Family Foundation maintains an extensive database of resources on Medicaid/CHIP along with state health facts and information regarding how reforms compare to prior policies. Available online at http://www.kff.org/medicaid/index.cfm. Site last visited 06/15/2012.

Chapter 4. The Privatization of Poverty Governance

1. See Table 1.1 in Appendix A.

2. See Michelle Wood, Jennifer Turnham, and Gregory Mills, "Housing Affordability and Family Well-Being: Results from the Housing Voucher Evaluation," *Housing Policy Debate* 19(2) (2008): 367–412.

3. *Wraparound services* refers to an intensive, holistic method of attempting to address the needs of people with complex needs, such as cognitive limitations, physical limitations, multiple mental health diagnoses, etc.

4. MAXIMUS is a private for-profit organization "helping government serve the people" through products and services for children and families, workforce development, TANF, and consulting related to the employer subsidies and tax credits available to business.

5. Florida law requires that the majority of each RWB be comprised of employers, and reports that RWBs around the state have awarded millions in contracts to businesses tied to or owned by the workforce board members are still under investigation.

6. Refer to Table 1.10 in Appendix A to see the breakdown by state over time.

7. Contracts for welfare services may be by type of service rather than being integrated in the manner that Wisconsin has chosen. Case management, employment services, support services, and specialized services may be contracted separately or in different combinations by area or agency. This may also vary by county in some states, creating a tremendous degree of variation.

8. Refer to Wacquant (2009) and Gustafson (2009) for compelling analyses of how state disciplinary operations have wed welfare systems with the penal logic that drives "get tough" criminal justice policies that contribute to mass incarceration. For a thorough assessment of how these patterns of practice fit into the broader practice of poverty governance, see Soss et al. (2011).

9. U.S. Census Bureau. 2000. "The Survey of Program Dynamics." Available online at http://www.census.gov/spd/. Site last visited July 21, 2014.

10. HHS provides status reports and updates on projects funded by federal appropriations to study welfare outcomes online at http://aspe.hhs.gov/_/office_specific/hsp.cfm. Site last visited July 21, 2014.

Chapter 5. Workfare Policies and the State of Self-Sufficiency

1. Table 2.1 in Appendix B outlines the source, measurement, and summary statistics for each variable in the analysis.

2. Data in the table reflect the budget gaps for a parent or parents working full time.

3. See Hotz and Schultz (2003), Hoffman and Seidman (2002), Meyer and Holtz-Eakin (2002), and Eissa and Hoynes (2006) for literature reviews on EITCs.

4. A dummy variable was also tested in place of the measure of the structure of IDA programs, and neither variable reached statistical significance.

5. It should be noted that the model was tested with a cross-section of data from the year 2002 replacing the federal prosecutions of corruption measure with the Boylan and Long (2003) measure of corruption, and the perceived levels of corruption across states were found to be a statistically significant (0.001 level)

factor contributing to impoverishment. In 2002, states with higher levels of corruption according to the survey of assessments by statehouse reporters of the priority of corruption in federal prosecutions had more intense poverty than states with lower levels of corruption.

Chapter 6. Philanthrocapitalism

1. It is important to note that poverty ventures can only be distinguished by the primary objective identified in the mission statement. Consequently, Corporate Social Responsibility (CSR) cannot be parsed by poverty objectives exclusively. Furthermore, the direct action of affinity groups (a small group of individuals engaging in direct action to address a cause) cannot be accounted for in these data, as affinity groups may address poverty but are less likely to form legally recognized organizations (e.g., some green anarchist providing food for communities) or may be a loosely organized group of grantmakers with common interests (see e.g., Council on Foundations Section on Affinity Groups available online at http://www.cof.org/about/affinitygroups.cfm. Site last visited July 22, 2014).

2. Refer to the works of Peter Dobkin Hall (2006, 2002, 1992) for a comprehensive overview of the history of voluntary action, philanthropy, and the development of the nonprofit sector in the United States.

3. See Brody (2006) for an outline of the legal framework for the nonprofit context, Brody (2010) for a comprehensive description of property tax exemptions for charities, Lynn, Heinrich, and Hill (2000) for a model of governance that outlines contracting relationships, and Gugerty and Prakesh (2010) for a model of voluntary regulation.

4. Table 3.4 in Appendix C identifies the states that have licensing and/or reporting requirements and those that have not passed legislation requiring licensing or registration.

5. This streamlined system developed from a collaborative effort on the part of the charitable community and the National Association of State Charity Officials (NASCO) and can be downloaded at www.nonprofits.org/library/gov/urs/. Site last visited July 23, 2014.

6. A list of the required supplementary forms specific to each of these states is provided by the National Association of Attorneys General (NAAG) and the National Association of State Charities Officials (NASCO) in collaboration with the Multi-State Filer Project (MFP). Available online at www.multistatefiling.org. Site last visited July 23, 2014.

7. Refer to IRS tax code 7.26.3.9.1 (11-19-1999) for the detailed requirements.

8. Experimental research shows that unethical behavior is more likely among wealthier classes but also demonstrates that exposure to "other" groups and a better understanding of the circumstances of poverty can elicit compassion (see Côté, Piff, and Willer 2013; Piff, Stancato, Côté, Mendoza-Denton, and Keltner 2012).

Conclusion

1. Jodie Levin-Epstein, *The IRA: Individual Responsibility Agreements and TANF Family Life Obligations* (Washington, DC: The Center for Law and Social Policy, 1998). Available online at http://www.clasp.org/admin/site/publications/files/0027.pdf. Site last visited July 24, 2014.

Appendix B

1. See Xu and Osberg (2002) for a review of axiomatic approaches to the measurement of poverty.

2. The poverty gap ratio is an expression of the total amount of money necessary to raise people who are poor from their present incomes to the poverty line.

References

Aaronson, Daniel, and Daniel Sullivan. 2001. "Growth in Worker Quality." *Federal Reserve Bank of Chicago Economic Perspectives* 25(4): 53–74.

Abayomi, Kobi, Andrew Gelman, and Marc Levy. 2008. "Diagnostics for Multivariate Imputations." *Journal of the Royal Statistical Society* 57(3): 273–91.

Abramovitz, Mimi. 1988. *Regulating the Lives of Women: Social Welfare Policy from Colonial Times to the Present*. Boston: South End Press.

———. 1999. *Regulating the Lives of Women: Social Welfare Policy from Colonial Times to the Present*. Cambridge: South End Press.

———. 2006. "Neither Accidental, Nor Simply Mean-Spirited: The Context for Welfare Reform." In *The Promise of Welfare Reform: Political Rhetoric and the Reality of Poverty in the Twenty-First Century*, eds. K. M. Kilty, and Elizabeth A. Segal. New York: Haworth Press.

AFSCME (American Federation of State, County, and Municipal Employees, AFL-CIO). 2006. *Government for Sale: An Examination of the Contracting Out of State and Local Government Services*. 8th Edition. Available online: http://www.afscme.org/news-publications/publications/privatization/pdf/GovernmentSale.pdf. Accessed July 24, 2014.

Aizer, Anna, and Sara McLanahan. 2006. "The Impact of Child Support Enforcement on Fertility, Parental Investments, and Child Well-Being." *Journal of Human Resources* 41(1): 28–45.

Akerlof, George. 1997. "Social Distance and Social Decisions." *Econometrica* 65(5): 1005–27.

Akerlof, George, and Janet Yellen. 1996. *An Analysis of Out-of-Wedlock Births in the United States*. Washington, DC: Brookings.

Alesina, Alberto, and Edward L. Glaeser. 2004. *Fighting Poverty in the US and Europe: A World of Difference*. Oxford: Oxford University Press.

Alesina, A., and E. La Ferrara. 2002. "Who Trusts Others?" *Journal of Public Economics* 85: 207–34.

Allard, Scott W., and Sheldon Danziger. 2003. "Proximity and Opportunity: How Residence and Race Affect the Employment of Welfare Recipients." *Housing Policy Debate* 13(4): 675–700.

Alter, Sutia Kim. 2006. "Social Enterprise Models and Their Mission and Money Relationships." In *Social Entrepreneurship: New Paradigms of Sustainable Social Change*, ed. Alex Nicholls. New York: Oxford University Press.

Andringa, Robert C., and Ted W. Engstrom. 2002. *Nonprofit Board Answer Book*. Washington, DC: Board Source.

Angel, Ronald J., Sonia M. Frias, and Terrence D. Hill. 2005. "Determinants of Household Insurance Coverage among Low-Income Families from Boston, Chicago, and San Antonio: Evidence from the Three-City Study." *Social Science Quarterly* 86(4): 1338–53.

Arrow, Kenneth. 1962. "Economic Welfare and the Allocation of Resources for Invention." *The Rate and Direction of Inventive Activity: Economic and Social Factors*. NBER. 609–626.

Austin, Curtis. 2005. *Workforce Investment Act Reauthorization: Hearing before the Subcommittee on Employment Safety and Training of the Senate Committee on Health, Education, Labor, and Pensions.* 108th Congress. (June 18, 2003) (testimony of Curtis C. Austin, President of Workforce Florida, Inc.).

Avery, James M., and Mark Peffley. 2003. "Race Matters: The Impact of News Coverage of Welfare Reform on Public Opinion." In *Race and the Politics of Welfare Reform*, eds. Sanford Schram, Joe Soss, and Richard Fording. Ann Arbor: University of Michigan Press, 131–50.

Bachrach, Peter, and Morton S. Baratz. 1962. "Two Faces of Power." *American Political Science Review* 56(4): 947–52.

Baden, S., and K. Milward. 2000. *Gender Inequality and Poverty*. Washington, DC: BRIDGE.

Baker, Ted, and Reed Nelson. 2005. "Creating Something from Nothing: Resource Construction through Entrepreneurial Bricolage." *Administrative Science Quarterly* 50(3): 329–66.

Bane, Mary Jo, and David Ellwood. 1994. *Welfare Realities: From Rhetoric to Reform*. Cambridge: Harvard University Press.

Banfield, Edward. 1970. *The Unheavenly City*. Boston: Little, Brown.

Bania, Neil, Claudia Coulton, and Laura Leete. 2003. "Public Housing Assistance, Public Transportation, and the Welfare-to-Work Transition." *Cityscape: A Journal of Policy Development and Research* 6(2): 7–44.

Barrett, Edith. 1995. "The Policy Priorities of African American Women in State Legislatures." *Legislative Studies Quarterly* 20(2): 223–47.

Bartels, Larry. 2008. *Unequal Democracy: The Political Economy of the New Gilded Age*. Princeton: Princeton University Press.

Bax, E., L. Blessing, A. Gurung, S. Harger, W. Lambe, and J. Wheeler. 2005. "Administering the Individual Development Account: A report for the North Carolina Department of Labor." Raleigh: NC: North Carolina Department of Labor.

Bennett, Michael, and Robert Giloth. 2007. *Economic Development in American Cities: The Pursuit of an Equity Agenda*. Albany: State University of New York Press.

Berner, Maureen, Sharon Paynter, and Emily Anderson. 2009. "When Even the 'Dollar Value Meal' Costs Too Much: Food Insecurity and Long Term Dependence on Food Pantry Assistance." Paper presented at the Midwest Political Science Association Annual Conference. Chicago, IL. April 3, 2009.

Bernstein, A. 1999. *Insurance Status and Use of Health Services by Pregnant Women*. Washington, DC: March of Dimes.

Bevir, Mark. 2012. *Governance: A Very Short Introduction*. Oxford: Oxford University Press.

Blank, Rebecca M. 1995. "Outlook for the U.S. Labor Market and Prospects for Low-Wage Entry Jobs." In *Social Safety Nets in the United States—Briefing Book*, eds. M. B. Demetra Nightingale and Pamela Holcomb. Washington, DC: Urban Institute Press.

———. 1997. "Policy Watch: The 1996 Welfare Reform." *Journal of Economic Perspectives* 11(1): 169–77.

Bornstein, David, and Susan Davis. 2010. *Social Entrepreneurship: What Everyone Needs to Know*. Oxford: Oxford University Press.

Boschee, Jerr. 2006. "Social Entrepreneurship: The Promise and the Perils." In *Social Entrepreneurship: New Paradigms of Sustainable Social Change*, ed. Alex Nicholls. New York: Oxford University Press, 356–90.

Bowles, Samuel, Herbert Gintis, and Melissa Osborne Groves. 2005. *Unequal Chances: Family Background and Economic Success*. Princeton: Princeton University Press.

Boylan, Richard T., and Cheryl X. Long. 2003. "A Survey of State House Reporters' Perception of Public Corruption." *State Politics and Policy Quarterly* 3(4): 420–38.

Brady, Henry E., Sidney Verba, and Kay Lehman Schlozman. 1995. "Beyond SES: A Resource Model of Political Participation." *American Political Science Review* 89(2): 271–94.

Brehm, John, and Wendy Rahn. 1997. "Individual Level Evidence for the Causes and Consequences of Social Capital." *American Journal of Political Science* 41: 888–1023.

Brodkin, Evelyn. 2006. "Bureaucracy Redux: Management Reformism and the Welfare State." *Journal of Public Administration Research and Theory* 17: 1–17.

Brodkin, Evelyn, and Malay Majmundar. 2010. "Administrative Exclusion: Organizations and the Hidden Costs of Welfare Claiming." *Journal of Public Administration Research and Theory* 20: 827–48.

Brodkin, Evelyn, Carolyn Fuqua, and Katarina Theron. 2002. "Contracting Welfare Reform: Uncertainties of Capacity-Building within Disjointed Federalism." *JCPR: Working Paper of the Project on the Public Economy of Work* 284.

Brody, Evelyn. 2006. "The Legal Framework for Nonprofit Organizations." In *The Nonprofit Sector*, eds. Walter Powell and Richard Steinberg. New Haven: Yale University Press, 243–66.

———. 2010. "All Charities are Property-Tax Exempt, but Some Charities are More Exempt Than Others." *New England Law Review* 44: 621.

Brophy-Baermann, Michelle, and Andrew Bloeser. 2006. "Stealthy Wealth: The Untold Story of Welfare Privatization." *Harvard International Journal of Press/ Politics* 11(3): 89–112.

Brown, David, Michael Touchton, and Andrew B. Whitford. 2011. "Political Polarization as a Constraint on Government: Evidence from Corruption." *World Development* 39(9): 1516–29.

Brown, Lawrence, and Lawrence Jacobs. 2008. *Private Abuse of the Public Interest: Market Myths and Policy Muddles.* Chicago: University of Chicago Press.

Brown, Robert D. 1995. "Party Cleavages and Welfare Effort in the American States." *American Political Science Review* 89(1): 23–33.

Brownson, Ross C., Elizabeth A. Baker, Terry L. Leet, and Kathleen N. Gillespie. 2003. *Evidence-Based Public Health.* New York: Oxford University Press.

Bruch, Sarah, Myra Max Ferree, and Joe Soss. 2010. "From Policy to Polity: Democracy, Paternalism, and the Incorporation of Disadvantaged Citizens." *American Sociological Review* 75(2): 205–26.

Bruen, B., and F. Ullman. 1999. *Children's Health Insurance Programs: Where States Are, Where They Are Headed.* In the series, New Federalism: Issues and Options for States, no. A-20. Washington, DC: Urban Institute.

Brush, Lisa D. 2006. "Safety and Self-Sufficiency: Rhetoric and Reality in the Lives of Welfare Recipients." In *The Promise of Welfare Reform: Political Rhetoric and the Reality of Poverty in the Twenty-First Century*, eds. K. M. Kilty, and Elizabeth A. Segal. New York: Haworth Press.

Caputo, Marc. 2004a. "Jobs Firm Probed for Fraud." *Miami Herald*, January 28.

———. 2004b. "Labor Records Sloppy." *Miami Herald*, January 31.

Carpenter, Emily. 2008. *Major Findings from IDA Research in the United States.* Washington University in St. Louis CSD Report No. 08-04.

Carrington, William J., and Bruce C. Fallick. 2001. "Do Some Workers Have Minimum Wage Careers?" *Monthly Labor Review* 124(5): 17–27.

Case, Anne, I-Fen Lin, and Sara McLanahan. 2003. "Explaining Trends in Child Support: Economic, Demographic, and Policy Effects." *Demography* 40(1): 171–89.

Chant, Silvia. 2009. "Dangerous Equations? How Female-headed Households Became the Poorest of the Poor: Causes, Consequences, and Cautions." *IDS Bulletin* 35(4): 19–26.

Chao, A., and J. Schor. 1998. "Empirical Tests of Status Consumption: Evidence from Women's Cosmetics." *Journal of Consumer Psychology* 19: 107–31.

Cherlin, Andrew, Karen Bogen, James M. Quane, and Linda Burton. 2002. "Operating Within the Rules: Welfare Recipients' Experiences with Sanctions and Case Closings." *Social Service Review* 76: 387–405.

Christner, A. M. 2003. *IDA Demonstration Project in Rhode Island Yielded Successful Outcomes and Lessons Learned.* Cranston, RI: A&M Consulting.

Cohen, Adam. 1998. "When Wall Street Runs Welfare." *Time*, March 23.

Cohen, Wesley, and Daniel A. Levinthal. 1990. "Absorptive Capacity: A New Perspective on Learning and Innovation." *Administrative Science Quarterly* 35(1): 128–52.

Collins, Jane, and Victoria Mayer. 2010. *Both Hands Tied: Welfare Reform and the Race to the Bottom of the Low-Wage Labor Market*. Chicago: University of Chicago Press.

Cooper, R., J. Kennelly, R. Durazo-Arvizu, H. Oh, G. Kaplan, and J. Lynch. 2001. "Relationship between Premature Mortality and Socioeconomic Factors in Black and White Populations of U.S. Metropolitan Areas." *Public Health Reports* 116(5): 464–73.

Costa, Dora L., and Matthew E. Kahn. 2006. "Public Health and Mortality: What Can We Learn from the Past?" In *Public Policy and Income Distribution*, eds. Alan Auerbach, David Card, and John Quigley. New York: Russell Sage Foundation.

Côté, S., P. Piff, and R. Willer. 2013. "For Whom Do the Ends Justify the Means? Social Class and Utilitarian Moral Judgment." *Journal of Personality and Social Psychology* 104: 490–503.

Coulton, Claudia, Younghee Lim, Thomas Cook, Nina Lalich. 2003. "Did Welfare Leavers Employment Levels and Job Characteristics Change During TANF Implementation: An Analysis Using SIPP 1996–2000." Joint Center on Poverty Research Working Paper Series. University of Chicago and Northwestern University. Available online at http://www.jcpr.org/. Retreived July 17, 2014. Site last visited on July 24, 2014.

Council on Foundations. 2008. Foundation basics. http://www.cof.org/templates/41.cfm?ItemNumber=17611. Accessed July 28, 2014.

Cunningham, Peter, and Michael H. Park. 2000. *Recent Trends in Children's Health Insurance Coverage: No Gains for Low-Income Children*. Issue Brief No. 29. Findings from HSC Washington, D.C.: Center for Studying Health System Change. Available online at http://www.hschange.org. Accessed July 24, 2014.

Czajka, John, and Cara Olsen. 2000. *The Effects of Trigger Events on Changes in Children's Health Insurance Coverage*. Washington, DC: Mathematica Policy Research.

Danziger, Sandra, and Kristin Seefeldt. 2002. "Barriers to Employment and the 'Hard to Serve': Implications for Services, Sanctions, and Time Limits." *Focus* 22: 76–81.

Danziger, Sheldon, and Peter Gottschalk. 1995. *America Unequal*. Cambridge: Harvard University Press.

Danziger, Sheldon, and Robert Haveman. 2001. "Introduction: The Evolution of Poverty and Antipoverty Policy." In *Understanding Poverty*, eds. Sheldon Danziger and Robert Haveman. New York: Russell Sage Foundation.

Danziger, Sheldon, Robert Haveman, and Richard Plotnick. 1981. "How Income Transfer Programs Affect Work, Savings, and the Income Distribution." *Journal of Economic Literature* 19: 975–1028.

Deaton, A., and D. Lubotsky. 2003. "Mortality, Inequality, and Race in American Cities and States." *Social Science and Medicine* 56(6): 1139–53.

DeHoog, Ruth Hoogland. 1985. *Contracting Out for Human Services: Economic, Political, and Organizational Perspectives*. Albany: State University of New York Press.

Delong, J., Lawrence Katz, and Claudia Goldin. 2003. "Sustaining U.S. Economic Growth." In *Agenda for the Nation*, eds. Henry Aaron, James Lindsay, and Pietro Nivola. Washington, DC: Brookings.

DeParle, Jason. 2004. "The 'Employment First' Welfare State: Lessons from the New Deal for Young People." *Social Policy and Administration* 37(7): 709–24.

Derthick, Martha. 1990. *Agency under Stress: The Social Security Administration in American Government*. Washington, DC: Brookings.

Dewees, S., and L. Florio. 2002. *Sovereign Individuals, Sovereign Nations: Promising Practice for IDA Programs in Indian Country*. Fredericksburg, VA: First Nations Development Institute.

Dias, Janice Johnson, and Steven Maynard-Moody. 2006. "For-Profit Welfare: Contracts, Conflicts, and the Performance Paradox." *Journal of Public Administration Research and Theory* 17: 189–211.

Druckman, Jacobs. 2011. "Segmented Representation: The Reagan White House and Disproportionate Responsiveness." In *Who Gets Represented?*, eds. Christopher Wlezien and Peter Enns. New York: Russell Sage.

Dubay, Lisa, and Genevieve Kenney. 2009. "The Impact of CHIP on Children's Insurance Coverage: An Analysis Using the National Survey of America's Families." *Health Services Research* 44(6): 2040–59.

Easterly, William, and Ross Levine. 1997. "Africa's Growth Tragedy: Politics and Ethnic Divisions." *Quarterly Journal of Economics* 112 (4): 1203–50.

Ehrenreich, Barbara. 1997. "The New Right Attack on Social Welfare." In *The Mean Season: The Attack on the Welfare State*, eds. Frances Fox Piven, Richard A. Cloward, Barbara Ehrenreich, and Fred Block. New York: Pantheon, 161–93.

Eissa, N., and H. Hoynes. 2004. "Taxes and the Labor Market Participation of Married Couples: The Earned Income Tax Credit." *Journal of Public Economics* 88(9–10): 1931–58.

———. 2006. "Behavioral Responses to Taxes: Lessons from the EITC and Labor Supply." In *Tax Policy and the Economy*, ed. J. Poterba. Cambridge: MIT Press, 74–110.

Emshoff, J., C. Courenay-Quirk, K. Broomfield, and C. Jones. 2002. *Atlanta Individual Development Account Pilot Program: Final Report*. Atlanta: United Way of Metropolitan Atlanta.

Etzioni, Amitai. 1994. *The Spirit of Community*. New York: Touchstone.

Fayolle, Alain, and Harry Matlay. 2010. *Handbook of Research on Social Entrepreneurship*. Northampton, MA: Elgar.

Fehr, Ernst, Simon Gächter, and Georg Kirchsteiger. 1997. "Reciprocity as a Contract Enforcement Device." *Econometrica* 65(4): 833–60.

Fehr, Ernst, and Simon Gächter. 2000. "Cooperation and Punishment in Public Goods Experiments." *American Economic Review* 90(4): 980–94.

Finkelman, Paul. 2002. *Slavery and the Law*. Lanham, MD: Rowman and Littlefield.

Finsel, C., and Russ, J. 2005. "Exploration and Use of Individual Development Accounts by Three American Indian Tribes in Oregon." (CSD Research Report). St. Louis: Washington University, Center for Social Development.

Fording, Richard. 1997. "The Conditional Effect of Violence as a Political Tactic: Mass Insurgency, Welfare Generosity, and Electoral Context in the American States." *American Journal of Political Science* 41: 1–29.

————. 2001. "The Political Response to Black Insurgency: A Critical Test of Competing Theories of the State." *American Political Science Review* 95(1): 115–31.

Fording, Richard, Joe Soss, and Sanford Schram. 2011. "Race and the Local Politics of Punishment in the New World of Welfare." *American Journal of Sociology* 116(5): 1610–57.

Foucault, Michel. 1988. "The Ethic of Care for the Self as a Practice of Freedom." In *The Final Foucault*, eds. J. Bernauer and D. Rasmussen. Cambridge: MIT Press, pp. 1–20.

————. 1991. "Governmentality." Trans. R. Braidotti and rev. C. Gordon. In *The Foucault Effect: Studies in Governmentality*, eds. G. Burchell, C. Gordon, and P. Miller. Chicago: University of Chicago Press, 87–104.

Frank, Deborah, Nicole Neault, Anne Skalicky, John Cook, Jacqueline Wilson, Suzette Levenson, Alan Meyers, Timothy Heeren, Diana Cutts, Patrick Casey, Maureen Black, and Carol Berkowitz. 2006. "Heat or Eat." *Pediatrics* 118(5): 1293–1302.

Freeman, Richard B., and Joel Rogers. 2007. "The Promise of Progressive Federalism." In *Remaking America: Democracy and Public Policy in an Age of Inequality*, eds. Joe Soss, Jacob Hacker, and Suzanne Mettler. New York: Russell Sage Foundation.

Fung, Archon. 2004. *Empowered Participation: Reinventing Urban Democracy.* Princeton: Princeton University Press.

Gainsborough, Juliet F. 2003. "To Devolve or Not to Devolve? Welfare Reform in the States." *Policy Studies Journal* 31(4): 603–23.

Galinsky, Adam D., and Gordon B. Moskowitz. 2000. "Perspective Taking: Decreasing Stereotype Expression, Stereotype Accessibility, and In-group Favoritism." *Journal of Personality and Social Psychology* 78: 708–24.

Galston, William. 1991. *Liberal Purposes: Goods, Virtues, and Diversity in the Liberal State.* Cambridge: Cambridge University Press.

Garand, James C. 2010. "Income Inequality, Party Polarization, and Roll-Call Voting in the U.S. Senate." *Journal of Politics* 72(4): 1109–28.

Garfinkel, Irwin, Daniel Gaylin, Chung Huang, and Sara McLanahan. 2003. "Will Child Support Enforcement Reduce Nonmarital Childbearing." *Journal of Population Economics* 16: 55–70.

Garrett, Bowen, and Alshadye Yemane. 2006. "Racial and Ethnic Differences in Insurance Coverage and Health Care Access and Use: A Synthesis of Findings from the 'Assessing the New Federalism Project.'" Washington, DC: Urban Institute Discussion Paper 06-01.

Gilens, Martin. 1996. "'Race Coding' and White Opposition to Welfare." *American Political Science Review* 90(3): 593–604.

————. 2000. *Why Americans Hate Welfare.* Chicago: University of Chicago Press.

————. 2005. "Inequality and Democratic Responsiveness." *Public Opinion Quarterly* 69: 778–96.

————. 2009. "Preference Gaps and Inequality in Representation." *PS: Political Science and Politics* 70(2): 335–41.

————. 2012. *Affluence and Influence: Economic Inequality and Political Power in America.* New York: Princeton University Press and the Russell Sage Foundation.

Gilliom, John. 2001. *Overseers of the Poor: Surveillance, Resistance, and the Limits of Privacy*. Chicago: University of Chicago Press.

Gittleman, Maury, and Edward N. Wolff. 2005. "U.S. Black-White Wealth Inequality." In *Social Inequality*, ed. K. M. Neckerman. New York: Russell Sage Foundation.

Goggin, Malcolm L. 1999. "The Use of Administrative Discretion in Implementing the State Children's Health Insurance Program." *Publius* 29(2): 35–51.

Gold, Rachel Benson, and Adam Sonfield. 2001. "Reproductive Health Services for Adolescents under the State Children's Health Insurance Program." *Family Planning Perspectives* 33(2): 81–87.

Golding, Peter, and Sue Middleton. 1982. *Images of Welfare*. Oxford: Martin Robertson.

Goldsmith, William, and Edward Blakely. 2013. *Separate Societies*. Philadelphia: Temple University Press.

Gonzalez-Baker, Susan. 1993. "Immigration Reform: The Empowerment of a New Constituency." In *Public Policy for Democracy*, eds. Helen Ingram and Steven Rathgeb Smith. Washington: Brookings.

Gordon, Linda. 1994. *Pitied But Not Entitled: Single Mothers and the History of Welfare*. New York: The Free Press.

Gordon, Linda. 2002. *The Arizona Orphan Abduction*. Cambridge: Harvard University Press.

Gorham, L., G. Quercia, W. Rohe, and J. Toppen. 2002. *Low Income Families Building Assets: Individual Development Account Programs Lessons and Best Practices*. Chapel Hill: University of North Carolina, Center for Urban and Regional Studies.

Gring-Pemble, Lisa M. 2001. "'Are We Going to Now Govern by Anecdote?': Rhetorical Constructions of Welfare Recipients in Congressional Hearings, Debates, and Legislation, 1992–1996." *Quarterly Journal of Speech* 87(4): 341–365.

Grinstein-Weiss, M., J. S. Lee, J. Greeson, C. Han, Y. Yeo, and K. Irish. 2008. "Fostering Low-Income Homeownership: A Longitudinal Randomized Experiment on Individual Development Accounts." *Housing Policy Debate* 19(4): 711–39.

Grogger, Jeffrey. 2004. "The Economy, Welfare Policy, and the EITC." *Journal of Policy Analysis and Management* 23(4): 671–95.

Grossback, Lawrence J., Sean Nicholson-Crotty, and David A. Peterson. 2004. "Ideology and Learning in Policy Diffusion." *American Politics Research* 32(5): 521–45.

Gugerty, Mary Kay, and Aseem Prakash. 2010. *Voluntary Regulation of NGOs and Nonprofits*. Cambridge: Cambridge University Press.

Guiso, Luigi, Paola Sapienza, and Luigi Zingales. 2000. "The Role of Social Capital in Financial Development." National Bureau of Economic Research Working Paper No. W7563.

Gunderson, Jill, and Julie Hotchkiss. 2007. "Job Separation Behavior of WOTC Workers: Results from a Unique Case Study." *Social Service Review* 8(2): 317–42.

Gustafson, Kaaryn. 2009. "The Criminalization of Poverty." *Journal of Criminal Law and Criminology* 99(3): 643–716.

Hacker, Jacob S. 2006. *The Great Risk Shift*. New York: Oxford University Press.

Hacker, Jacob S., and Paul Pierson. 2010a. *Winner-Take-All Politics: How Washington Made the Rich Richer—and Turned Its Back on the Middle Class*. New York: Simon and Schuster.

———. 2010b. "Winner-Take-All Politics: Public Policy, Political Organization, and the Precipitous Rise of Top Incomes in the United States." *Politics & Society* 38(2): 152–204.

Hall, Peter Dobkin. 1992. *Inventing the Nonprofit Sector: Essays on Philanthropy, Voluntarism, and Nonprofit Organizations*. Baltimore: Johns Hopkins University Press.

———. 2002. "Philanthropy, the Welfare State, and the Transformation of America's Public and Private Institutions, 1945–2000." In *Charity, Philanthropy, and Civility in American History*, eds. Lawrence Friedman and Mark McGarvie. Cambridge: Cambridge University Press.

———. 2006. "A Historical Overview of Philanthropy, Voluntary Associations, and Nonprofit Organizations in the United States, 1600–2000." In *The Nonprofit Sector*, eds. Walter W. Powell and Richard Steinberg. New Haven: Yale University Press.

Hamersma, Sarah. 2005. "The Effects of an Employer Subsidy on Employment Outcomes: A Study of the Work Opportunity and Welfare-to-Work Tax Credits." Institute for Research on Poverty Discussion Paper No. 1303-05.

———. 2011. "Why Don't Eligible Firms Claim Hiring Subsidies? The Role of Job Duration." *Economic Inquiry* 49(3): 916–34.

Hamersma, Sarah, and Carolyn Heinrich. 2007. "Temporary Help Service Firms' Use of Employer Tax Credits: Implications for Disadvantaged Workers' Labor Market Outcomes." Upjohn Institute Working Paper No. 07-135. Kalamazoo: W. E. Upjohn Institute for Employment Research.

Han, C. K., M. Grinstein-Weiss, and M. Sherraden. 2007. "Assets beyond Saving in Individual Development Accounts." CSD Working Paper No. 07-25. St. Louis: Center for Social Development.

Handler, Joel, and Yeheskel Hasenfeld. 1991. *The Moral Construction of Poverty*. Newbury Park, CA: Sage.

———. 2007. *Blame Welfare, Ignore Poverty and Inequality*. Cambridge: Harvard University Press.

Hasenfeld, Yeheskel, Toorjo Ghose, and Kandyce Larson. 2004. "The Logic of Sanctioning Welfare Recipients: An Empirical Assessment." *Social Service Review* (June): 304–19.

Hays, Sharon. 2004. *Flat Broke with Children: Women in the Age of Welfare Reform*. New York: Oxford University Press.

Heclo, Hugh. 1994. "Poverty Politics." In *Confronting Poverty: Prescriptions for Change*, eds. Sheldon Danziger, Gary Sandefur, and Daniel Weinberg. New York: Russell Sage Foundation, 396–437.

———. 2001. "The Politics of Welfare Reform." In *The New World of Welfare*, eds. Rebecca Blank and Ron Haskins. Washington, DC: Brookings.

Heidenheimer, Arnold J. 1970. *Political Corruption: Readings in Comparative Analysis.* New York: Holt, Rinehart and Winston.

Hero, Rodney E. 1998. *Faces of Inequality: Social Diversity in American Politics.* New York: Oxford University Press.

Herrick, John Middlemist, and Paul H. Stuart. 2005. *Encyclopedia of Social Welfare History in North America.* New York: Sage.

Heymann, J. 2000. *The Widening Gap: Why America's Working Families Are in Jeopardy—and What Can Be Done About it.* New York: Basic Books.

Hodge, Graeme A. 2000. *Privatization: An International Review of Performance.* Boulder: Westview.

Hoffman, S., and L. Seidman. 2002. *Helping Working Families: The Earned Income Tax Credit.* Washington DC: W. E. Upjohn Institute.

Holahan, John, and A. Bowen Garrett. 2009. *Rising Unemployment, Medicaid, and the Uninsured.* Washington, DC: Urban Institute.

Holtgrave, D., and R. Crosby. 2003. "Social Capital, Poverty, and Income Inequality as Predictors of Gonorrhea, Syphilis, Chlamydia, and AIDS Case Rates in the United States." *Sexually Transmitted Infections* 79(1): 62–64.

Hotz, V., and J. Scholz. 2003. "The Earned Income Tax Credit." In *Means-Tested Transfer Programs in the United States,* ed. R. Moffitt. Chicago: University of Chicago Press.

Howard, Christopher. 1999. "Field Essay: American Welfare State or States?" *Political Research Quarterly* 52(2): 421–42.

Hurst, Erik, and James Ziliak. 2005. "Do Welfare Asset Limits Affect Household Saving? Evidence from Welfare Reform." *Journal of Human Resources* 41(1): 46–71.

Iyengar, Shanto. 1990. "Framing Responsibility for Political Issues: The Case of Poverty." *Political Behavior* 12(1): 19–40.

Jacobs, Lawrence R., and Benjamin I. Page. 2005. "Who Influences U.S. Foreign Policy?" *American Political Science Review* 99: 107–24.

Jacobs, Lawrence R., and Theda Skocpol, eds. 2005. *Inequality and American Democracy: What We Know and What We Need to Learn.* New York: Russell Sage Foundation.

Jacobs, Lawrence R., and Joe Soss. 2010. "The Politics of Inequality in America: A Political Economy Framework." *Annual Review of Political Science* 13: 341–64.

Johnston, Joslyn, and Barbara Romzek. 1999. "Contracting and Accountability in State Medicaid Reform: Rhetoric, Theories, and Reality." *Public Administration Review* 59(5): 383–99.

———. 2000. *Implementing State Contracts for Social Services: An Assessment of the Kansas Experience.* Washington, DC: The PricewaterhouseCoopers Endowment for the Business of Government.

Jordan-Zachery, Julia S. 2007. "Let Men Be Men: A Gendered Analysis of Black Ideological Response to Familial Policies." *National Political Science Review* 11: 177–92.

———. 2009. *Black Women, Cultural Images, and Social Policy.* New York: Routledge.

Kabbani, Nader, and Myra Kmeid. "The Role of Food Assistance in Helping Food Insecure Households Escape Hunger." *Review of Agricultural Economics* 27: 439–45.

Kalil, Ariel, Kristin Seefeldt, and Hui-chen Wang. 2002. "Sanctions and Material Hardship under TANF." *Social Service Review* (December): 642–62.

Katz, Michael. 1989. *The Undeserving Poor: From the War on Poverty to the War on Welfare*. New York: Pantheon.

———. 1996. *In the Shadow of the Poorhouse: A Social History of Welfare in America*. New York: Basic.

———. 2001. *The Price of Citizenship: Redefining America's Welfare State*. New York: Metropolitan Books.

Keiser, Lael R., Peter R. Mueser, and Seung-Whan Choi. 2004. "Race, Bureaucratic Discretion, and the Implementation of Welfare Reform." *American Journal of Political Science* 48(2): 314–27.

Keiser, Lael R., and Joe Soss. 1998. "With Good Cause: Bureaucratic Discretion and the Politics of Child Support Enforcement." *American Journal of Political Science* 42(4): 1133–56.

Kelly, Nathan J. 2005. "Political Choice, Public Policy, and Distributional Outcomes." *American Journal of Political Science* 49(4): 865–80.

———. 2009. *The Politics of Income Inequality in the United States*. New York: Cambridge University Press.

Kettl, Donald F. 1988. *Government by Proxy: (Mis?)Managing Federal Programs*. Washington, DC: Congressional Quarterly Press.

———. 1993. *Sharing Power: Public Governance and Private Markets*. Washington, DC: Brookings Institution.

Khademian, Anne M. 2002. *Working with Culture: The Way the Job Gets Done in Public Programs*. Washington, DC: CQ Press.

Kim, HeeMin, and Richard Fording. 2010. "Second-Order Devolution and the Implementation of TANF." *State Politics and Policy Quarterly* 10(4): 341–67.

Klawitter, M., Stromski, L., and Holcomb, T. 2006. *United Way of King County IDA Program: Progress Report*. Seattle: United Way of King County.

Kluegel, James R., and Eliot R. Smith. 1986. *Beliefs about Inequality*. New York: Aldine de Gruyter.

Knack, Stephen, and Philip Keefer. 1997. "Does Social Capital Have an Economic Payoff? A Cross-Country Investigation." *Quarterly Journal of Economics* 112(4): 1251–88.

Kohler-Hausmann, Julilly. 2007. "The Crime of Survival: Fraud Prosecutions, Community Surveillance, and the Original 'Welfare Queen.'" *Journal of Social History* 41(2): 329–54.

Koralek, Robin. 2000. "South Carolina Family Independence Program Process Evaluation." Prepared for the South Carolina Department of Social Services. Washington, DC: Urban Institute.

Kunicova, Jana, and Susan Rose-Ackerman. 2005. "Electoral Rules and Constitutional Structures as Constraints on Corruption." *British Journal of Political Science* 35: 573–606.

Ladd, Everett Carll, ed. 1993. "Public Opinion and Demographic Report: Reforming Welfare." *Public Perspective* 4(6): 86–87.

Lagendijk, Arnoud, and Päivi Oinas. 2005. "Proximity, External Relations, and Local Economic Development." In *Proximity, Distance and Diversity. Issues on*

Economic Interaction and Local Development, eds. Arnoud Lagendijk and Päivi Oinas. New York: Ashgate, 3–22.

La Porta, Rafael, Florencio Lopez-de-Silanes, Andrei Shleifer, and Robert W. Vishny. 1997. "Trust in Large Organizations." *American Economic Review* 87(2): 333–38.

Larson, Anita M., Shweta Singh, and Crystal Lewis. 2011. "Sanctions and Education Outcomes for Children in TANF Families." *Child & Youth Services* 32(3): 180–99.

Lawrance, Emily. 1991. "Poverty and the Rate of Time Preference: Evidence from Panel Data." *Journal of Political Economy* 99(1): 54–77.

Leigh, Andrew. 2010. "Who Benefits from the EITC? Incidence among Recipients, Coworkers, and Firms." *B.E. Journal of Analysis and Policy* 10(1): 1–41.

Lens, Vicki, and Susan E. Vorsanger. 2005. "Complaining after Claiming: Fair Hearings after Welfare Reform." *Social Service Review* 79: 430–53.

Levin-Epstein, Jodie. 1998. *The IRA: Individual Responsibility Agreements and TANF Family Life Obligations.* Washington, DC: The Center for Law and Social Policy.

Levy, Barry S., and Victor W. Sidel. 2005. *Social Injustice and Public Health.* New York: Oxford University Press.

Lieberman, Robert. 1998. *Shifting the Color Line: Race and the American Welfare State.* Cambridge: Harvard University Press.

Light, Paul. 2003. "The Illusion of Smallness." In *Classics of Public Personnel Policy*, ed. Frank J. Thompson. Belmont, CA: Wadsworth, 157–77.

Lineberry, Robert L. 1977. *American Public Policy: What Government Does and What Difference It Makes.* New York: Harper and Row.

Lobmayer, P., and R. Wilkinson 2002. "Inequality, Residential Segregation by Income, and Mortality in U.S. Cities." *Journal of Epidemiological and Community Health* 56(3): 183–87.

Losby, J. L., M. L. Hein, J. R. Robinson, and J. F. Else. 2002. *Program Evaluation of Year One of the Michigan IDA Partnership.* Newark, DE: ISED Consulting and Research.

Losby, M., J. R. Robinson, and J. F. Else. 2004. *Michigan IDA Partnership: Year 3 Program Evaluation Report.* Newark, DE: ISED Consulting and Research.

Lynn, Laurence E., Carolyn J. Heinrich, and Carolyn J. Hill. 2000. "Studying Governance and Public Management: Challenges and Prospects." *Journal of Public Administration Research and Theory* 10(2): 233–61.

Mair, Johanna, and Ignasi Marti. 2006. "Social Entrepreneurship Research: A Source of Explanation, Prediction, and Delight." *Journal of World Business* 41(1): 36–44.

Mann, Cindy, Diane Rowland, and Rachel Garfield. 2003. "Historical Overview of Children's Health Care Coverage." *The Future of Children* 13(1): 30–53.

March, James, and Johan Olsen. 2006. "The Logic of Appropriateness." In *The Oxford Handbook of Public Policy*, eds. Michael Moran, Martin Rein, and Robert E. Goodin. Oxford: Oxford University Press, 689–708.

Marcotte, Dave E. 2000. "Continuing Education, Job Training, and the Growth of Earnings Inequality." *Industrial and Labor Relations Review* 53(4): 602–23.

Marston, Sallie A. 1993. "Citizen Action Programs and Participatory Politics in Tucson." In *Public Policy for Democracy*, eds. Helen Ingram and Steven Rathgeb Smith. Washington, DC: Brookings, 119–35.

Martin, Joanne. 1992. *Cultures in Organizations: Three Perspectives*. New York: Oxford University Press.

Martindale, Carolyn. 1996. "Newspaper Stereotypes of African Americans." In *Images That Injure*, ed. Paul Martin Lester. Westport, CT: Praeger.

Massey, Douglas, and Mary Denton. 1993. *American Apartheid: Segregation and the Making of the Underclass*. Cambridge: Harvard University Press.

Maynard-Moody, Steven, and Michael Musheno. 2003. *Cops, Teachers, Counselors: Stories from the Front Lines of Public Service*. Ann Arbor: University of Michigan Press.

Mayo, E., and H. Moore. 2001. *The Mutual State*. London: New Economics Foundation.

McCarty, Nolan M., Keith T. Poole, and Howard Rosenthal. 2006. *Polarized America: The Dance of Ideology and Unequal Riches*. Cambridge: MIT Press.

McEvily, Bill, Vincenzo Perrone, and Akbar Zaheer. 2003. "Trust as an Organizing Principle." *Organization Science* 14(1): 91–103.

McKernan, S., C. Ratcliffe, and Y. Nam. 2007. "The Effects of Welfare and IDA Program Rules on the Asset Holdings of Low-Income Families." In *Poor Finances: Assets and Low-Income Households*. Washington, DC: U.S. Department of Health and Human Services, Office of the Assistant Secretary for Planning and Evaluation.

McLanahan, S., A. Sorenson, and D. Watson. 1989. "Sex Differences in Poverty, 1950–1980." *Signs* 15(1): 13–27.

McLaughlin, D., and C. Stokes. 2002. "Income Inequality and Mortality in U.S. Counties: Does Minority Racial Concentration Matter?" *American Journal of Public Health* 92(1): 99–104.

Mead, Lawrence. 1992. *The New Politics of Poverty*. New York: Basic.

———. 1997. *The New Paternalism: Supervisory Approaches to Poverty*. Washington, DC: Brookings Institution Press.

———. 1998. "Telling the Poor What to Do." *Public Interest* 132: 97–112.

Meier, Kenneth J. 1993. *Politics and the Bureaucracy*. Pacific Grove, CA: Brooks/Cole.

Meier, Kenneth J., and Thomas M. Holbrook. 1992. "'I Seen My Opportunities and I Took 'Em': Political Corruption in the United States." *Journal of Politics* 54: 135–55.

Mendelberg, Tali. 2001. *The Race Card*. Princeton: Princeton University Press.

Mettler, Suzanne. 1998. *Dividing Citizens: Gender and Federalism in New Deal Public Policy*. Ithaca: Cornell University Press.

Meyer, B. 2002. "Labor Supply at the Extensive and Intensive Margins: The EITC, Welfare, and Hours Worked." *American Economic Review* 92(2): 373–79.

Meyer, B., and D. Holtz-Eakin. 2002. *Making Work Pay: The Earned Income Tax Credit and Its Impact on America's Families*. New York: Russell Sage Foundation.

Meyer, B., and D. Rosenbaum. 2001. "Welfare, the EITC, and the Labor Supply of Single Mothers." *Quarterly Journal of Economics* 116: 1063–1114.

Mikhail, Blanche. 2000. "Prenatal Care Utilization among Low-Income African American Women." *Journal of Community Health Nursing* 17(4): 235–46.

Miller, Carol. 2001. "State Jobs Agency under Fire." *Miami Herald*, December 31.

Miller, Gary J., and Andrew B. Whitford. 2002. "Trust and Incentives in Principal-Agent Negotiations: The 'Insurance/Incentive Trade-off.'" *Journal of Theoretical Politics* 14 (2): 231–67.

Milward, H. Brinton, and Keith Provan. 2003. "Managing the Hollow State: Collaboration and Contracting." *Public Administration Review* 66(1): 33–43.

Montinola, Gabriela, and Robert Jackman. 2002. "Sources of Corruption: A Cross-Country Study." *British Journal of Political Science* 32(1): 147–70.

Mosher, Frederick C. 1980. "The Changing Responsibilities and Tactics of the Federal Government." *Public Administration Review* 40(9): 541–48.

Moskowitz, Gordon B., and Peizhong Li 2011. "Egalitarian Goals Trigger Stereotype Inhibition: A Proactive Form of Stereotype Control." *Journal of Experimental Social Psychology* 47(1): 103–16.

Moskowitz, Gordon B., and Jeff Stone. 2011. "Egalitarian Goals Trigger Stereotype Inhibition: A Proactive Form of Stereotype Control." *Journal of Experimental Social Psychology* 47: 103–16.

Mosley, Jane, and Laura Tiehen. 2004. "The Food Safety Net after Welfare Reform: Use of Private and Public Food Assistance in the Kansas City Metropolitan Area." *Social Service Review* 78: 267–83.

Mulgan, Geoff. 2006. "Cultivating the Other Invisible Hand of Social Entrepreneurship: Comparative Advantage, Public Policy, and Future Research Priorities." In *Social Entrepreneurship: New Paradigms of Sustainable Social Change*, ed. Alex Nicholls. New York: Oxford University Press, 74–98.

Murray, Charles, and Richard J. Herrnstein. 1994. *The Bell Curve: Intelligence and Class Structure in American Life*. New York: Free Press.

Naples, Nancy A. 1997. "The New Consensus on the Gendered Social Contract: The 1987–1988 US Congressional Hearings on Welfare Reform." *Signs* 22(4): 907–45.

Neckerman, Kathryn M. 2004. *Social Inequality*. New York: Russell Sage Foundation.

Newacheck, Paul, Yun Yi Hung, M. Jane Park, Claire Brindis, and Charles Irwin Jr. 2003. "Disparities in Adolescent Health and Health Care: Does Socioeconomic Status Matter?" *Health Services Research* 38(5): 1235–52.

Nicholson-Crotty, Sean. 2007. "The Impact of Program Design on Enrollment in State Children's Health Insurance Programs." *Policy Studies Journal* 35(1): 23–35.

Nord, Mark. 2009. "Food Insecurity in Households with Children: Prevalence, Severity, and Household Characteristics." Economic Research Service Bulletin No. EIB-56. Washington, DC: USDA.

Nord, Mark, and Marie Golla. 2009. "Does SNAP Decrease Food Insecurity? Untangling the Self-Esteem Effect." Economic Research Report (ERR 85). Washington, DC: USDA Economic Research Service.

Nord, Mark, Kyle Jemison, and Gary Bickel. 1999. "Prevalence of Food Insecurity and Hunger by State, 1996–1998." Food Assistance and Nutrition Research Report No. 2. Washington, DC: USDA.

Nye, John V. C. 2002. "Economic Growth and True Inequality." The Library of Economics and Liberty January 28, 2002. Online publication available at http://econlib.org/library/Columns/Nyegrowth.html. Last visited July 27, 2014.

Ochs, Holona LeAnne. 2012. "Philanthropic Social Ventures: A Framework and Profile of the Emerging Field." *Journal of Public Management and Social Policy* 18(1): 3–26.

Oliver, Thomas R., and Pamela Paul-Shaheen. 1997. "Translating Ideas into Actions: Entrepreneurial Leadership in State Health Care Reforms." *Journal of Health Politics, Policy, and Law* 22(3): 721–88.

Olson, Laura Katz. 2010. *The Politics of Medicaid.* New York: Columbia University Press.

Ore, Tracy. 2003. *The Social Construction of Difference and Inequality.* New York: McGraw-Hill.

Orr, Larry. 1976. "Income Transfers as a Public Good: An Application to AFDC." *American Economic Review* 66(3): 359–71.

Osbourne, David, and Ted Gaebler. 1992. *Reinventing Government: How the Entrepreneurial Spirit Is Transforming the Public Sector.* Reading, MA: Addison-Wesley.

Pavetti, LaDonna, Michelle Derr, and Heather Hesketh. 2003. *Review of Sanction Policies and Research Studies: Final Literature Review.* Report prepared for the Office of the Assistant Secretary for Planning and Evaluation, Mathematica Policy Research, Washington, DC.

Pearce, Diane. 1978. "The Feminization of Poverty: Women, Work, and Welfare." *Urban and Social Exchange Review* 11(1): 28–36.

Peck, Jamie. 2001. *Workfare States.* New York: Gilford Press.

Peffley, Mark, and Jon Hurwitz 1999. *Perception and Prejudice: Race and Politics in the United States.* New Haven: Yale University Press.

Perrini, Francesco, and Clodia Vurro. 2006. *The New Social Entrepreneurship: What Awaits Social Entrepreneurship Ventures.* Northampton, MA: Edward Elgar.

Persson, Torsten, and Guido Tabellini. 2003. *The Economic Effects of Constitutions.* Cambridge: MIT Press.

Piff, P., D. Stancato, S. Côté, R. Mendoza-Denton, and D. Keltner. 2012. "Higher Social Class Predicts Increased Unethical Behavior." *Proceedings of the National Academy of Sciences* 109: 4086–91.

Pinder, J., J. Yagley, S. Peck, and C. Moore. 2006. *Designing and Implementing Rural Individual Development Account Programs.* Washington, DC: Housing Assistance Council.

Piven, Frances Fox, and Richard A. Cloward. 1971. *Regulating the Poor: The Functions of Public Welfare.* New York: Vintage Books.

———. 1993. *Regulating the Poor: The Functions of Public Welfare.* New York: Vintage Books.

Plotnick, Robert, and Richard Winters. 1985. "A Politico-Economic Theory of Income Redistribution." *American Political Science Review* 79: 458–73.

Primus, Richard A. 1999. *The American Language of Rights, Ideas in Context; 54.* Cambridge and New York: Cambridge University Press.

Quadagno, Jill. 1996. *The Color of Welfare: How Racism Undermined the War on Poverty*. New York: Oxford University Press.

Quigley, William P. 1999. "Five Hundred Years of English Poor Laws, 1349–1834: Regulating the Working and Nonworking Poor" *Akron Law Review* 73: 82–92.

Radin, Beryl. 2006. *Challenging the Performance Movement: Accountability, Complexity, and Democratic Values*. Washington, DC: Georgetown University Press.

Ratcliffe, Caroline. 2007. "The Effect of State Food Stamp and TANF Policies on Food Stamp Program Participation." Washington, DC: Urban Institute.

Raymond, Susan U. 2004. *The Future of Philanthropy: Economics, Ethics, and Management*. Hoboken: John Wiley and Sons.

Reese, Ellen. 2005. *Backlash against Welfare Mothers: Then and Now*. Berkeley: University of California Press.

Reichman, Nancy E., Julien O. Teitler, and Marah A. Curtis. 2005. "TANF Sanctioning and Hardship." *Social Service Review* (June): 215–36.

Reingold, David, and Helen Liu. 2009. "Do Poverty Attitudes of Social Service Agency Directors Influence Organizational Behavior?" *Nonprofit and Voluntary Sector Quarterly* 38(2): 307–32.

Ridzi, Frank. 2009. *Selling Welfare Reform: Work-First and the New Common Sense of Employment*. New York: New York University Press.

Rigby, Elizabeth, and Gerald C. Wright. 2011. "Whose Statehouse Democracy? State Policy Responsiveness to Rich vs. Poor Constituents in Rich vs. Poor States." In *Who Gets Represented?* eds. Peter Enns and Christopher Wlezien. New York: Russell Sage Foundation, 189–222.

———. 2013. "Political Parties and Representation of the Poor in the American States." *American Journal of Political Science* 57(3): 552–65.

Robinson, Jeffrey. 2006. "Navigating Social and Institutional Barriers to Markets: How Social Entrepreneurs Identify and Evaluate Opportunities." In *Social Entrepreneurship*, eds. Johanna Mair, Jeffrey Robinson and Kai Hockerts. New York: Palgrave Macmillan, 95–120.

Romzek, Barbara S., and Melvin J. Dubnick. 1987. "Accountability in the Public Sector: Lessons from the Challenger Tragedy." *Public Administration Review* 47(3): 227–38.

Rossi, P. H., and H. E. Freeman. 1993. *Evaluation: A Systematic Approach*. Newbury Park, CA: Sage.

Rothstein, Jesse. 2010. "Is the EITC as Good as an NIT? Conditional Cash Transfers and Tax Incidence." *American Economic Journal: Economic Policy* 2(1): 177–208.

Rowett, M. 2006. *Arkansas' Individual Development Account Program*. Little Rock: Southern Good Faith Fund.

Sabatier, Paul A. 1999. *Theories of the Policy Process*. Boulder: Westview.

Salamon, Lester M. 1989. "Beyond Privatization: The Tools of Government Action." *Public Policy* 29(3): 255–75.

Sanger, M. Bryna. 2003. *The Welfare Marketplace: Privatization and Welfare Reform*. Washington, DC: Brookings Institution Press.

Sawyer, Rachel. 2010. *Community Assistantship Program: Family Assets for Independence in Minnesota*. Minneapolis: Center for Urban and Regional Affairs.

Schattschneider, E. E. 1960. *The Semi-Sovereign People*. New York: Holt, Rinehart and Winston.

Schlozman, Kay Lehman, Sidney Verba, and Henry E. Brady. 2012. *The Unheavenly Chorus: Unequal Political Voice and the Broken Promise of American Democracy.* Princeton: Princeton University Press.

Schneider, Anne, and Helen Ingram. 2005. *Deserving and Entitled: Social Constructions and Public Policy*. Albany: State University of New York Press.

Scholz, John T., and Mark Lubell. 1998. "Trust and Taxpaying: Testing the Heuristic Approach to Collective Action." *American Journal of Political Science* 42: 398–417.

Schott, Liz, and LaDonna Pavetti. 2011. "Many States Cutting TANF Benefits Harshly Despite High Unemployment and Unprecedented Need." Center on Budget and Policy Priorities.

Schram, Sanford F. 2005. "Contextualizing Racial Disparities in American Welfare Reform: Toward a New Poverty Research." *Perspectives on Politics* 3(2): 253–68.

———. 2006a. "That Old Black Magic? Welfare Reform and the New Politics of Racial Implication." In *The Promise of Welfare Reform: Political Rhetoric and the Reality of Poverty in the Twenty-First Century*, eds. K. M. Kilty, and Elizabeth A. Segal. New York: Haworth Press.

———. 2006b. *Welfare Discipline: Discourse, Governance, and Globalization*. Philadelphia: Temple University Press.

Schram, Sanford, Joe Soss, and Richard Fording. 2006. *Race and the Politics of Welfare Reform*. Ann Arbor: University of Michigan Press.

Schram, Sanford, Joe Soss, Linda Houser, and Richard Fording. 2009. "The Third Level of U.S. Welfare Reform: Governmentality under Neoliberal Paternalism." *Citizenship Studies* 14(6): 739–54.

Schram, Sanford F., and J. Patrick Turbett. 1983. "Civil Disorder and the Welfare Explosion: A Two-Step Process." *American Sociological Review* 48(3): 408–14.

Schreiner, M., M. Clancy, and M. Sherraden. 2002. *Saving Performance in the American Dream Demonstration: Final Report*. St. Louis: Washington University, Center for Social Development.

Schreiner, M., and M. Sherraden. 2007. *Can the Poor Save? Saving and Asset Building in Individual Development Accounts*. New Brunswick, NJ: Transaction Publishers.

Sen, Amartya Kumar. 1976. "Poverty: An Ordinal Approach to Measurement," *Econometrica* 44: 219–31.

———. 1982. *Choice, Welfare, and Measurement*. Cambridge: MIT Press.

Shapiro, Thomas. 1995. *Black Wealth/White Wealth*. New York: Routledge.

———. 2004. *The Hidden Cost of Being African American: How Wealth Perpetuates Inequality*. New York: Oxford University Press.

Shepsle, Kenneth. 1991. "Discretion, Institutions, and the Problem of Government Commitment." In *Social Theory for a Changing Society*, eds. Pierre Bordieu and James S. Coleman. New York: Westview.

Sherraden, Michael. 1991. *Assets and the Poor*. New York: Sharpe.

———. 2001. *Asset-Building Policy and Programs for the Poor, Assets for the Poor: The Benefits of Spreading Asset Ownership*. New York: Russell Sage Foundation.

Sherraden, M. S., A. M. McBride, and S. Beverly. 2010. *Striving to Save*. Ann Arbor: University of Michigan Press.

Sherraden, M. S., A. M. McBride, E. Johnson, S. Hanson, F. Ssewamala, and T. W. Shanks. 2005. *Saving in Low Income Households: Evidence from Interviews with Participants in the American Dream Demonstration*. Research report. St. Louis: Washington University, Center for Social Development.

Shi, Leiyu, Thomas R. Oliver, and Virginia Huang. 2000. "The Children's Health Insurance Program: Expanding the Framework to Evaluate State Goals and Performance." *The Milbank Quarterly* 78(3): 403–46.

Shone, Laura P., Andrew W. Dick, Cindy Brach, Kim S. Kimminau, Barbara J. LaClair, Elizabeth A. Shenkman, Jana F. Col, Virginia A. Schaffer, Frank Mulvihill, Peter Szilagyi, Jonathan D. Klein, Karen VanLandeghem, and Janet Bronstein. 2003. "The Role of Race and Ethnicity in the State Children's Health Insurance Program (SCHIP) in Four States: Are There Baseline Disparities, and What Do They Mean for SCHIP?" *Pediatrics* 112(2): 521.

Shorrocks, A. 1995. "Revisiting the Sen Poverty Index." *Econometrica* 63: 1225–30.

Sidel, Ruth. 1996. *Keeping Women and Children Last*. New York: Penguin Books.

Skocpol, Theda. 1995. *Protecting Soldiers and Mothers: The Political Origins of Social Policy in the United States*. Cambridge: Harvard University Press.

Smith, Kathleen. 1997. "How to Cover Our Nation's Uninsured Children." *Pediatric Nursing* 23: 625.

Smith, Rogers. 1993. "Beyond Tocqueville, Myrdal, and Hartz: The Multiple Traditions in America." *American Political Science Review* 87(3): 549–66.

Smith, Steven Rathgeb. 2007. "Transforming Public Services: Contracting for Social and Health Services in the U.S." *Public Administration* 74(1): 113–27.

Smith, Steven Rathgeb, and Michael Lipsky. 1993. *Nonprofits for Hire: The Welfare State in the Age of Contracting*. Cambridge: Harvard University Press.

Solt, Frederick. 2008. "Economic Inequality and Democratic Political Engagement." *American Journal of Political Science* 52(1): 48–60.

Sommers, Benjamin. 2009. "Enrolling Eligible Children in Medicaid and CHIP: A Research Update." *Health Affairs* 29(7): 1350–55.

Soss, Joe. 2000. *Unwanted Claims: Politics, Participation, and the U.S. Welfare System*. Ann Arbor: University of Michigan Press.

Soss, Joe, Richard C. Fording, and Sanford F. Schram. 2011a. *Disciplining the Poor: Neoliberal Paternalism and the Persistent Power of Race*. Chicago: University of Chicago Press.

———. 2011b. "The Organization of Discipline: From Performance Management to Perversity and Punishment." *Journal of Public Administration Research and Theory* 21: 203–32.

Soss, Joe, Jacob S. Hacker, and Suzanne Mettler. 2007. *Remaking America: Democracy and Public Policy in an Age of Inequality*. New York: Russell Sage Foundation.

Soss, Joe, and Lawrence R. Jacobs. 2009. "The Place of Inequality: Non-participation in the American Polity." *Political Science Quarterly* 124(1): 95–125.

Soss, Joe, and Sanford Schram. 2007. "A Public Transformed? Welfare Reform as Policy Feedback." *American Political Science Review* 101(1): 111–27.

Soss, Joe, Sanford Schram, Thomas Vartanian, and Erin O'Brien. 2001. "Setting the Terms of Relief: Explaining State Policy Choices in the Devolution Revolution." *American Journal of Political Science* 45(2): 378–95.

Stegman, Michael A. 1999. *Savings for the Poor: The Hidden Benefits of Electronic Banking*. Washington, DC: Brookings Institution.

Stegman, M. A., and R. Faris. 2005. "The Impact of IDA Programs on Family Savings and Asset Holdings." In *Inclusion in the American Dream: Assets, Poverty, and Public Policy*, ed. M. W. Sherraden. New York: Oxford University Press, 216–37.

Stern, Ken. 2013. *With Charity For All*. New York: Doubleday.

Stöhr, Walter B. 1990. *Global Challenge and Local Response: Initiatives for Economic Regeneration in Contemporary Europe*. Vol. 2. United Nations University Press.

Stoll, Michael A. 2010. "Race, Place, and Poverty Revisited." In *The Colors of Poverty: Why Racial and Ethnic Disparities Persist*, eds. David Harris and Ann Chih Lin. New York: Russell Sage Foundation, 201–31.

Stone, Deborah A. 2002. *Policy Paradox: The Art of Political Decision Making*. New York: Norton.

———. 2008. *The Samaritan's Dilemma: Should Government Help Your Neighbor?* New York: Nation.

Lévi-Strauss, Claude. 1967. *The Savage Mind*. Chicago: University of Chicago Press.

Super, David A. 2004. "Offering an Invisible Hand: The Rise of the Personal Choice Model for Rationing Public Benefits." *Yale Law Journal* 113: 815–93.

Thaler, Richard H., and Cass R. Sunstein. 2008. *Nudge: Improving Decisions about Health, Wealth, and Happiness*. New York: Penguin.

Thon, D. 1979. "On Measuring Poverty." *Review of Income and Wealth* 25: 429–40.

Ullman, F., B. Bruen, and J. Holohan. 1998. "The State Children's Health Insurance Program: A Look at the Numbers." Occasional paper no. 4: Assessing the New Federalism Program. Washington, DC: Urban Institute.

Van Slyke, David. 2003. "The Mythology of Privatization in Contracting for Social Services." *Public Administration Review* 63(3): 296–315.

———. 2006. "Agents or Stewards: Using Theory to Understand the Government-Nonprofit Social Service Contracting Relationship." *Journal of Public Administration Research and Theory* 17: 157–87.

Veblen, Thorstein. 1994 [1899]. *The Theory of the Leisure Class*. New York: Penguin.

Verba, Sidney, Kay Lehman Schlozman, and Henry Brady. 2006. *Voice and Equality: Civic Voluntarism in American Politics*. Cambridge: Harvard University Press.

Vestal, Christine. 2006. "States Stumble Privatizing Socail Services." *Stateline*, August 4.

Volden, Craig. 2006. "States as Policy Laboratories: Emulating Success in the Children's Health Insurance Program." *American Journal of Political Science* 50(2): 294–312.

Wacquant, Loic. 2009. *Punishing the Poor: The Neoliberal Government of Social Insecurity*. Durham: Duke University Press.

Waldron, T., B. Roberts, and A. Reamer. 2004. *Working Hard, Falling Short: America's Working Families and the Pursuit of Economic Security*. A national report by the

Working Poor Families Project, sponsored by the Annie E. Casey, Ford, and Rockefeller Foundations. Baltimore: The Annie E. Casey Foundation.

Ward, Deborah E. 2005. *The White Welfare State: The Racialization of U.S. Welfare Policy*. Ann Arbor: University of Michigan Press.

Watkins-Hayes, Celeste. 2009. *Race, Poverty, and Policy Implementation: Inside the Black Box of Racially Representative Bureaucracies*. Paper presented at the Symposium on Welfare States in Transition, University of Chicago, Chicago, IL, May 15, 2009.

Wei-Skillern, Jane, James Austin, Herman Leonard, and Howard Stevenson. 2007. *Entrepreneurship in the Social Sector*. Los Angeles: Sage.

Weick, Karl. 1995. *Sensemaking in Organizations*. Thousand Oaks, CA: Sage.

White, Lucie. 2002. "Care at Work." In *Laboring Below the Line*, ed. Frank Munger. New York: Russell Sage Foundation.

Whitford, Andrew, and Soo-Young Lee. 2008. "Exit, Voice, Loyalty, and Pay: Evidence from the Federal Workforce," *Journal of Public Administration Research and Theory* 18(4): 647–71.

Whitford, Andrew, and Gary J. Miller. 2007. "The Principal's Moral Hazard: Constraints on the Use of Incentives in Hierarchy," *Journal of Public Administration Research and Theory* 17(2): 213–33.

Whitford, Andrew B., William P. Bottom, James Holloway, Gary Miller, and Alexandra Mislin. 2006. "Pathways to Cooperation: Negotiation and Social Exchange between Principal and Agent." *Administrative Science Quarterly* 51(1): 29–58.

Whitford, Andrew B., Jeff Yates, and Holona LeAnne Ochs. 2006. "Ideological Extremism and Public Participation." *Social Science Quarterly* 87(1): 36–54.

Wilkinson, Richard G., and Kate Pickett. 2010. *The Spirit Level: Why Greater Equality Makes Societies Stronger*. New York: Bloomsbury Press.

Wilson, James Q., and John J. DiLulio. 2007. *American Government: The Essentials*. 11th Edition. New York: Houghton Mifflin.

Wilson, William J. 1978. *The Declining Significance of Race: Black and Changing American Institutions*. Chicago: University of Chicago Press.

———. 1987. *The Truly Disadvantaged: The Inner City, the Underclass, and Public Policy*. Chicago: University of Chicago Press.

Wilson, William Julius. 2011. "Being Poor, Black, and American: The Impact of Political, Economic, and Cultural Forces." *American Educator* (Spring): 10–26.

Winston, Pamela, Andrew Burwick, Sheena McConnell, and Richard Roper. 2002. *Privatization of Welfare Services: A Review of the Literature*. A Report Submitted to the U.S. Department of Health and Human Services Contract No. HHS-100-01-0011. Washington, DC.

Winters, Jeffrey A., and Benjamin I. Page. 2009. "Oligarchy in the United States?" *Perspectives on Politics* 7(4): 731–51.

Wood, Michelle, Jennifer Turnham, and Gregory Mills. 2008. "Housing Affordability and Family Well-Being: Results from the Housing Voucher Evaluation." *Housing Policy Debate* 19(2): 367–412.

Wright, Gerald. 1976. "Racism and Welfare Policy in America." *Social Science Quarterly* 57(1): 718–730.

Wright, C. 1992. *The Transformation of Charity in Post Revolutionary New England.* Boston: Northeastern University Press.

Wu, Chi-Fang. 2008. "Severity, Timing, and Duration of Welfare Sanctions and the Economic Well-Being of TANF Families with Children." *Children and Youth Services Review* 30(1): 26–44.

Wu, Chi-Fang, Maria Cancian, Daniel R. Meyer, and Geoffrey L. Wallace. 2006. "How Do Welfare Sanctions Work?" *Social Work Research* 30(1): 33–50.

Xu, Kuan, and Lars Osberg. 2002. "On Sen's Approach to Poverty Measures and Recent Developments." Paper presented at the Sixth International Meeting of the Society for Social Choice and Welfare.

Zahra, S., E. Gedajlovic, D. Neubaum, and J. Shulman. 2009. "A Typology of Social Entrepreneurs: Motives, Search Processes, and Ethical Challenges." *Journal of Business Venturing* 24(5): 519–34.

Ziliak, James. 2005. "Understanding Poverty Rates and Gaps: Concepts, Trends, and Challenges." *Foundations and Trends in Microeconomics* 1(3): 127–99.

Index

Act for the Relief of the Poor (1597; 1601), 13

Administration for Children and Families (ACF), 45, 59, 68, 85, 87; data source, 195, 247, 256, 257, 285, 287

Aid to Families with Dependent Children (AFDC), 1, 19, 31, 43, 44, 49, 55, 58, 78, 84, 86, 107, 125, 126, 163, 186, 229–47

Aid to Families with Dependent Children-Unemployed Parent (AFDC-UP), 58

American Recovery and Reinvestment Act (ARRA) (2009), 44–45; (2005) 45, 93. *See also* Recovery Act

Asset building approaches, 6, 8, 79–84, 129–32, 137, 157, 165–66, 217–24, 225–28, 259, 287, 289

Assets for Independence Act (AFI), 80–81

Basic Needs and Emergency Assistance (BNEA). *See* Emergency Assistance (EA)

charitable disposition, 9, 139, 144–45, 148, 161, 169, 271–74

Child Care and Development Block Grant (CCDB or CCDBG), 43, 45, 56. *See also* Child Care Development Fund (CCDF). *See also* Supplemental Grants

Child Care Development Fund (CCDF), 104

child support enforcement, 45–46, 57, 59, 64, 84–88, 110, 168, 229–47

Children's Health Insurance Program (CHIP), 52, 73, 98–100, 288. *See also* State Children's Health Insurance Program Reauthorization Act (CHIPRA) (2009)

Community Development Block Grant (CDBG), 56, 66, 80, 205

Deficit Reduction Act (DRA) of 2005, 44, 49, 53, 59, 72, 76, 87, 125, 194, 256

devolution, 1–2, 5, 7–8, 15–17, 21, 25–27, 31, 37–38, 41–88, 96, 98, 102, 106, 109, 113, 116–17, 121,